Ethical Wills
& How to
Prepare Them

A Guide to Sharing Your Values from Generation to Generation

Edited by
Rabbi Jack Riemer & Dr. Nathaniel Stampfer
Foreword by Rabbi Harold S. Kushner

For People of All Faiths, All Backgrounds
JEWISH LIGHTS Publishing
Woodstock, Vermont

Ethical Wills and How to Prepare Them:
A Guide to Sharing Your Values from Generation to Generation

2015 Quality Paperback Edition, First Printing

Previous Jewish Lights edition published as *So That Your Values Live On: Ethical Wills and How to Prepare Them* (1991).

A number of ethical wills in Sections I–IV appeared in *Ethical Wills: A Modern Jewish Treasury*, edited and annotated by Jack Riemer & Nathaniel Stampfer (Schocken Books, 1983).

The Library of Congress has catalogued the previous edition, published as *So That Your Values Live On*, as follows:
So that your values live on: ethical wills and how to prepare them, edited and annotated by Jack Riemer & Nathaniel Stampfer.
Collection of wills originally written in English, German, Hebrew, and Yiddish.
     Rev. ed. of: Ethical wills. 1983.
     Includes index.
     ISBN-13: 978-1-879045-34-7 (quality pbk.)
     ISBN-10: 1-879045-34-6 (quality pbk.)
     1. Wills, Ethical. I. Riemer, Jack. II. Stampfer, Nathaniel. III. Ethical wills.
BJ1286.W59S6 1991
396.3'85—dc20

                            91-28039

Revised edition
ISBN 978-1-58023-827-4 (quality pbk.)
ISBN 978-1-58023-829-8 (eBook)

10 9 8 7 6 5 4 3 2 1

Manufactured in the United States of America

Cover and Interior Design: Tim Holtz
Cover Art: © ideldesign/Shutterstock

Published by Jewish Lights Publishing
A Division of LongHill Partners, Inc.
Sunset Farm Offices, Route 4, P.O. Box 237
Woodstock, VT 05091
Tel: (802) 457-4000   Fax: (802) 457-4004
www.jewishlights.com

To Nathan, Lisa, Naomi, and Sterling,
May you be your own person—and ours too.
J.R.

To my nine grandchildren—
Find grace and good favor
in the eyes of God and man (Prov. 3:4).
N.S.

Contents

Foreword   xi
    Rabbi Harold S. Kushner

Preface   xiii
    Dr. Nathaniel Stampfer

Acknowledgments   xvii

Introduction to the Revised Edition   xix
    Rabbi Jack Riemer

What I Have Learned Since I Began Collecting Ethical Wills   xxiii
    Rabbi Jack Riemer

PART ONE

Traditional Wills   1

Solomon Kluger   3
    "Preparing provisions for the journey"

Moshe Yeshoshua Zelig Hakohen   9
    "A guide for the practices of piety"

Benjamin M. Roth   18
    "A letter to a departing son"

Mordekhai Mottel Michelsohn   25
    "I shall give you some useful advice"

Shmuel Tefilinsky   28
    "Put your trust in God and He will sustain you"

Hayyim Elazar Shapira (The Munkatcher Rebbe)   34
    "We merit redemption by virtue of our choices"

Yehuda Leib Graubart (The Stashever Rav)   38
    "Return the borrowed books in my possession"

PART TWO

Wills from the Holocaust   39

Hirsch Moshe Zaddok   41
"They treated us like animals"

A Mother's Will   42
"A struggle for the sanctification of the human heart"

Zippora Birman   43
"No choice but to die with honor"

Among the Embers: Martyrs' Testaments   45
The last twelve Jews in Chelmno

David Elster, on the synagogue wall

The members of "Dror"

Gina Atlas, on the synagogue wall

A young woman, on the synagogue wall

Berl Tomshelski, on a wooden board

A Polish Jew, to the Blozhever Rebbe

The Chief Rabbi of Grodzisk   47
"Let him come, but let me not see him"

On the Walls of Bialystok Prison   48

Shulamit Rabinovitch   50
"Don't mourn for us with tears and words, but rather with deeds"

Shulamit Rabinovitch's Husband   52
"Our fate lies in wait for us"

PART THREE

Wills from the Land of Israel   53

Elijah David Rabinovitz (Teomim)   55
"Always have I received more honor than I deserved"

Theodor Herzl   59
"I wielded my pen as an honest man"

Edmond James de Rothschild   61
"My eldest son James ... will further my work"

Abraham Isaac Kook   64
"Help your holy people"

Ben Zion Meir Hai Uziel   66
The shepherd thanks his flock

Alter Ya'akov Sahrai   68
"Loyal to his people, its Torah, and its land"

Meir Dizengoff   70
To the new life beyond Awareness

Yitzhak Ben Nehemia Margalit   73
"Come, I will show thee where earth meets heaven"

Naftali Swiatitsky   75
"I have only one request"

Hannah Senesh   78
"There are events without which one's life becomes unimportant"

Noam Grossman   81
"Do not eulogize me; I did my duty"

Avraham Kreizman   82
"When I die, for you I shall continue to live"

Eldad Pan   83
"Life by itself is worth little unless it serves something greater than itself"

Dvora Waysman   84
"I am leaving you an extended family"

PART FOUR

Wills of Modern and Contemporary American Jews   87

Nissen Sheinberg   89
  "From me, your friend and father"

Emil Greenberg   94
  "A wisp, a whisper of immortality becomes mine, and yours"

Yitschak Kelman   96
  "The Holy Presence is with the sick"

Bernard L. Levinthal   101
  "Be bound by the oath taken at the foot of Mount Sinai"

David De Sola Pool   104
  An affirmation of life

Sholom Aleichem   107
  "Bury me ... among the common Jewish folk"

Mordkhe Schaechter   110
  "Have no fear of being in the minority"

Dora Chazin   112
  "Find favor in the eyes of God and man"

William Schulder   114
  "Never consider yourself greater than the next man"

Hayim Greenberg   116
  "I have erred not out of love of sin"

Rafael L. Savitzky   117
  "In America the women are the saintly souls"

Samuel Lipsitz   120
  "Live together in harmony"

Sadie S. Kulakofsky   122
  "The principles of Judaism and the basis of civilization"

Sidney Rabinowitz   123
  "I wanted to do something to make the world better"

Samuel Furash   125
  "You are the nearest stars in my heaven"

Harold Katz   128
"So that all mankind could live in a free and peaceful world"

Madeline Medoff   130
"They carry something of me in their lives"

Allen Hofrichter   135
"An ineffable peace entered our house"

Jennie Stein Berman   137
"You should always be together"

Leonard Ratner   138
"Don't forget your seats at Park Synagogue"

Harold   139
"Be forever vigilant for those in need"

Randee Rosenberg Friedman   141
"Open your hearts and your homes"

Rosie Rosenzweig   144
"Your good character will earn you your way"

William Joseph Adelson   147
"What I consider really important"

Hayyim and Esther Kieval   150
"We have both loved the United States"

Nitzah Marsha Jospe   152
"What is important is to make each day good"

William Lewis Abramowitz   156
"Ritual is only a tool to remind us who we are"

Marcia Lawson   159
"As Jews within the human family"

Sam Levenson   161
"I leave you ... some four-letter words for all occasions"

Richard J. Israel   163
"With a love that has been well seasoned"

Rabbi Herbert A. Friedman   175
"From Vilna to Connecticut to Jerusalem"

Stanley J. Garfein   183
"Finish your final business"

Rabbi Monroe Levens   193
"Life here is a great and wonderful adventure"

PART FIVE

Three Wills from Classics of Modern Jewish Literature   195

Zvi Kolitz   197
Yossel Rakover Speaks to God

Y. L. Peretz   203
Four Generations—Four Wills

Avraham Sutzkever   208
The Will of Nissim Laniado

PART SIX

A Guide to Writing Your Own Ethical Will   213

Topical Index   221
Credits   222
Notes   225

Foreword

Each of us is several people over the course of our lifetime. We all start out as someone's child. Then we grow up to be someone's friend and classmate, someone's serious romantic partner, and then someone's husband or wife, leading in the normal course of events to becoming someone's father or mother, and perhaps someone's grandparent. At each of these stages, we learn something—usually several important somethings—about life, and at each of these stages, we come to realize that what we previously believed may have been incorrect, or at least seriously flawed. By the time we approach the last stages of our lives, we have gathered all those life-lessons, including the errors we have outgrown and the mistakes we are embarrassed to recall, under the rubric of "wisdom."

By the time we come to realize that the years ahead are far fewer than the years we have already lived we confront the discouraging truth that, unless we do something about it, all that hard-won wisdom will disappear with us when we die. So, over time, the custom arose of composing an ethical will, bequeathing our wisdom to our descendants even as we bequeath to them our hard-earned material assets.

It is probably too much to hope that our children will avoid the mistakes that we made and tried to warn them about, but at least we can assure them that those mistakes of youth and impatience are survivable. More importantly, we can point them to what we found to be of lasting value. All of this has to be done carefully, lest we convey an impression of "nagging from the grave," of wishing not only to enlighten but to control. A lot will depend on your having had a good relationship with the next generation during your years together.

But done right, an ethical will can be seen as a gift of love, a way of saying "this is what I found gave me satisfaction and gave my life meaning. It animated my relationship to you and to your mother (or father). May it do the same for you. I send this to you with much love."

Rabbi Harold S. Kushner

Preface

The tradition of bequeathing a spiritual legacy either in the form of a codicil to a conventional will or as a separate document has its roots in the Bible and the Talmud. The biblical and talmudic examples, however, are invariably shown to have been conveyed orally while later generations committed their ethical wills to writing. As a result of this practice, numerous examples of *tzavaot* (wills, instructions) of the medieval and Renaissance periods have been preserved. Some of the older ethical wills possess a high literary quality. Others that are not noteworthy in form are exquisite in their content.

But literary integrity was not primary in the intentions of the writers of ethical wills. Deeply cherished was the desire to bequeath to their descendants an instructive account of the ideals and *midot* (traits, measures of refinement) closest to their hearts. They sought to write and transmit not philosophical treatises but personal reflections on their lives as Jews and on the motivating values and events in their life's experience. They hoped to impart the precepts of God's Law refracted through the prism of a parent's life. While the writing of ethical wills is not unknown to the Christian tradition, this volume is devoted exclusively to Jewish ethical wills.

As with material possessions, parents often conveyed the ethical inheritance during their lifetimes. In this context, an ethical testament may be referred to as an *iggeret* (letter, missive). The term is thus used in the present volume. Many ethical wills are thought to have been conveyed during the lifetimes of their authors. Clearly these are ultimately identical to those conveyed posthumously and may be so regarded for all purposes; they too speak from "beyond the grave" and become *tzavaot* upon the death of the writer. The intentions are certainly identical and for these reasons no distinction is made between *igrot* (plural of *iggeret*) and *tzavaot* in this collection.

The first collection of ethical wills, *Hebrew Ethical Wills*, was published in America by the British scholar Israel Abrahams.[1] The present collection differs from the pioneer work of Professor Abrahams in several respects. A major distinction lies in the intent of the authors of this anthology: to compile a representative sample of the ethical wills literature of the modern period. Thus this collection contains wills by rabbis and prominent leaders as well as those of unknown or relatively obscure individuals. Further, the wills in this collection are drawn entirely from the modern period (i.e. post–French Revolution); the Abrahams work closes with the will of R. Joel ben Avraham Shemaria, published in 1799 or 1800.

The ethical wills presented here fall under five headings: traditional testaments, wills from the Holocaust, from Israel, by contemporary American Jews, and wills from classics of modern Jewish literature. The reader will quickly discover that the difference in historical time frames and the events they brought produces significant additions and changes in the concerns expressed by the writers of ethical wills, and in the languages used as well. Wills of the modern period are written in the vernacular more often than in Hebrew, notably Yiddish, German, and English. Last but no means least, women in the modern period have begun to make contributions that deserve to be treasured as part of Jewish ethical wills literature.

Several points need to be made about the rabbinical ethical wills in this collection. Whether in the form of *hanhagot*—rules for daily ritual and ethical conduct—or as essays on ethical behavior woven about a mosaic of biblical and talmudic passages, rabbinical wills are not written for the families of the writers alone. The rabbis' commitments extend beyond their immediate family circles, and most often are not limited even to the extended family of the congregation. Rabbis and bnei Torah, scholars whose lives are devoted to the sacred lore and its observance, often speak to all the Congregation of the Children of Israel in all generations. Hence their testaments include, in addition to messages directed to their own kindred, ethical insights addressed to Jews everywhere. As rabbinical wills tend to be lengthy (the complete will of Reb Shmuel Tefilinsky contains forty-five pages), meaningful selections from their contents often tend to be lengthy. The authors have not hesitated to present these longer selections where necessary to preserve the structure of *tzavaot* that are classic examples of the genre.

When I began teaching a course entitled "Jewish Ethical Wills" at Spertus College, Chicago, more than two decades ago, it was one course in the Jewish philosophy sequence. The ethical wills read and analyzed were traditional and rabbinic in the main. Gradually, as the result of research, (and an "Author's Query" in the *New York Times* book section), a full range of masterpieces, large and small, of this burgeoning genre came to light. With heightened appreciation for the depth and scope of the ethical wills literature of the recent past and the immediate present, I originally approached the publishers of the first edition of this book with a manuscript. It was the publishers who then introduced us, Rabbi Jack Riemer and me, to each other. We learned then of our mutual respect and love for this beautiful Jewish custom and its literature.

This relationship has been developed further with the publication of this revised edition by Jewish Lights, whose publishers suggested to us further enhancements, many of which we had thought about previously, to make the book even more desirable and useful. We have had the opportunity to add much material to the book since it was first published: a major new introduction explaining the value and importance of writing ethical wills today; over thirty new wills of significant merit and interest; and, most important of all, a major section on how to write your own ethical will—a step-by-step guide. This section, along with the addition of a topical index, makes the original "treasury" of wills into a "treasure" that is useful and easily used by its readers.

Today, I feel every ethical will I encounter or receive to be a part of my own spiritual legacy. I thrill with the recipients as they press to their hearts the beloved letters from loved ones. Each time this occurs, I am doubly moved by the wisdom of our tradition that clothes a human impulse in the sacred garments of mitzvah, and by the power vested in each of us to bestow such blessings on our future generations.

Dr. Nathaniel Stampfer

Acknowledgments

Deep gratitude is expressed to the late Rabbi Dr. David Graubart for suggestions and comments about the traditional materials in this volume; to Marcia Lawson for careful reading of the text and for preparing the topical index; to Richard Tennes for his helpful suggestions regarding special papers and inks in the preparation of ethical wills; to the Kohl Education Foundation and the Kohl Jewish Teacher Center of Wilmette, Illinois, especially to Mrs. Dolores Kohl Solovy, founder and chairman of the board, and to her staff for pioneering efforts in bringing the concept and process of ethical wills to a wide public through the workshop "Generation to Generation" to parents and children in synagogues throughout the Chicago metropolitan area and elsewhere in the Midwest; to Rabbi Gedaliah Dov Schwartz, Av Beth Din (head of the rabbinic court) of the Chicago Rabbinical Council, for his guidance regarding some of the sources cited in the will dealing with organ transplantation; to the research staff of the Norman and Helen Asher Library at Spertus College of Judaica; to the Yiddish seminar members at Spertus College for valued assistance in reviewing the Yiddish translations for this volume; and to all those who shared the ethical wills in their possession with a wide and interested public through publication here.

Introduction to the Revised Edition

Most writers would kill to find a great publisher. But Nathaniel Stampfer, now of blessed memory, and I have had a different experience. First, Theodore Schocken, who was the scion of a noble publishing house whose branches have had an enormous effect on Jewish life, first in Germany and then in Israel and America, called us out of the blue and asked us to do a book of ethical wills. He reached out to us because of an article we had written on the subject that he had seen in *Hadassah Magazine*. Then some years later, after the book had a very respectable run in its first edition, we were contacted by Stuart M. Matlins, who was just starting Jewish Lights at the time and who has since become one of the major figures in the world of Jewish publishing. He asked us to do a revised and expanded edition geared to the needs of a new generation. And now Jewish Lights is printing a third edition, guided by Emily Wichland, who as vice president of editorial and production at Jewish Lights has helped bring many important books into being.

Most books do not enjoy three lives, and I have wondered why this one has. This is my explanation: this book and the subject of ethical wills struck a chord in the hearts of two generations, and it is positioned to do the same for a third generation as well.

What are these chords?

In the 1980s, a generation of American Jews was concerned that their children would not know, except from books, what the Holocaust meant or how Israel came into being. They had a sense of responsibility for the Jewish past that was expressed most eloquently by twentieth-century Jewish theologian Rabbi Abraham Joshua Heschel, when he wrote, "we will either be the last of the Jews or else we will be those who will hand over the heritage we have received to those who come after us."[1] This generation responded to the first edition of this book because they wanted their children to learn from those who had lived through the Holocaust and those who had laid the foundation of the State of Israel.

Then at the turn of the millennium, a new generation arose who wanted their children to be a part of—and yet to be apart from—the rest of American society. This was the challenge that drew them to reading and writing ethical wills: they wanted to teach their children who they were and what they stood for, and what they wanted their children and their grandchildren to care about and to continue after they were gone. It was Stuart M. Matlins who insisted on including in that second edition a step-by-step guide to writing an ethical will so that readers would not only have the ethical wills of their ancestors to transmit to their descendants but also have some guidance on how to write their own messages to their loved ones.

Now American Judaism has a third generation who feels the need for this book. We live in an age in which there is enormous diversity in the Jewish family. It is now not uncommon to find children from the former Soviet Union or the Far East who have been adopted by Jewish parents and who go to Jewish schools. Families have fewer children, people marry at a later age, they intermarry, or they don't marry at all. But while the makeup of the family may have changed, the questions that keep many of us awake at night are the same:

- Who are we and who will we be in the memories of those that come after us?
- What are the values that give meaning to our lives and how shall we convey these values to a generation who will not share our nostalgia?
- What will they remember of us and what will they know of the values that shaped our lives?
- Will our values be cherished or will they disappear when we do?

So we offer this book to a third generation who needs it at least as much as the previous two generations did. For the first generation of its readers, this book was a gateway into the world of our ancestors. It showed its readers how the pious among our people held on to their faith despite the Holocaust. It taught them how some of these brave souls sent messages to their children who were fortunate enough to live on the other side of the walls of the hell within which their parents were confined, asking them to be Jews and to be human beings despite what their parents were going through. For the second generation, for whose children Israel was a place to visit on Birthright, on vacation, or during a gap year, this book became the way to explain to them what the Land meant to those pioneers who created it by their own sweat and struggle. For this new, third generation, this book is a way for North American Jews living through a major transition in the Jewish community to influence sociological trends in a positive direction. They are struggling to keep their children involved in Jewish life—both religious and secular—and to see Israel as an important component of their Jewish identity. Parents and children are asking themselves:

- Why be Jewish?
- Why support Israel?
- Why become involved (or stay involved) in the Jewish community?

For this generation, at a critical time for American Judaism, ethical wills are an opportunity to answer these questions.

This edition begins a third life, in which it will strive to be the voice through which a new generation of parents can convey the innermost truths of their existence to those who will live on beyond us. May it succeed a third time.

Rabbi Jack Riemer

What I Have Learned Since I Began Collecting Ethical Wills

For the last few years I have taught classes in synagogues and churches, in schools and hospices, in colleges and high schools in how to read and how to write ethical wills. In the process I have learned at least as much as I have taught. Here are some of the lessons that I have learned.

I have learned that many people have ethical wills in their possession, many more than I originally thought. I was on the *Today Show*, talking about this custom. And for the two weeks after the broadcast, I was inundated with letters from all over the country, from people who wanted to tell me that they had ethical wills in their possession that they had received from their parents. Many of them told me that they had not known that this was a Jewish tradition or even that it had a name, but they all said that they treasured these wills and took them out and reread them often.

I have learned that when you write such a will you learn a great deal about yourself in the process. I met one man who said to me: "I tried to write a letter to my family and found that I couldn't because we aren't really a family. We have so little to do with each other. So I had to write three separate letters, one to my wife and one to each of my children. That is a pretty sad thing to realize about yourself and your family," he said, "but I guess it is better to learn it now while you can still do something about it than it is to learn later when it is too late."

One family told me that the parents decided that instead of leaving a letter behind to be opened up afterwards, they would read the letter to their children while they were still alive. The children who heard the letter told their parents that they were surprised to find out that some of the things in it were of such great importance to their parents, and the parents replied that they were surprised to find that the children did not know how strongly they felt about these things. The experience brought them closer together and led to a much better understanding between them. Things that the parents thought they had said had never really been communicated to the children, and the children felt as if their parents had expected them to be mind readers, instead of saying what was on their minds and in their hearts.

I have met some rabbis who teach their confirmation classes how to write wills and who encourage the parents to write them to their teenage children. Then they meet and compare what they have written. One rabbi I know asks the children in his confirmation class to do an exercise in which they try to write down what they think their parents would say to them if they were writing an ethical will, and then they compare what they think their parents would say to them with what the parents actually write. Sometimes it is surprising to see how far off the children are in guessing what their parents would say. And I know one rabbi who takes these ethical wills that her students have written at the age of sixteen and puts them away in a safe deposit box. She gives them back to their authors ten years later, so that they can see how much they have grown and how they have changed during the decade.

I have learned that if we don't tell our children our stories and the stories of those from whom we come, no one else ever will. The stories will disappear and our kids will be deprived. I have learned this truth from the meetings that I have with the children in my synagogue who are going to be Bar or Bat Mitzvah. One of the questions that I always ask them is: What is your Hebrew name? They all know. Then I ask them: What is your father's Hebrew name? Most know. Then I ask them: What is your mother's Hebrew name? Less know. Then I ask them: Who are you named for? They have some vague idea that it was for great uncle so-and-so or for great aunt such-and-such. And then I ask them: *What was that person like? What qualities did that person have that were so important that your parents saw fit to name you for him or her?* Hardly any of them know the answer to that question. And so their first homework assignment from me is to go home and interview their parents and anyone else they can find who knew that person, so that they can find out who he or she was, what he or she stood for and lived through, and what it means to be named for them.

Can you imagine what a precious gift it would have been if those people had left behind a sound recording or video or a letter in which they had told this not-yet-born-namesake something about their lives? I suppose that it is wiser to do this autobiography on paper instead of in a recording, because we can't know how the technology of the future will change. It may be that our current recording devices will be as outdated in the next generation as reel-to-reel cassettes or 78 rpm records are today, but words that are written on paper, if it is acid-free paper and if they are written in a clear hand and with the right ink, will probably still be decipherable a century from now.

I have learned that an ethical will can do harm as well as good. If it becomes a desire to control instead of to teach, if it becomes "a grudge from the grave," then it can cripple the recipient and destroy his capacity to live a good life. There is one ethical will, perhaps the most famous of all, that I think falls into this category. It is the will that was written by Judah ibn Tibbon to his son, Samuel, sometime in the twelfth century.

The will is well known because of the famous line that it contains about books. He writes: "Let books be your companions; let book-cases and shelves be your pleasure grounds and gardens. Bask in their paradise, gather their fruit, pluck their roses, enjoy their spices and their myrrh. If your soul be sated and weary, change from garden to garden, from furrow to furrow, from prospect to prospect."

Everyone knows this passage. It is seen on posters for Jewish Book Month every year. It is quoted in hundreds of sermons. But what most people do not know is that this is only one passage from the will. The will itself runs to over fifty pages! And with the exception of this passage, most of it is full of rebukes and chastisements and laments and self-pity. The father tells his son at great length just how much he has done for him, how hard he has worked for him, how nobly he has sacrificed for him, and how much aggravation the son has given him in return. He goes on for page after page after page after page, rebuking his son for neglecting his studies, for having bad penmanship, for not writing Arabic more elegantly, etc. And he ends by asking his son to read this will twice a day for the rest of his life!

You would think that a child who received a will like this would grow up to be rebellious, resentful, or spiritually crippled. Surely that is what all the experts in child upbringing would predict. And yet, this child grew up—I can't explain how—to be a gifted translator like his father, a skilled physician like his father. So much for all the educational theories!

I have learned that ethical wills have the power to make people confront the ultimate choices that they must make in their lives. They can make people who are usually too preoccupied with earning a living stop and consider what they are living for. There is one will that I often read, especially when I am speaking to powerful and prosperous people. It is a work of fiction, but it speaks with such authenticity that I have seen it stir many a listener into making an accounting of what she is doing with her days. This is the will.[1]

Dear Willie,

By the time you read this letter, I think I will be dead.

I am sorry to startle you, but I suppose there is no pleasant way to break such news. The trouble I've been having is due to a rather vicious disorder, malignant melanoma. The prognosis is 100 percent bad. I have known about my condition for a long time, and figured that I would probably die this summer, but the body has begun to go a bit sooner. I suppose I should be in a hospital at this moment, but I hate to spoil your departure. And since there is no hope anyway, I have postponed it. I am going to try to stall until I know you have left San Francisco. Your mother doesn't know anything yet. My guess is that I won't last more than three or four weeks now.

I am a little too young to go, according to the insurance tables, and I must say I don't feel ready, but I dare say that that is because I have accomplished so little. I look back on my life, Willie, *and there's not much there.*

Your mother has been a fine wife, and I have no regrets on that score, but I seem to have led such a thoroughly second-rate life, not only compared to my father, but in view of my own capabilities.

I had a feeling for research. When I fell in love with your mother, I thought I couldn't marry unless I undertook general practice in a high-income community. It was my plan to make a pile in ten or fifteen years of such work, and then go back to research. I really think I might have done something in cancer research. I had a theory, a notion, you might say, nothing I could put down on paper. It needed three years of systematic investigation. Nobody has touched it to this day—I've kept up with the literature. My name might have meant as much as my father's, but now there's no time even to outline the procedure. The worst of it is, that I now feel your mother would have stood by me and lived modestly, if I had only asked her.

But I've had a pleasant time, I can truthfully say that. I've loved reading and golf, and I've had all of that that I wanted. The days have gone by all too fast.

I wish I might have met this girl of yours. It seems to me that she, or the Navy, or both, are having quite a good effect on you. And believe me, Willie, that is by far the brightest thought I take with me into the hospital.

I've let slide my relationship with you, as I have so many other things, through plain sloth; particularly since your mother seemed anxious to take charge of you. It is too bad that we had no more children. Just bad luck. Your mother had three miscarriages, which you may not know about.

I'll tell you a curious thing. It seems to me that I have a higher opinion of you than your mother has. She regards you as a helpless baby who will have to be coddled through life. But I am coming to believe that though you are spoiled and soft at the surface, you are tough enough at the core. After all, I see that you have always done pretty much as you pleased with your mother, while giving her the idea she was ruling you. I'm sure this was no plan on your part, but you have done it anyway.

You have never had a serious problem in your life, up to this Navy experience. I watched you in the forty-eight demerits business very closely. It had its silly side, but it really was a challenge. You rose to it in an encouraging way.

Perhaps, because I know that I'll never see you again, I find myself sentimentalizing over you, Willie. It seems to me that you are very much like our country—young, naive, spoiled, softened by abundance and good luck—but with an interior hardness that comes from sound stock. This country of ours consists of pioneers. After all, these new Poles and Italians and Jews, as well as the older stock, were all people who had the gumption to get up and go, and make themselves better lives in a new world. You're going to run into a lot of strange men in the Navy, some of them pretty low, by your standards. I dare say, though I won't live to see it, that they are going to make the best navy the world has ever seen. And I think you're going to make a good naval officer too, after a while. Perhaps after a great while, but you will.

This is not criticism, Willie. God knows, I am pretty soft myself. Perhaps I'm wrong, you may never make a naval officer at all, and we may lose the war. But I don't believe that. I think we are going to win, and I think you are going to come back with more honor than you believed possible.

I know you're disappointed at having been sent to a ship like this one. Now, having seen it, you're probably disgusted. Well, remember this: you've had things your own way too long, and all of your immaturity is due to that. You need some stone walls to batter yourself against. I strongly suspect that you'll find plenty of them there on board that ship. I don't envy you the experience itself, but I do envy you the strengthening you're going to derive from it. Had I had such experiences in my younger years, I might not be dying a failure.

These are strong words, but I won't cross them out. They don't hurt too much, and besides, my hand is not the one to cross them out anymore. I'm finished now, but the last words of my life rest with you. If you turn out well, I can still claim some kind of success in the afterworld, if there is one.

About your singing versus comparative literature—you may have a different outlook when the war is over. Don't waste brain power now over the far future. Concentrate on doing well now. Whatever assignment they give you on the ship, remember that it's worth your best efforts. It is your way of fighting the war.

It's surprising how little I have to say to you in these last words. I ought to fill up a dozen more sheets, and yet I feel you are pretty good at getting your way, and in other matters, any words I might write would make little sense, without your own experience to fill them with meaning. Remember this, if you can:—*THERE'S NOTHING, NOTHING, NOTHING MORE PRECIOUS THAN TIME.* You probably feel you have a measureless supply of it, but you haven't. Wasted hours destroy your life just as surely at the beginning as at the end, only at the end it's more obvious. Use your time while you have it, Willie. Use it to make something of yourself.

Religion: I'm afraid we haven't given you much, not having much ourselves. But I think after all I will mail you a Bible, before I go into the hospital. There is a lot of dry stuff in the Bible, stuff about wars and rituals that may put you off, but don't make the mistake of skipping the Old Testament. It is the core of *all* religions, I think, and there's a lot of everyday wisdom in it. You have to be able to recognize it. That takes time. Meantime, get familiar with the words; you won't regret it. I came to the Bible, as I did to everything in life, too late.

About money matters: I'm leaving all my property to your mother. Uncle Lloyd is the executor. There is a ten-thousand-dollar policy of which you're the beneficiary. If you want to get married, or go back to school, that should be enough to enable you to carry out your plans. Money is a very pleasant thing, Willie, and I think you can trade almost everything for it—except the work you really want to do. If you sell out your time for a comfortable life, and give up your natural work, I think you lose in the exchange. There remains an inner uneasiness that spoils the comfort.

Well, Willie, it's 3:00 A.M. by my old desk clock. A waning moon is shining through the library window, and my fingers are stiff from writing. So it is sleeping pills and bed for me now. Thank God for barbiturates.

Take care of your mother, if she lives to be very old. And be kind to her if you come back from the war with enough strength to break away from her. She has many faults, but she is good, and she has loved you, and me, very truly.

Think of me, and of what I might have been, Willie, at the times in your life when you come to a crossroads. For my sake, for the sake of the father who took the wrong turn, take the right one. And carry my blessing and my justification with you.

I stretch out my hand to you. We haven't kissed in many years. I used to like to kiss you when you were a baby. You were such a sweet good-natured child, with wonderful large eyes. God! Long ago!

Good-bye, my son. Be a man.

Dad

One of the things that I have learned is that you do not have to be a professional writer in order to prepare an ethical will. "Words that come from the heart enter the heart," and so some of the most moving wills that I know come from plain ordinary people. For example, one of my favorite ethical wills is this one which was written by Rose Weiss Baygel, who came to Cleveland from Riga as a small child. She had little formal education and worked in a sweat shop in her teens. She walked a picket line in the early years when the Garment Workers Union was being formed. She married Sam Baygel, also an immigrant, and together they worked unceasingly to raise and educate their three children.

She left behind an ethical will, written on plain ordinary tablet paper. It has spelling mistakes and grammatical mistakes, but they don't really matter: the point gets through. I reproduce it here exactly as she wrote it:

My dear children:

I am writing this in the bank. This is what I want from you children: Evalyn, Bernice and Allen to be to one another— good sisters and brother. Daddy and I love the three of you very much, and we did our best raising you and gave you the best education we could afford. Be good to each other. Help one another if "God forbid" in need. This is my wish.

Love all of you,
Your mother

"Daddy" had been dead some time already when she wrote this will, and yet she speaks of him in the present tense. That may be because she did not know grammar well, or it may be because to her he was still alive. She was not able to acquire much formal education herself, but she made sure that her children did. And she was concerned about only one thing in her last letter—that her children get along. She had seen examples of children who fought with each other in court over the estate, and she did not want that to happen to her children. Children who get a last request like this one—"to love one another and to help each other"—are not likely to end up fighting with each other in court.

Why don't more people write ethical wills nowadays? Many do, of course, but why don't more people keep this tradition? I think that there are at least three reasons.

One is that in order to write an ethical will, one must come to terms with one's own mortality. If you think that you are going to live forever, you need not write one. The trouble is that everyone understands in their minds, but no one really believes in their gut, that they are mortal, and so it is hard for us to contemplate a time when we will no longer be.

Judaism is not a morbid religion, but it is a realistic religion. So Jews would buy plots and prepare their shrouds and write their ethical wills just in case, just so as to be ready. They lived with their emotional bags packed. They understood that death is a constant companion and possibility within life, that we live all our days in the shadow of death. We moderns use a host of different devices by which we try to deceive ourselves about the coming of old age and the inevitability of death. Dr. Heschel once said that in our society it is less rude to ask a person about his income or about the intimate details of his sex life than it is to ask his age. We have a multi-million-dollar industry devoted to helping us cover up the signs of aging. We have memorial gardens instead of cemeteries. We have rouge and makeup with which we paint the dead, and we have many other techniques by which we try to deny the reality of death—futile ways in which we try to deceive ourselves.

There is a story told about a tourist who came from America to visit the renowned scholar and saint who was known as the Chafetz Chaim. He came in, and he saw a bed, a chair, a table, a cupboard, a closet, and a bookcase. The tourist was shocked, and asked the sage:

"Where are your possessions?"

The Chafetz Chaim replied: "And where are *your* possessions?"

The tourist said: "What kind of a question is that? I'm a visitor here."

The sage replied: "I am too."

Jews lived with the awareness that we are all strangers and sojourners on this earth, we are all visitors here. This is one of the reasons why they were able to write ethical wills, while we find it difficult to do so.

There is a second reason why we have trouble writing an ethical will. We live in a relativistic culture. Everything is a matter of opinion. You are entitled to your opinion, and I am entitled to mine. I have no right to impose my values on you, and you have no right to impose your values on me. I may happen to like carrots and you not. You may happen to be in favor of abortion rights and I not. You may like being a cannibal and I may not—but each of us is entitled to our own opinion. If this is the way you feel, then you have no convictions, and therefore you cannot write an ethical will in which you share your convictions with those who come after you.

The mentality that says that everything is a matter of opinion, and that all opinions have equal value, has to have some limits. If the teacher asks the class: "Who was the first president of the United States?" you cannot say: "Let's vote on it." Some things are simply not up for voting. They are either right or wrong.

In Judaism, some things are right and some things are wrong, and to be a Jew is to know some truths, to affirm them and care about them so passionately that you want to persuade those whom you love to affirm them too. We do not want to cripple our heirs by imposing a burden of guilt. We do not want to impose our beliefs and values upon them by threats or by manipulating their emotions. That would be wrong. But we do want a vote, if not a veto, in their lives. We want the chance to convey to them, in words as well as by our deeds, who we are and what we stand for and what are the things that mean the most to us. To do this is our right as parents, and our duty too.

There is one more reason why ethical wills are not as widely known in our time as they should be, and that is because all of Judaism is so little known and understood in our time. This truth came home to me in an extraordinary experience that I had when my first book on this subject came out. The congregation that I served was kind enough to have a reception in honor of the event, and there was some publicity about it in the local newspapers. An hour before the dedication party was to begin, a man came knocking at my door, obviously distraught. He introduced himself to me this way:

"I am a therapist. And I make use of this very technique of having people sum up their innermost values and their convictions by writing a letter. I use it in my work with terminally ill patients and in my counseling with married couples. Why didn't anyone ever tell me that this was a part of Judaism *BACK WHEN I WAS JEWISH?*"

That therapist's question has haunted me ever since I heard it. This man did not really reject Judaism—*he never had it to reject!* He may have had a smattering of Jewish education at a child's level, but he was never really exposed to it in any serious or substantive way as a grown-up. As Dr. Heschel used to lament: "Judaism is one of the world's least known religions," and the question this therapist asked me is proof of that.

These are, in my judgment, the three main reasons why many people are reluctant to write ethical wills. To do so requires coming to terms with one's own mortality. It requires having clear convictions that you really believe in deeply. And it requires some knowledge of the Jewish tradition.

Writing an ethical will is not an easy thing to do for these reasons and for many more, and yet I would urge you try it. The examples in this book prove that one need not be a professional writer in order to write one. Many of these wills come from plain, ordinary fathers and mothers, and yet they touch the hearts of all who read them. And so I suggest that you read these wills, and then that you try your hand at writing one of your own. If you do, you will leave a gift to the future, and the not-yet-born children of your children's children will thank you and bless you for it.

Rabbi Jack Riemer

Part One
Traditional Wills

The designation of the wills in the following section as "traditional" does not imply uniformity in form or content, as even a cursory reading reveals. The unifying element is their focus on the traditional precepts and values of Judaism, including Torah study, observance of rituals and the socioethical precepts, and striving for perfection by developing the virtues exemplified in the lives of biblical and historic Jewish personalities and through imitation of the Divine Attributes. The exhortations toward these values, however, take various forms—letters to loved ones (*igrot*), rules for the daily conduct of the pious (*hanhagot*), elaborate suggestions for ideal methods of study, and others. A unifying geographic thread appears to prevail in that most of the wills in this section were written by Jews in Europe.

Solomon Kluger

Rabbi Solomon Kluger (1785–1869), one of the most gifted talmudists and halakhists of the modern era, was the rabbi of Brody for nearly fifty years. Brody (also Brod) was a substantial city and a Jewish center on the border between Russia and Austrian Galicia. During the 1880s it was the transfer point for Jews seeking to settle in the West, much like Vienna a century later for Soviet Jews emigrating westward. Rabbi Kluger's career coincided with decades of intense activity of the Haskalah (Enlightenment) Movement. His strong support of tradition against changes sought by proponents of *haskalah* is reflected in the sections of his will translated here. As a youth, following the death of his father, rabbi of Komarov, he studied in Zamosc under Rabbi Jacob Kranz, the renowned Maggid of Dubno. Rabbi Kluger, known also by the mnemonic Maharshak, was a remarkably prolific author—his known writings include 175 works in addition to hundreds of responsa. The younger son, Abraham Benjamin, mentioned in the first addendum to the following will, succeeded his father as rabbi of Brody. The provision for the ritual of stoning described in the final codicil is uncommon but not unique in the ethical wills literature.

Because this year I enter my Jubilee [fiftieth] Year, I have thought perhaps the Almighty will cleanse me of my transgressions through His love and mercy and not through suffering; by His mercies let Him purify me as I was at birth, and thus restore my soul to its pristine inheritance, as Scripture states, "In this year of jubilee ye shall return every man unto his possession" (Lev. 25:13). Who knows whether I shall be clear-minded when my time comes and responsible for my actions. I have decided, therefore, to plan my journey now. "The preparations of the heart are man's, but the answer of the tongue is from the Lord" (Prov. 16:1).

Let me begin by discussing how to prepare "provisions for the journey,"[1] may the Almighty in His kindness guide me toward good.

When those who stand near me sense that the departure of my soul is imminent, let them assemble ten pious men, and let them prevent anyone, including my wife and children, from approaching my bed closer than four cubits.

Afterward, remove my body directly onto the earth, if I am near bare earth at the time. But if there is a wooden or stone floor, let them bring earth from somewhere (preferably from the synagogue courtyard or from the house of study, or another clean, pure place nearby) and sprinkle it on the floor. Then place my body directly on the earth with nothing intervening.

Take two books of mine that I wrote with the skills with which God endowed me, whichever two chance first to come to hand. Open them, place them face down, one over my heart and one on my head, covering my eyes and forehead. Then cover over everything the same as is customarily done for everyone.

For the time of *teharah* [ritual cleansing of the body] I shall consider it a true kindness if those who perform it go first to the mikvah [ritual pool]. After the *teharah*, let them try to obtain some earth from Eretz Yisrael [the Land of Israel]. Perhaps God will enable me to prepare some for myself by then. If not, let them seek some. First let them place some on the sign of the sacred covenant; if any remains, let them sprinkle some on my heart; if some remains, place some on my eyes; then if any is left, sprinkle it on my forehead, on the place of the tefillin [phylacteries]. If, God forbid, they cannot find any earth from Eretz Yisrael, let them take earth from the floor of the synagogue and put it on the above places, and let them recite: "May it be Thy will, O Lord our God, that this may serve in place of earth from the Holy Land to atone for this person, Shlomo Ya'akov Yosef ben Yehuda." It would be good if this earth is from the place in the synagogue where the reader stands.

Before removing me outdoors, announce a prohibition forbidding my wife and child from accompanying me to my grave and against their approaching closer than four cubits to my grave during the first twelve months. Afterward, this prohibition is nullified. I hereby instruct my wife and son to observe the above in keeping with the rules of reverence for parents and under the most stringent injunction.

When they have taken me outside, announce that I gave instructions before my death to ask forgiveness from all against whom I may have erred, in word or deed, whether in the course of rendering judgments or in business affairs; and if I aggravated anyone in any way, I ask them to forgive and pardon me. Then let each one say quietly that he forgives me for everything. And I do the same regarding them.

As for a eulogy, I do not restrain anyone from the mitzvah [divine commandment, or any worthy deed] of eulogizing who may be moved to do so. But only on condition that no specific praise be said referring expressly to me. Only in a general way, mentioning some sayings of the sages and mentioning the great merit of speaking about and weeping over the death of a worthy human being. But avoid mentioning me directly in connection with words of praise or worthiness. Just say, "This man served the public for many years, and now it is fitting that we perform these services for him," and "We beseech the Almighty in his behalf to forgive his transgressions and set him on the path of goodness and life."

Now you, my comrade, my son, of you I request that you recite the Kaddish for me with great devotion and deliberation. Make every effort to serve as reader morning and evening in the synagogue, pray with devotion, and be sure to study a regular lesson in Mishnah or Gemara, then to recite the "Yehi Ratzon" for the uplift of my soul, as it is printed in the prayerbooks; then recite the Rabbis' Kaddish with deliberation and heartfelt devotion.

Be very careful to honor your mother, and certainly never to irritate her, as the Torah requires of you. And likewise teach your wife to honor your mother.

Seek also to honor me after my death in every way possible, and for Heaven's sake, tread the paths of righteousness, be God-fearing, depart from evil, and do good [Pss. 34:15, 37:27].

Do not be among those erring moderns, neither of this extreme group or another; just walk in the path of moderation, the way of our fathers.

But in one thing put forth great effort—do not depart from the Code of Religious Law—right or left; then will you prosper and succeed, and merit seeing your children and your children's children engaged in Torah pursuits.

Let your heart be perfect with the Almighty; do not engage in philosophical probings, but recite daily the Thirteen Principles with utmost devotion, and thereby will you be strengthened and not falter; you will know that the ways of God are beyond us, and that all is created by Him, blessed be He, so it is not for man to investigate His deeds. So do not be envious of this group or the other that pursue such a course with apparent success, for so it is foreordained, that before the coming of the Redeemer, falsehood is allowed to triumph just prior to its final extinction, the same as a candle flame flares brightest just before it goes out. All this is a true test for those who stand firm in their faith in God and in the principles of His Torah.

Do not turn aside right or left for the sake of illusory success. Give heed to all these matters about which I instruct you briefly here, because it is impossible to elaborate it fully in writing.

May the Lord be your help to guide you in paths straight and good in His eyes; and may you live to one hundred twenty years and live to see the Redeemer soon and in our day. Amen.

On my tombstone let no virtues be inscribed, nor any titles, only:

> Here lies our teacher, Rabbi Shlomo, judge in the community of Brody, son of the Light of the Exile, our saintly teacher Rabbi Judah, his memory for eternal life, judge in Komarov.

Do not inscribe "righteous judge" because God alone knows whether I judged aright; therefore merely inscribe "judge." Avoid writing about virtues,[2] because what is the good of a Song of Ascents? It is the purpose of man to be an acceptable offering on God's altar. It is written too, "Neither shalt thou ascend by steps unto my altar…" (Ex. 20:23), for it is not because of praises said of him in this world that a man ascends to the altar of God, blessed be He. On the contrary, "… that thy nakedness be not uncovered thereon" (Ex. 20:23); excessive extolling here may cause more [scrutiny of] shortcomings on high. Therefore avoid mentioning in a eulogy or inscribing on a tombstone any praise of virtues; and I pray that my shortcomings may be overlooked and my transgressions covered over by His love.

These are the words of the writer, whose sighs pour forth from a breaking heart, Thursday, I Adar 4, 5594 [February 14, 1834], in Brody.

This ends the text of the original will of Rabbi Kluger. Codicils were added to the original in 1848 and 1852 of which the following are excerpts. A third codicil, added in 1854, deals with material bequests and is not represented here.

Added in 5608 (1848)

I have already written a will, with God's help, in 1834. But conditions have changed, since my first wife has died and I have since remarried. Also, I have a child with her, thank God; may He enable him to attain to Torah study, to marriage, and to good deeds. For these reasons I must alter some of the material provisions enumerated there.

My books as well as my unpublished manuscripts shall be divided equally between my two sons. I beg my [elder] son Hayyim Yehuda, and enjoin him with the admonition of paternal reverence never to vex my wife nor my son, the lad Master Avraham Binyamin, and to fulfill the dictum of the sages, "'Honor thy father and thy mother' is to include the father's wife as well." Be as a father to the lad and watch over him in every way necessary, for as you know, the lad was my delight, "brought up in scarlet" [Lam. 4:5], and I cannot endure the thought of his suffering pain or distress, God forbid. And I promise my [elder] son that should I succeed in being a spokesman for him on high, I shall certainly be an advocate in his behalf.

So too do I ask of all my loved ones and my friends to be alert in every way possible in watching over the child and guiding him along the proper path and toward worthy objectives. For this may the Almighty reward them, as this is an act of true kindness.[3]

Let all other matters be carried out as explained in my original will.

Added 5613 (1852)

Sunday, Heshvan 18, 5613 [Oct. 31, 1852]

I further request that my grave be next to anyone at all, so long as it is someone known to be a thoroughly upright man and poor; and do not bury me next to a wealthy person even if he is known to be completely upright. Also, do not bury a wealthy person next to me [later] even if he is known to be upright, but only a poor man known to be upright; and attired as Jews are supposed to be;[4] and also, he should not be an enemy to me nor I to him.

I also prohibit my wife and children from approaching my grave closer than four cubits. But my grandchildren, both male and female, and my daughters-in-law are permitted to approach my grave.

Be aware that there is [prepared] a piece of rock, and it is of earth from Eretz Yisrael. See that it is crushed and placed on the organs listed in my will. But purchase some soil from Eretz Yisrael as well, because who knows which is truly from there. So put them both on, and if you mix them both together it would be better still.

I instruct my sons to recite the Kaddish in the twelfth month as well; and if it should be a leap year, then the thirteenth month as well, up until the date of the anniversary.[5]

When they remove my body [from the deathbed] to place me on the earth, let them throw me down from the bed onto the ground. Then let them take a large stone and throw it on my heart, not gently but forcefully, as they recite, "Lord, full of compassion, have mercy upon this deceased; let this be accounted unto him as though he were subject to stoning by the Sanhedrin, by virtue of his intention while writing [his will] in conjunction with this present act. Let this be accounted unto him as though the Sanhedrin sentenced him to all four capital punishments [stoning, burning, slaying, strangling] for we have it on the authority of the rabbis that the punishment of stoning is the most severe. Thus may this man be purified of all his defects.[6] In the Name of the Four Letters of the Tetragrammaton, may it be His will."

Moshe Yehoshua Zelig Hakohen

Rabbi Moshe Yehoshua Zelig Hakohen (c. 1790–1855) was head of the Rabbinic Court in Ayzpute and Kuldiga, in Latvia. His will is written in the form of *hanhagot*, rules for daily conduct of the God-fearing, incorporating rituals, ethical behaviors, and commonsense guidelines for the conduct of one's secular affairs. In the eighty-nine items enumerated in this will we find the religious and secular rules intermingled and presented in no particular order. This suggests that the list of *hanhagot* was written down over a period of years, and that the writer saw no sharp distinction between sacred duties and ethical conduct. The first sixty-six of the rules appear here.

Tenth of Tevet, 5609 [January 4, 1849]

Praise unto the Creator and blessings unto Him Who creates all, Who enjoined our father Abraham to instruct his children after him that they keep the path of God. We may ask: But after that, when at the revelation of Sinai, He conveyed to us all the observances and admonitions, both the Written Law and the Oral Law which are pertinent unto the end of all time, from which there is nothing to detract and to which nothing may be added, what, then, can we say after that in instructing our children to follow the path of God, for what can we add to the Torah?

Still, I perceive it as an obligation for every individual to instruct his children, to caution them, to remind them to be alert against forgetting aught of God's will in His Torah, or these traits of the righteous:

1. To strengthen oneself to arise in the morning to the service of the Creator.
2. To cleanse the body thoroughly.
3. To recite the Torah benedictions with true devotion and to study Torah for its own sake, each according to his God-given endowments.
4. To pray with utmost devotion, as described in *Nefesh Hahayyim*, section 2, page 7.
5. To control oneself.

9

6. To be long-suffering—among the insulted, never the insulters; among those who are insulted but never respond in kind, even when it is by one's wife or household member.

7. If possible, to eat to somewhat less than full satiety.

8. Ceasing to eat while still desiring food is even more meritorious than fasting.

9. To avoid ingesting any excessive food and drink, because these excesses cause many problems, God forbid.

10. To avoid vows and oaths and all things doubtful.

11. To beware of deceit.

12. To write a will at a time when one is well and strong, in the clarity of mind, in proper order and as appropriate.

13. Prepare burial garments.

14. Avoid any sharp business transactions and whatever is contrary to the law and honesty.

15. Write down all items and subjects that require improvement either in matters of personal traits or good deeds, each according to the requirement, in order to remember it constantly and correct it with all possible speed.

16. Do not walk too straight and tall [haughtily].

17. Never worry about any worldly matter, but rather do everything in a rational way, according to the teachings of Torah.

18. Trust in God, that He will certainly do everything for your benefit—for "What is past is no more, and the future's still in store."

19. After listening to what one's fellow says, one should think through well in his own mind how to answer carefully and pleasantly ("with milk and honey") whether to answer yes or no, or to say, "I don't remember ... I don't know ... I forgot ... or give me time to recall it."

    Never answer what was not asked, but only to clarify according to the need. *Before* answering, one can still reply and say what he wants, but after he speaks the utterance is master over the speaker.

    If one does not wish to accede to the wishes of another, let him reply in a manner of utmost courtesy.

20. Write down any and all miraculous and wondrous occurrences that happen to you.

21. Avoid doing a task that is beyond your physical strength.

WIN A $100 GIFT CERTIFICATE!

Fill in this card and mail it to us—
or fill it in online at

**jewishlights.com/
feedback.html**

—to be eligible for a
$100 gift certificate for
Jewish Lights books.

JEWISH LIGHTS PUBLISHING
SUNSET FARM OFFICES RTE 4
PO BOX 237
WOODSTOCK VT 05091-0237

Fill in this card and return it to us to be eligible for our quarterly drawing for a $100 gift certificate for Jewish Lights books.

We hope that you will enjoy this book and find it useful in enriching your life.

Book title: _____

Your comments: _____

How you learned of this book: _____

If purchased: Bookseller: _____ City _____ State _____

Please send me a free JEWISH LIGHTS Publishing catalog. I am interested in: (check all that apply)

1. ☐ Spirituality
2. ☐ Mysticism/Kabbalah
3. ☐ Philosophy/Theology
4. ☐ History/Politics
5. ☐ Women's Interest
6. ☐ Environmental Interest
7. ☐ Healing/Recovery
8. ☐ Children's Books
9. ☐ Caregiving/Grieving
10. ☐ Ideas for Book Groups
11. ☐ Religious Education Resources
12. ☐ Interfaith Resources

Name (PRINT) _____

Street _____

City _____ State _____ Zip _____

E-MAIL (FOR SPECIAL OFFERS ONLY) _____

Please send a JEWISH LIGHTS Publishing catalog to my friend:

Name (PRINT) _____

Street _____

City _____ State _____ Zip _____

JEWISH LIGHTS PUBLISHING

Tel: (802) 457-4000 • Fax: (802) 457-4004

Available at better booksellers. Visit us online at www.jewishlights.com

22. Avoid a business transaction that appears difficult to complete successfully.

23. Do not pay before receiving the item of purchase: do not lend money in a questionable situation except to a poor *ben Yisrael*; lend only with a pledge [collateral], but even if he fails to repay, do not foreclose on him.

24. Avoid entering into partnerships unless absolutely necessary.

25. Remove yourself from anger and pride to the utmost possible extreme.

26. Conduct yourself in the way of modesty to the utmost extent possible, as explained by the revered Shalah [Rabbi Shlomo Halevi Horowitz], p. 7, column 2: Each person whose inclination moves him to right his ways and his deeds, let him pursue humility to perfection, accept abuse but never give any, hear himself denigrated but never react, then will the Divine Presence rest upon him immediately.

27. At home wear the plainest of garments; elsewhere, respectably, and in honor of Sabbath and festival, according to one's station, the best affordable.

28. Do not think or talk about things that may bring on the slightest conceit, even in matters of Torah.

29. Throughout the weekdays keep to a minimum eating, drinking, and use of elegant utensils.

30. Never seek after luxuries, but only for absolute necessities; except for the requirements of hospitality and the needs of religious observances.

31. Fulfill "Know Him in all your dealings" [Prov. 3:6].

32. Perform your good deeds in private when possible, in order to observe the scriptural "... and walk humbly with your God" [Mic. 6:8].

33. Revere your father and mother in every conceivable matter.

34. If there should befall some anxiety or difficult circumstance, God forbid, immediately eliminate anguish from your heart and thoughts, and think instead how insignificant this is compared to all the troubles that are possible, God forbid. For instance, having to go begging from door to door, naked and lacking in everything; having creditors while lacking even necessities; illness; being tortured with iron instruments; being sentenced to cruel flogging;

being condemned to hard labor in Siberia; having many children while the household is without food or raiment, and lacking a dwelling; and other troubles of various kinds as have befallen some of our contemporaries. And even if, God forbid, all one's days are pain-filled or, on the contrary, if one's days are passed in rejoicing and happiness and pleasant times, let him think: What is all this worth next to the delights and benefits of eternal life in the hereafter, where it is all perfect without end? Then it will be easy to tolerate all the suffering of this world, just as it is easier to suffer the various tribulations of the journey because of the serenity and rest within his own home, because all our earthly days are like unto the shadow of a bird in flight, and one hour of pleasure in the hereafter is worth an entire lifetime in this world.

35. Have faith that the Almighty, praised be He, will do all for your benefit—everything God does is only for good.

36. Arrange all matters pertaining to both social and divine relations diligently and with utmost dispatch, in keeping with our religious law.

37. Send your children to a proper tutor, one who is God-fearing, to instruct them in Torah and in good habits to age eighteen; and if beyond that, so much the better.

38. Wed your sons to wives who are daughters of Torah scholars, and give your daughters in marriage to devout Torah scholars; give them in marriage before the age of sixteen.

39. Deal faithfully.

40. Recite all benedictions with devotion.

41. Tithe the principal, then tithe the profit; and if you wish to give double, one-fifth, then may blessings overtake you.

42. Before each daily morning worship give a half-kopek to charity. It is good to keep charity money in a separate pocket so that it is available at all times for a mitzvah.

43. Do everything possible to maximize the amount of time free of all concerns, both for sacred service and for the sake of limiting worldly occupation.

44. Seclude yourself for a short period every day to contemplate the ultimate purpose of man's existence in the world, and to strive with the greatest diligence possible to be fit for the service of the Creator, praised be He.

45. Remember all the good the Creator does for us despite our vexing Him constantly; therefore we too are duty-bound to imitate His traits and act kindly even to those who vex us. But for evil do not return good, as explained in Midrash Rabba.

46. Remove yourself from anything that may lead to transgression and sin, heaven forbid.

47. Teach yourself a specific tractate or other Torah source until you know it by heart, in order to be able to study and contemplate it en route, at mealtime, in the darkness, and at work in places where it is not possible to use books. Or, at least, think always of God's name, as it is written in the *Book of the Covenant*, under Love, "… except in a place where it is prohibited to contemplate Torah subject matter."

48. Other than essential things, do not think or talk about subjects other than Torah matters, as written in *Nefesh Hayyim*, page 15, section 4, citing *Avot D'Rabbi Nathan*, "whoever keeps the words of the Torah on his heart, is exempt from ten things," etc.

49. A kilogram of bread per day and a little water are adequate for a man in good health; for raiment, linen garments or wool cloth.

50. Avoid listening to any obscene speech.

51. Keep your possessions out of sight.

52. Learn a trade that is honest and simple.

53. Do not make a halakhic ruling, even on fully familiar matters, without consulting the *Shulhan Arukh*, at least.

54. Train yourself in the habit of balance, expecting in equal amounts criticism and praise, sadness and joy, pain and pleasure. Supervise your children so they make progress in their studies; have them review what they have learned, act according to the laws of Torah and good manners. Also, oversee the members of your household and community, insofar as possible, to guide them in good and righteous paths, according to the laws of Torah.

55. If you should have a falling-out with another person, make every effort to settle it between yourselves. But if it is impossible to do so, then go before an arbitrator in good faith, without resorting to squabbles or strife, God forbid.

56. Anything we imagine to be good and proper at a given time may alter in the course of changes brought on by events. But

the statutes and judgments of the Torah, the precepts, the commandments, and the virtues in both the written and oral Law, in the Talmud, in the Midrash, in the sacred *Zohar*, and in the responsa, all these remain true and applicable, immutable eternally without change, for "... the word of the Lord is tried" [2 Sam. 22:31, Ps. 18:31], so depart not from it right or left.

57. At times when not studying Torah or performing mitzvot, read and reread all that is written here; and your eyes will discern even more than is written in it; and may God be with you.

58. Do everything according to the will of the Creator, blessed be He, and ignore the evil inclination who blinds man, showing the light as darkness and the darkness as light, diverting him from truth, devouring his days with the vanities of the times, not having any time for thought to sacred service as is fitting and right. For these reasons I have written these brief notes, small in size but of high quality, that one can review quickly and recall, and thus escape the machinations of the evil inclination.

59. Learn a little penmanship, arithmetic, language, and the outside sciences, but do not waste too much valuable time on these trifles; and even this small amount of time should be in the privacy of your home with a good tutor who is also God-fearing. In this way you avoid the slightest calumny and heretical ideas contrary to the Torah, God forbid; and restrict your review of these [outside] studies to those places where it is forbidden to think about Torah.

60. Beware of all falsehood because "He that speaketh falsehood shall not be established before mine eyes" [Ps. 101:7]. Indeed, falsehood is the greatest *kelippa*[1] of all, heaven forbid.

61. Hearken, my friends, my children, to the instruction of your father, and take pity upon me, yourselves, and your offspring—I enjoin you by the parental decree to observe and to perform all that is written and received in the Torah of Moses our teacher, of blessed memory; and just as it is obligatory for a child to obey his father during the father's lifetime, so is it obligatory *after* his death. As it is written in the *Zohar* (*Behukotai*), that a child's reverence for a parent applies both during the parent's lifetime as well as afterward. Also in Midrash Rabba, chapter 67.

You know from your youth that I have given you as many benefits as possible, so let these words be engraved in your hearts. Do not deviate from them under any circumstance, and act only in accordance with religious law; never embarrass anyone, because "he who embarrasses anyone in public loses his share in the hereafter" [Jerusalem Talmud, Tractate *Hagiga* 2:1].

Every day after my death, for the first thirty days or so, you should read this will in order to mark and perform everything in it without omission.

If you should be inclined to practice asceticism, do thus: abstain from idle talk for a day or two, according to your willpower, not allowing any idle utterance to escape your lips. This will benefit the soul more than any affliction from fasting or other afflictions, particularly in this weakened generation.

62. Don't become involved in flattery even when it seems permissible; it stupefies the feelings of a person.

63. This is a time schedule for each twenty-four-hour day:

> For midnight prayers[2]—½ hour
> Mishnah—1 hour
> Pentateuch—1 hour
> Cantillation—1 hour
> Midrash—½ hour
> Grammar—½ hour
> Eyn Ya'akov—½ hour
> Kabbala—½ hour
> Morning prayers (public worship)—1 hour
> Responsa—1 hour
> Talmud—3 hours
> Ethics—1 hour
> Research study—½ hour
> Homily—½ hour
> Preparation—½ hour
> Writing and arithmetic—½ hour
> Bodily care—½ hour
> Afternoon prayers—½ hour
> Labor or business—3 hours
> All meals—1 hour
> Evening prayers—½ hour
> Rest—½ hour
> Sleep—5 hours

After this fashion everyone should divide his twenty-four-hour day, according to his concerns and needs, his energy, health, and knowledge. Probably to this the *Gemara* alludes when it states "Set you times for study" [*Avot* 1:15], that everyone should establish regular times for daily sacred service.

64. Seclude yourself daily for a brief period to meditate and to correct whatever requires improvement in the sacred service for the purpose of which you were placed in this world.

65. Ask forgiveness from every person and be forgiving of everyone both in speech and deed, as set forth in *Bet Avraham*.

66. If you need to train yourself in a desirable trait, then practice this trait to the utmost extreme until you are habituated to it. Afterward, practice it in the normal [moderate] way, as described by Maimonides, of blessed memory.

At the end of his will, Reb Moshe Hakohen lists miraculous events in the lives of his family members. This is in keeping with the suggestion made in paragraph 20 of his will. The following are examples from his list acknowledging his debt to Providence:

These are some of the miracles and wonders I am aware of that the Almighty performed in my behalf in His great mercy and compassion:

In the year 1809 I was gravely ill, critically, and the Almighty in His compassionate mercy restored me to health after six weeks.

In 1822 my wife Rachel was ill for three weeks, and thanks to God Who healed her in His kindness.

In winter 1824 a severe, unexplained palsy afflicted my son Dov Ber in his left arm, and he recovered from it, thanks to God.

In 1825 a heavy weight struck me, and as I fell, the beam of the well fell upon me; from all this I emerged safely, praise to the Almighty's compassion.

In 1826 I suddenly had no source of income whatever, and the Almighty sent salvation through the intervention of Mr. Nahum ben Hayyim of Lebau, who established me in a respectable post in Meinegin.

On January 14, 1828, a fire broke out in the middle of the night, and praised be God, the fire extinguished itself within the hour.

In summer 1828 a large piece of plaster fell from the ceiling on my head and, thank God, it did not injure me at all.

On April 30, 1829, my four sons fell very ill, three with very high fever, and thanks to the Almighty's mercies, within six weeks they were all cured.

On May 30, 1839, I fell from the carriage and struck my head and leg on a stone and, thank the Almighty, in three days I was well.

In 1840 one of my sons suffered deliriums and the Almighty sent him healing through Physician Barr of Talesin.

On February 19, 1845, one of my daughters suffered deliriums and due to God's mercy she was restored to health in a short time, without the aid of a human healer.

On January 6, 1848, my son Solomon reported to the military authorities for military service in behalf of my family and, thank God, he was declared exempt.

On January 3, 1849, at 3:00 o'clock after midnight, the heavy wall closet fell and crushed the table and bed next to me, and it missed me by a hair's-breadth and, blessed be God and blessed be His name, I was not injured.

Benjamin M. Roth

This unusual ethical letter (*iggeret*) was written in 1854 by Benjamin M. Roth to his son Solomon, just prior to the latter's leaving for the United States from the family home in Hechingen, Württemberg, Germany. The letter was handed to the son by his father. Solomon and his brother Moses settled in Milwaukee, and later in Cincinnati.

Hechingen, June 1854

My Dear Son:

It is doubtful whether we shall see each other again in life; and from afar I cannot warn you against such dangers as often threaten youth. Yet even from the furthermost distance I shall think of you only with fatherly love and tenderness, and will at all times do everything in my power to help you. No sacrifice is too great for a father's love to bring willingly. In whatever situation you may find yourself, turn to me; and I will always show you that I am yours with an unending love, now and forever. Always have confidence in me. Before you give your confidence to a stranger—trust your father.

At this moment of our parting, since I can no longer be near you, let me give you the following precepts for life to take with you. Obey them, follow them, and you will never be unhappy. Whatever situations you may enter into, you will be able to take hold of yourself, to comfort yourself; and God, to Whom I pray daily for your welfare, will let it be well with you.

1. Always seek to keep your conscience clear, i.e., never commit an action which you will have to regret afterward. Think carefully about everything you contemplate doing before its execution, and consider its consequences, so that you will act only after due consideration. A sure test of a clear conscience is an unclouded temperament and a cheerful spirit. Since you have received both from nature, seek to preserve them.

2. Consider what you possess as a trust given you by God. Be thrifty with it, and seek to enlarge it in an honest manner. Consider it

just as much the possession of your brothers and sisters, and therefore ... let no sacrifice appear too great for you. Wealth should never come to diminish your honor and your clear conscience. Also, never say in the manner of the cold Englishman or American: "Help your own self!" Instead, aid rather to the full extent of your powers every poor man and anyone who needs your help. In short, be thrifty for yourself, that you may be able to aid a suffering humanity with your wealth.

3. Never leave the religion that is yours by birth, the faith of your parents and ancestors. Neither wealth, nor friendship, nor the possibility of a brilliant career in life, nor seduction, nor even the love of a girl should move you or have the power to make you change your religion. Should you be forced, partly through circumstances, partly because of the dictates of reason, to omit the ceremonial observances, you must nevertheless under no circumstances depart from the basis of religion: "The Eternal, your God, is one, unique, single being." Reason and conviction can never force you to desert Judaism, since the Jewish religion is really the only one whose basic teachings can be brought into harmony with philosophy. Therefore desertion would be for worldly advantages, and these are never valuable enough to sacrifice the Eternal One or our conscience. I feel I must recommend this to you doubly, since you have a tendency toward frivolity which could lead you to an easier acceptance of this type of seduction.

Also, never have any contact with missionaries. You do not have enough knowledge of the Holy Scriptures. That way, you cannot engage in disputations with them; for they could easily lead you astray. Consider them therefore only as self-seeking cheats, or as ranting visionaries, as I have come to know them. And indeed in my conversations with them I frequently exhibited them as such in the presence of company, something I could do since I have studied Scripture from my childhood days. And yet even then it was a difficult task.

4. Do not become acquainted—not to mention closer relationships—with women. Be polite and well-mannered toward them; for the rest, as far as it is possible, keep your distance. Consider them like a sharp, pointed toy, with which one can play only occasionally—and then with the greatest of care. Seek to keep

your heart free; guard it; and be not seduced by the tempting, destructive speech and actions of your contemporaries. This last demands your closest attention.

Have no relations with a prostitute. Her breath is poison, her word the bite of a snake; and they are all alike. However, let me add here, in praise of Jewish womanhood, that with a few exceptions they have preserved much purer morals than the girls of other races; and they have contained themselves from selling their charms for money.

I recommend the above to you in particular as injunctions to be followed. With your fine appearance and cheerful temperament you will be exposed to many temptations and opportunities in regard to women. And I do not want to say much on this point, leaving it rather to your wisdom and unspoiled instincts. My deepest prayer is that you may guard the latter; and if it is your firm intention to remain pure, the good Lord will aid you in this task.

5. Do not trust a stranger; and certainly do not confide in him, particularly if he flatters you. In general, be reserved and discreet toward all. For many a wolf wears lamb's garments, and a true, honest friend can be recognized only after years of close acquaintance, and after he has passed many tests. But then, value him as a jewel—and a rare jewel, at that. If someone confides a secret to you, guard it; but do not make him your confidant in return. Again, this is a point which I must emphasize to you, since you are a trusting soul. But you yourself have already had experiences of this nature in your travels. Young as you are, you yourself know that men do not always mean what they say.

6. Never exhibit money or articles of value in front of a stranger, in an inn, or in any public place where strangers may be found. Even when you are with your acquaintances, do not act boastfully in regard to your possessions. On the contrary, rather claim to be poorer than you actually are. For there is no greater lure to crime than the great god Mammon; and needless bragging has brought misfortune to many a man.

7. Throughout life, whether you are in good or evil circumstances, keep your parents and your home in your mind. Guard firmly your resolution to return to them, even if only after many years

(unless they are able to come to visit you). No matter when, no matter what the circumstances surrounding you, they long for you; and they will receive you with open arms.

8. Do not try to see everything because of an overwhelming curiosity. Avoid any locations or places that threaten danger. Do not place yourself in danger through willfulness, carelessness, or excessively brave or needless action. However, be brave and determined where danger cannot be avoided, and at the critical stage, keep your presence of mind, for presence of mind has often turned away the gravest dangers, and has saved others when the danger seemed overwhelming.

9. Avoid the company of drunkards and merrymakers. Should you, by accident or because of unavoidable circumstances, find yourself in their presence, leave the room and the location they occupy. Suffer an insult rather than get into an argument with them, for such people cannot really insult a man of honor. As a general rule, let yourself be insulted rather than insult others. Be particular to avoid all quarrel and argument. Meet everyone in a polite and friendly fashion. If you believe that someone has slighted you, lock your sensitivity and your anger into your heart; and forgive the offender.

10. Avoid gambling; and seek to occupy your time with useful things. Any occupation is better and more honorable than gambling; for before one becomes aware of it, one may become an inveterate gambler. Gambling is the most destructive of vices. Much as I must criticize the excessive reading of novels, which damages one's sensibilities and the heart, and makes one weak and woman-like, if time must be killed which could be used for so many pleasant and useful occupations, such reading is preferable to gambling.

11. Be frugal and economy-minded. Save each heller as you would a gulden; for he who needlessly spends a kreutzer will never save a gulden. Seek to acquire wealth in an honest manner; and preserve it through economy. But let not this economy turn to miserliness. Be very saving in regard to your own needs, and limit your needs to the utmost. Avoid unnecessary luxuries, unless it be a matter of doing good. If you save without being miserly, no one will be able to entice you into acts of dishonor or crime.

12. Be meek and patient, and seek to acquire the character and patience of your mother. Through many years of continual suffering and pain she showed herself, in this manner, to be a true angel of patience. Be, as she was, forgiving when injustice or misfortune seeks you out; and strive in this to emulate your all-forgiving God.

13. Sunlight and moonshine are powerful lamps. But the light of your reason must eclipse them; i.e., do nothing in haste, nothing without due thought.

14. Passions are the mightiest of all tyrants. Give them one finger and they will at once take all of your body and soul. Seek, therefore, to keep free of them; and give them no opportunity to rule you.

15. Those who hate and envy us can bring much evil upon us; but the greatest evil can be brought upon us through our own soul when it walks the paths of foolishness and error. Therefore seek to avoid them in every way of life; strive to set yourself against their power.

16. Great tribulations bring us into bad habits; and once we become accustomed to a habit, it becomes second nature to us. Therefore do not learn any vices; and let no habit become a passion to you.

17. The lying tongue of viciousness can do us great damage, but our own tongue can be still worse. Therefore guard your mouth and tongue. Consider each word before it crosses your lips, for he who guards his mouth and lips is exposed to no danger. Particularly guard yourself against saying what you think during revolutionary times—no matter to which faction you belong. Do not enter into political discussions, and always remain in the background on such occasions. Live a private rather than a public life.

18. Do not count too much on the favor of a personage, whether he be highly placed or of low rank. But least of all rely on the favor of a great man. Their promises are an empty sound, their words a gust of wind. They prefer you as long as they need you; once the need is gone, they do not know you anymore.

19. Give in to necessity, and patiently bear what fate has in store for you. That which is done cannot be changed; and what has been decided on high cannot be nullified or avoided.

20. Despise and avoid the man of invectives, the calumniator, and the hypocrite. They would entice you and then use your words against you; and avoid a fool the way you would avoid a mad dog.

21. Long have I pondered, searched, and examined as to what constitutes man's true happiness. I have found only one bliss for him: virtue and fear of God. Hold fast to both of them, if you desire to attain happiness.

And thus I transmit to you, my beloved son, these rules for life. Seek to follow them. I particularly recommend to you that you seek to emulate your brother Moses and that you obey him; partly because he is your older brother, partly because he has an excellent, steadfast, and firm character. I do not censure you for the fact that big-city life and your growing up among strangers have in some ways been detrimental to you. This is the reason why you have almost discarded by now that steadfastness of spirit which you took with you from your parents' home. It remained longer in Moses, who stayed at home till he was seventeen, and whose character could therefore develop further. Really, you could not give me more pleasure than by living together peacefully and in brotherly harmony, as you could also give me no greater pain and sorrow than by not doing this. I do not doubt that both of you will follow my wishes, and in that way you will also fulfill the words of our sages [Hebrew]: "How good and how pleasant it is for brethren to live together in unity."

I assure you that my whole happiness exists in the happiness of my children. Believe me, no sacrifice would be too great for me to bring willingly if I could make you happy. It was a great inward struggle for me (and I had to conceal my feelings from you as from mother) to send you away from me while you were yet so young. But it was your firm desire—and I did not want to take it from you. For all eternity my feelings toward you will be those of the deepest love.

And with this I give you, now, my blessing; may it follow you on all your paths with the words [Hebrew]:

The angel who hath redeemed me from all evil bless thee; and let my name be named in thee, and the name of my fathers, Abraham and Isaac; and mayest thou grow into a multitude in the midst of the earth.

The Lord bless thee, and keep thee.

The Lord make His face to shine upon thee, and be gracious unto thee.

The Lord lift up His countenance upon thee, and give thee peace.

God make thee as Ephraim and Manasseh, like Moses in his humility, like Solomon in his wisdom, like Samson in his strength, like Absalom in his beauty, like Hezekiah in his righteousness, and like David in his reverence.

Mordekhai Mottel Michelsohn

Mordekhai Mottel Michelsohn (1800–1872), surnamed "Kalushiner" after the Polish city that was the center of his activities, was a highly accomplished man, thoroughly versed in Torah and in the complex economic and political affairs of his time. Conditions in nineteenth-century Poland were chaotic following the Third Partition (1795), administration of the country being for the most part by absentee Russian officials or their agents. Out of these conditions emerged leaders like Mordekhai Mottel Kalushiner to manage aspects of Poland's economic life, collect taxes, and often to serve as intermediaries between Jewish communities and the authorities. In the reign of Nicholas I, when Jewish boys were forcibly taken at age twelve for long-term military service (with the intent to convert them), Mordekhai Kalushiner helped restore countless boys to their families by interceding in their behalf. The text of this will is almost unique in the harshness with which the writer castigates his sons, although he forgives them their shortcomings.

"Man that is born of woman is of few days, and full of trouble" (Job 14:1). Few and troubled have been the years of my life. As a lad diseases and illness wracked me, distress and suffering from the start. From the day I reached manhood I have had no rest, no tranquility. While I have achieved success, it was only with great effort, anguish, pain, and stress that I accomplished any task. Now I have advanced in years and "It is time for the Lord to work ..." [Ps. 119:126]. Is there a man who lives forever and sees not death? Therefore listen, my children to that which I admonish you: "I have meditated on the books ..." [Dan. 9:2] and know that it is a father's religious duty to instruct his children, and that doing so is a means of perfecting the soul; and this is the meaning of Scripture, "... in order that he may instruct his children and his household after him" [Gen. 18:19].

What shall I instruct you about? If about Torah and its commandments, these things are well explained already. If your hearts are inclined toward them, you will meditate on them, obey them, observe them, and benefit from them. If not, of what use are my words? For if the teachings of Torah and the books of sainted scholars abounding in the world, permanently recorded and published, do not bear fruit for you, how can I expect to do more? You will forget both me and my words.

For all that, I shall give you some useful advice: Beware of these two vices—intoxication and lying. Both of these are vile in the eyes of God and man; they are among the most despicable of habits. "Looking upon the cup when it is red" [Prov. 23:41] leads to crooked paths seeming straight. The sages comment on this verse: "The entire world seems to him as a plain; he is viewed as a laughing-stock by all who see him and his end is to be cut off" (Talmud *Yoma* 75a).

As to lying, "He that speaketh falsehood shall not be established" [Ps. 101:7] before God, nor does anyone heed his words.

In these words are included the entire Torah and its commandments, as the sages comment on the verse, "Keep thee far from a false matter ..." [Ex. 23:7].

Thus all your utterances on every subject, including business, should be spoken in truth.

These two traits have felled many victims. Since these are well expounded and much of Torah is based on them as fundamental to what is good and ill in life, what do I add to your knowledge about them by telling you this? I tell you this day that these are habits that I have despised during my lifetime, and that doing so has proven most effective for me (besides fulfilling the biblical admonitions regarding them) for success in commercial enterprise in our day.

Furthermore, I beseech you, be soft-spoken and let your words be few in number because "In the multitude of words there wanteth not transgression" [Prov. 10:19]; "Multiply not exceeding proud talk; let not arrogance come out of your mouth" [1 Sam. 2:3]. "For as the crackling of thorns under a pot" [Eccles. 7:6], so are the words of fools.

This too you ought to practice for your own good: Daily recite a number of *Tehillim* [Psalms]; a lesser number, with devotion, is to be preferred.

I would that you desire daily study; on days when I studied I was happy and my mind was clear in conducting all my affairs. I know this because I experienced it so.

Avoid miserliness for it is a nasty trait. They speak nonsense who maintain that stinginess leads to wealth; it doesn't work that way. On the contrary! A miser never stops trying to amass a fortune; he is dead in the midst of life. When he dies, others despoil the results of his labors.

On the other hand the generous giver gains more—he enjoys his life and bequeaths a blessing at his death. Generosity should, of course, be sensible: never for the sake of honor or recognition, but according to means and specific need. That is, as appropriate to the giver and to the beneficiary.

Never take the offensive in a quarrel; avoid disputes, but in all cases "be rather of the persecuted than of the persecutors" (Talmud *Baba Kamma* 93a). Whenever I attempted to gain the upper hand over my adversaries, even though justice was on my side, I never managed to prevail. But whenever I was the target, I prevailed over them. Also, avoid communal politics, even when you are in the right because the Evil Inclination will cast his net to deny truth and to show good as evil in accusing you. If at such times you keep your peace and do not seek to prevail, then those tidal waves will ebb as quickly as they surged.

And now, my children, obey the instruction of your father. Know that you have been rebellious for as long as I have known you. You have not been obedient and have not appreciated the benefits I have given you. Your personal conduct and your business practices have caused me vexation and pain. I was abhorrent in your eyes; my ways were not followed.

But why should I cry out against you for wrongdoing? All men are lacking in wisdom. We all are God's children, one God created us; have we not one father?[1] Yet though we see all the benefits that God grants us and His kindnesses to us at all times and at every hour, still we transgress. Nevertheless God, our faithful Father, in His mercies continues to spare us, forgives us, and does not withhold His kindnesses from us.

I am no more than human. I therefore forgive and pardon you; and so may God forgive you for unintended transgressions, causing them to vanish and be forgotten. Only this I entreat you: that you fulfill all that I ask with a good will; as I have instructed, so shall you do. Then will you enjoy long life and it will go well with you.

Your father, Mottel Michelsohn of Kalushin.

Thus have I directed you, my children; obey and let your souls live.

Concluded on the eve of Shabbat Nahamu, 5627 [1867], here at Kalushin.

Reb Shmuel Tefilinsky

Among the Torah sages of twentieth-century Jerusalem, Reb Shmuel Tefilinsky (1888–1945) was one of the most highly respected. Born in Jerusalem, he left the precincts of the Old City only two or three times during his lifetime; one of those occasions is mentioned in his will. He was recognized in Jerusalem for piety, devotion to Torah, and profound talmudic scholarship. As a *ben Torah*, or *ben yeshiva*, his entire life was spent in the ceaseless toil of learning and teaching Torah.

The term *ben Torah* (pl. *bnei Torah*) requires elucidation if the will of Reb Shmuel is to be understood. In every generation there have been Jews who were drawn to Torah study as their sole calling. Jewish tradition encourages other Jews to provide support for these *bnei Torah* (scholars). The sustenance thus gained was quite meager despite the relatively small number of these *bnei Torah*; but it must be remembered that the lot of the average Jew in the Old World was one of grinding poverty. Reverence for the sacred lore and for the scholars who devoted their lives to its maintenance impelled them to contribute what they could to *ezras Torah* ("maintaining Torah").

Bnei Torah, as a rule, pursued their studies under the auspices of an institution—a yeshiva (hence, *ben yeshiva*) or *kolel*—which allocated stipends to the scholars. In his will the author urges his sons, should they elect to follow his vocation, to avoid appealing to the institutional leaders for added sums. Basing himself always on appropriate traditions and verses, he suggests also that *bnei Torah* view themselves as the spiritual heirs of the Levites of old, consecrated to learning and teaching, eschewing all worldly occupations.

The ethical will of Reb Shmuel Tefilinsky is designed as a practical guide for his children, whether or not they choose the life of the *ben Torah*. The will is divided into clear sections: faith in God, maximizing learning, fixing times for study, methods of study, *musar* learning, educating sons and daughters, tithing incomes, and general rules of conduct. Excerpts are presented here.

Minimize Business and Engage in Torah

1. Endeavor to the utmost to cleave to God's teachings day and night, to devote yourselves all the days of your life to Torah and to the service of God, and to labor in the Torah in order to perceive and understand, to hearken, to learn and to teach and to "cast your burden on the Lord and he will sustain you"

[Ps. 55:23] in the manner of the tribe of Levi. These are the words of Maimonides, of blessed memory, chapter 13 in the *Laws of Fallow Year and Jubilee*: "Why were the Levites not allotted land in Eretz Yisrael or a share in its booty along with their brethren? Because they were singled out to serve the Lord and minister to Him, to teach His upright ways and just laws to many people, as it is written: 'They shall teach Jacob Thine ordinances, and Israel Thy law....' [Deut. 33:10]. For this reason, they were separated from worldly affairs; they fought no battles like the rest of Israel; they inherited no land; they won nothing by means of their physical ability. They are indeed the Lord's army, as it is written: 'Bless, O Lord his substance' [Deut. 33:11]. The Lord, blessed be He, has won them for Himself, as it is written: 'I am your portion and your share'" [Num. 18:20].

Not only the tribe of Levi, but each well-informed, thinking person whose spirit moves him to devote himself to the service of the Lord, to know the Lord, and to walk uprightly after casting off his neck the yoke of many a cunning wile that men contrived, is indeed divinely consecrated, and the Lord will forever and ever be his portion. God will provide sufficiently for his needs, as He did for the priests and the Levites. David, may he rest in peace, declared: "The Lord is my allotted portion and my cup; thou maintainest my lot" [Ps. 16:5].

2. If it should be your lot to be among the students of the academy and to receive an institutional stipend as customary here in Jerusalem, you should consider and understand what the nature of such a stipend is, what the nature of a Torah academician is, and what is the essence of the ideal of establishing Torah academies [yeshivot] in Jerusalem.

Experience has taught that in every land, city, or community where there are yeshivot and Torah scholars, Judaism is at a high level, the place is suffused with the spirit of Torah, and Jewish life is strong. In lands where yeshivot are lacking, Judaism is at a low level, the condition of Jewish life and faith deteriorates day by day, and the Torah is almost forgotten there, along with Jewish identity.

It is precisely for this ideal that Torah centers and institutions are established among our people—to provide insofar as possible for the needs of those who wish to commit their lives to study of Torah and whose spiritual existence is dependent on its pursuit. Ensuring the survival of these people and their families underlies the idea of a yeshiva. This also defines the concept of a true *ben yeshiva*, who cannot be lured even by a thousand thousand denarie of gold [*Avot* 6:9] from his Torah study, his reason for being and the sole aspiration of his life.

Let this principle be engraved on your soul, in every aspect of your lives: that the purpose and rationale of study for the *ben Torah* is *not* to earn the stipend and support of the academy, as many think. On the contrary the academy's support makes possible the study and preservation of Torah, since "without flour [i.e., basic necessities] there can be no Torah" [*Avot* 3:17].

3. Now, my sons, whoever among you will choose to enter the divine service dedicated to God's Torah and to His word, and seeks to be counted among the hosts of the Almighty, blessed be He, must carefully consider and realize the significance of the sacred role he takes upon himself. He must be ever alert, constant, and courageous in his Torah pursuit. In terms of *time*, he must keep to a maximum the time at the academy, day and night; guard each moment of time to avoid wasting a single minute on extraneous matters, like a day laborer at his tasks. In terms of *achievement*, he must enhance and add to his skill in the realm of Torah knowledge through continual review until it is thoroughly mastered; and he must labor and struggle with all his might to penetrate the depths of the law, to discern the basis and reason of each issue, "to search out through debate, then arrive at conclusions in keeping with tradition" [*Sota* 21a].

4. One further detail must be kept in mind seriously even though one is a *ben Torah* already fully devoted to Torah learning. That is, let him not forget at appropriate times the duty of *every* Israelite to set times for Torah study. For there are times and seasons when one is especially burdened, like the eves of festivals, ritual celebrations, or on journeys away from home and from studies for a period of time. At such times let his attention not be diverted from the duty of setting specified times for Torah study, several hours during the day and at night. Let him not think for an instant that a *ben yeshiva* is exempt from setting

aside definite times for study. For on the occasions when he cannot meditate on the Torah the entire day, he is no less duty-bound to pursue Torah than any other Jew. This feeling I first had during the World War in 1915 when there was a locust plague. The government required everyone to assist in eliminating the locusts. All of us *bnei yeshiva* traveled to the settlements in Judea, to the vineyards and orchards of the area, where we spent entire days exterminating the locusts. At that time I called it to the attention of my group that we are not exempt from setting times for Torah study.

Fix Regular Times for Torah Study

There may be among you or your children those whose inclinations or aptitudes do not permit them to devote full time to study of Torah, "like the ox to the yoke or the mule to the burden" [*Aboda Zara* 5b] but rather seek to engage in worldly endeavor in keeping with the dictum "It is best for Torah to be accompanied by a worldly occupation" [*Avot* 2:2]. If so, then let the words of Maimonides (chapter 1 in *Laws of Torah Study* and cited in the *Shulhan Arukh*) be inscribed on their *hearts* and familiar on their lips:

> Every Jew is responsible for Torah study
> be he rich or poor, in bodily health or
> suffering pain, both in youthful vigor and
> in feebleness of advanced age, even he who is
> supported by charity or begs for alms,
> and even one who has wife and children,
> is obliged to set regular times for Torah
> study—during the day and during the evening—
> as it is written,
> "Thou shalt meditate on it
> by day and by night."

On Scheduling Studies

My dearest ones, if you wish to attain the Crown of Torah, if you seek to preserve your studies and truly be in possession of Torah learning and gain knowledge and understanding in Talmud and the Law, resolve firmly to form the habit of very copious amounts of review.

Know and realize that the idea of review is not for the sake of memory alone. Rather, it is for the purpose of comprehension and profundity, in order to plumb the depths of the Law and its underlying rationale.

As to the best manner of review, according to my observation and from what I have learned from experience and from others, one must give attention to the "near and far." That is, several times the immediate location; three, four times the page or the topic; then from one Mishnah to the next (or four, five pages) at one stretch; then the chapter three or four times, after that, three or four chapters all the way through three or four times, finally, the entire tractate all the way through three or four times.

You should also resolve to concentrate on at least one particular Talmud volume for special mastery besides all your other schedules of study. Ideally, mastery of the volume should also be by heart; at least the *mishnayot* should be committed to memory. One benefit of this is in being able to fulfill the verse, "Thou shalt talk of them ... when thou walkest on the way," and if, on occasion, one happens to be where there are no books, he can avoid neglecting his Torah studies.

On Set Times for Moral Instruction (*Musar*)

My dear and beloved ones, resolve firmly to set regular, frequent times for studying and meditating on *musar* books, the men and women alike; convey moral instruction to your children and offspring constantly, especially on Sabbath and festival days around the table at mealtime. Tell them stories about our ancestors and our heroes, from the narratives of the Talmud and the midrash that are appealing, in order to implant in their hearts good and honest traits, love of Torah, reverence for God and respectful conduct.

On Education of Sons and Daughters

"Oh, our travail," refers to the children (Passover Haggadah). A valuable allusion and a profound meaning is given us by the author of the Passover Haggadah in these few words, namely, that throughout all the travail of a human being in this world and all the pain and toil endured in life, the main object of his aim and hopes are his children. To leave behind him a generation of righteous, praiseworthy offspring, offspring who are good in the eyes of God and man. This is his reward for all his toil which he toiled on earth; and he regards as worthwhile all the suffering, misery and mishaps that overtake one at various times, so long as he knows that there remains after him a blessing—that is, that he leaves behind him genuine human beings, sanctified offspring, descendants of whom he need not be ashamed either in this world or in the next. For beside this, what other expectation does one have, and of what benefit is his travail and what remains to him of all his toil? "For whom then do I labor and deprive my soul of pleasure?" [Eccles. 4:8]. *Oh, our travail*—refers to the children!

So, dear children, I ask you to guide yourselves according to Torah teachings as taught us by our sages; and similarly teach your own children diligently, as we are commanded to do [Deut. 6:7]. For if one does not learn, one cannot properly perform what is required of him. How can he rise to an ever-higher level of sanctity if he does not know how to ascend the "ladder of mitzvot?" Raise up generations of God-fearing descendants who will find favor in the eyes of God and man, so that it may be said of them, "By you shall Israel invoke blessings" [Gen. 48:20].

Hayyim Elazar Shapira
(The Munkatcher Rebbe)

Reb Hayyim Elazar Shapira (1869–1937) was the official rabbi of the city of Munkatch (till World War I in Hungary, then Czechoslovakia) and the surrounding communities. In an exceptional combination of roles, Reb Hayyim Elazar Shapira was also the "Munkatcher Rebbe," head of a large hasidic following. A highly erudite scholar, he wrote a dozen volumes of responsa and other Torah works. In addition, he was an able administrator: he supervised the *Darekhei Teshuvah* yeshiva in Munkatch, and headed a full-time *bet din*, consisting of five rabbis, which sat in daily session. Reb Hayyim Elazar was an extraordinarily charitable man who gave away most of his earnings. At his death, he left no material estate whatever.

Sunday, Vayakhel-Pekudei, 5688 [1928]

It is written of Abraham our father, the first of our progenitors, "For I have known him, to the end that he may command his children and his household after him, that they may keep the way of the Lord, to do righteousness and justice ..." [Gen. 18:19] and it is written that "no man knows his time ..." [Eccles. 9:12]. From my elders, I have learned [to do] like the great scholar, our revered teacher Rabbi Shlomo Kluger, of blessed memory, who wrote his first will when he was but fifty years of age. He wrote in support of it this allusion: "In this year of jubilee ye shall return every man unto his possession" [Lev. 26:13]. Especially since I am, thank God, fifty-seven years old and I have passed a full jubilee plus another sabbatical year after the jubilee, I shall note down a number of things, with directions for good, in earnest entreaty and by full authority of the law of such testaments, that all of it be executed without any changes. With all this, I pray the Almighty, blessed be He, for length of days to fulfill His Torah and commandments and continue to benefit the public properly and, by light of day, await the coming of the Redeemer of Zion, speedily in our day, all of us together. And may I be preserved in life, together with the members of my family; may they have length of days in the midst of all Israel, Treasured People, let us merit salvation and redemption speedily.

1. First, I bow and bend the knee to the Almighty, blessed be He, Who formed and created me; and I confess all my many sins and transgressions, asking for forgiveness and a full repentant return. I hereby declare that the whole and sole intent in my innermost heart has been to serve Almighty God according to His will, to help bring about the perfection of the polity and hasten the coming of the Redeemer of Zion speedily and in our days, for this is the ultimate desire of the Almighty in creating the worlds—"last in creation, first in design"—that we merit redemption by virtue of our choices and life's tests, etc., as made known in the sacred books. And all intentions or words contrary to this are vanity, motivated by the Evil Inclination, and null and void in their very essence, as written in our prayerbooks in the Declaration [*moda'a*] following the *hatarat nedarim* on the eve of Rosh Hashanah about the practices of our holy sages and forefathers, may their merit protect us.

2. To all my household, including my daughter Frima and my students (whom I never called by this term in writing—and, as I explained in my essay, *Dibrei Torah*—not orally either; because they are to me like sons, like comrades, like *teachers*. "From my students I learned more than from anyone else" [*Ta'anit* 7a] as our talmudic sages state it. Considering all this, it is a mark of special affection for many when I refer to them as "my students," so I shall accede to their wishes this once, but even so, for the sake of expressing affection only), I pray you be careful to tread the path that is the path of our fathers, may their merit shield us, to adopt not the modern vogues, heaven forbid, but only reverence for God, all your lives; not to join any groups or organizations, including those who kick up their heels, the hypocrites and flatterers, like the *agudisten* [political Zionists] and the *yishuvisten* [those who settled in the Land of Israel or who believed in doing so], and their like. For their end is bitter, heaven protect us, and all contain heresy (God save us from their views), and postpone the redemption by reason of our sins, as we have already warned in concert with many of the great and saintly rabbis of this generation.

3. So also in matters of obscenity in dress and lewd uncovering of parts that should be covered: woe and alas, there is no

obscenity or breach more serious than this, and these acts cause great harm to Israel and postponement of Jerusalem's reestablishment. Pray, then, take heed, in particular our followers enumerated above, and my own offspring, may they attain to an old and good age, they, their sons, their daughters and wives. And my daughter Frima, may she achieve length of days and years, I caution strongly (and she will doubtless heed my words, God willing, to her benefit) with emphatic warning, to go about with kerchief on your head (begin doing so immediately after the twelve-month period) in the tradition of our ancestors, and as your mother does, may she flourish; and follow all seemly, modest ways. Even on weekdays, do not go, God forbid, with a "frisset," or with a "fall" resembling hair (because this is also forbidden according to the regulation cited in *Dibrei Hayyim* by our rabbi, may his merit protect us).

4. So, too, with the help of God, I trust that the remnant of Israel will do no injustice and on my [rabbinic] chair no outsider will sit, so that others will not inherit my honor, which is the honor of Torah, which is the honor of the Almighty, blessed be He and His faith. But rather that they will act in accordance with our tradition in general and in all details. This is my request and my behest in this matter; and may it be God's will that the source will not disappoint, the tree not be cut off but put forth worthy fruit.

5. Also, I emphatically caution my offspring, our followers, and our townspeople, may they all flourish, not to alter our sacred custom in matters pertaining either to public Torah study and the large, excellent group *Mahzikei Torah*, or in all other religious matters like matzos for Pesach. So also the many other matters, and especially in my *Bet Hamidrash*, regarding the traditional ritual of our revered forefathers, may their merit shield us. So also our followers and comrades, wherever they are able to practice it, should establish the ritual of our fathers, together with the published prayer ritual. So also in all communal religious matters that I instituted, make efforts to maintain them with the extra fervor and strength of Torah.

Pertaining to burial arrangements:

Wrap me in the tallis which I was accustomed to wearing for the Sabbath afternoon service. It was my revered father's, may his merit preserve us; do not render any of the fringes unfit [as is customarily done].

Do not let my bier stay overly long; as written in the sacred *Zohar*, only as long as absolutely necessary. In all events, at the very longest only close to twenty-four hours from the time of expiration to the closing of the grave.

Do not eulogize me either over my bier or away from it. Especially do not say about me "righteous ... pious ... Torah genius ..." for I am none of these. May the Almighty yet grant that I might return in true repentance, meditate on His Torah in fine detail, for length of days and years.

Earth of the Holy Land shall be placed on my knees, on my body, and some on my abdomen, but none on my face; only the customary pottery shards on my eyes.

I am as one who follows after giants; nonetheless, as was done for my revered father and master, place at the bottom of the grave under my body, on the ground, only a single board.

Let my bier be made out of the boards of my Shabbos table, just as our forefathers did, may their merit protect us.

Yehuda Leib Graubart (The Stashever Rav)

Rabbi Yehuda Leib Graubart, chief rabbi of Toronto, Canada, from 1922 to 1936, was renowned both in Europe and America as a great halakhic scholar and author. An eloquent orator and an influential leader of Mizrahi, he was a strong proponent of Eretz Yisrael in the decades before Zionism was widely accepted among Orthodox Jews. Note the concern Rabbi Graubart expresses about the return of borrowed books. In general, remaining a debtor, in money or any tangibles, at death is a serious concern for the ethically scrupulous; books are a special concern too, because in Jewish tradition one may not refuse to lend a book.

Regarding the will which I wrote on the 14th of Menahem-Ab 5694 [July 26, 1934], and the several details added to it on Nisan 19, 5696 [April 11, 1936]: Both are written in the language of the land [English], devised in accordance with the law in the most effective manner, and let no heir contest it.

Please return the borrowed books in my possession: the volumes belonging to the Etz Hayyim school. Also, return these volumes to the *Bet Hamidrash* in Stashov (*Magen Avraham* published in Johannesburg, *Hoq Ya'akov, Ikkarei Arha'ah Turim*); to Notte Meir of Stashov (*Sidre Teharah*), to the rabbi there, Rabbi Yitzhak Meir (*Sha'ar Mishpat*, two volumes *Shoshanat Ya'akov*); to Asher Nussbaum there (*Sefer Derush Ashre Hatzevi*).

I caution you in strongest terms not to eulogize me (except if my sons are here). [Place] my grave only beside a poor, honest man who earned his living by the work of his hands. The gravestone should be of utmost simplicity; inscribe no titles, only my name, the name of my sainted father, of blessed memory, and the family name.

On the eve of Nisan 20, 5696 [April 12, 1936]
(The year and the Sidre Tzav)
Distribute charity on that day [of burial]

Part Two

Wills from the Holocaust

The Holocaust poured out on the world a measure of malevolence and bestiality unprecedented in human history. Its martyred victims, like their more fortunate brethren elsewhere, wished to leave an expression of their inmost thoughts to survivors and coming generations. Even the pitiably few surviving wills and letters reveal a wide range of individual response to the unbelievable catastrophe which overtook their writers. Some demand vengeance and a continuing fight to the death with the cruel oppressor and all that he represents. Others, to our everlasting wonder, reveal a struggle to maintain the author's divine image and human dignity in the face of incomparable evil.

Hirsch Moshe Zaddok

This will was written by the last Jew of Kovno, Hirsch Moshe Zaddok. It was written inside the cover of a book, and was discovered by the writer's brother, who escaped Kovno at the start of the war and returned with the victorious Soviet forces.

To every man and woman! They treated us like animals in the forest. Seven days and nights we hid in an attic with no food or water. The heat was fierce. On the eighth day they rained grenades on us and torched the building. We managed to reach the cellar but the entire building was engulfed in flames over our heads.

Brothers! Avenge us! We were once more than fifty thousand souls in Kovno and now there remain but a few. We too await the end. Our revenge will come when you destroy the very last of the wild beasts!

Show them no mercy, just as they had no pity on us. Repay them for all their crimes on behalf of all those they tortured and killed. Only then will mankind be rid of these snakes who dare call themselves humans. Brothers! *Vengeance*—this must be your sacred mission in life.

Hirsch Moshe Zaddok
One of the Jewish victims

A Mother's Will

Published in the ghetto newspaper *Warsaw-Krakow*, 1940, this will was signed only "Your Mother."

Judaism, my child, is the struggle to bring down God upon earth, a struggle for the sanctification of the human heart. This struggle your people wages not with physical force but with spirit, with sincere, heartfelt prayers, and by constant striving for truth and justice.

So do you understand, my child, how we are distinct from others and wherein lies the secret of our existence on earth?

Knowing this, will your heart still be heavy, my child? Will you still say you cannot stand your fate? But you must, my child, for so were you commanded; it is your calling. This is your mission, your purpose on earth.

You must go to work alongside people of other nations ... and you will teach them that they must come to a brotherhood of nations and to a union of all nations with God.

You may ask, "How does one speak to them?" This is how: "Thou shalt not murder; thou shalt not steal; thou shalt not covet; love thy neighbor as thyself...." Do these things and through their merit, my child, you will be victorious.

Zippora Birman

The writer, a member of the Jewish fighting group in the Bialystok ghetto, fell in the defense of the ghetto in August 1943. Her notes were discovered after the war.

All is lost. This is our fate, to atone for the sins of the preceding generations.

We mourned all of them, we grieved over their loss; the most horrible possibility in history has happened to us. We witnessed, we heard, we anguished; and now we have been sentenced to be silenced forever. Our bones will not even be brought to decent Jewish burial. Unbearable. There is no choice but to die with honor, along with the thousands who go to their deaths without fear, without fright. We *know*: the Jewish people will not disappear. It will return to life, grow and bloom again, and will avenge our blood that is spilled.

So I address you, comrades, wherever you may be: You have the obligation to avenge. Day and night, take no rest from this charge—avenge the blood that is spilled—just as we have no respite here, face-to-face with death.

Cursed is he who reads this, mournfully sighs, and returns to his daily tasks.

It is not mourning that we demand of you! We did not even mourn our own parents, but speechless and silent we viewed the heaped corpses of our loved ones who were shot like dogs.

We call upon you: Vengeance, vengeance—with no mercy, with no sentimentality, with no "good" Germans. For the "good" German let it be an easier death; let him be killed last. That is what they promised the Jews of whom they approved: "You will be shot last."

This is our demand, the demand of all of us. This is the burning appeal of human beings who likely will be among the fallen, who will fight with courage and die with dignity.

To vengeance do we call you, you who were not imprisoned in Hitler's hell; this is our summons, and you are compelled to fulfill it, even at the risk of death.

Our crushed bones, scattered to all corners of Europe, will know no repose and the ashes of our corpses, scattered to the winds, will have no rest until you avenge us.

Remember this and do it. It is our plea—it is your duty.

Among the Embers: Martyrs' Testaments

These five wills, brief and hurriedly written, speak for themselves. All five appeared in *Mime Hashoah Vehagevura*, published by Yad Vashem in Jerusalem.

Written by the last twelve Jews to be murdered at the death camp at Chelmno, in January 1945. Before their deaths, they defended themselves and killed a number of Germans.

If any relatives or friends of these individuals are left alive, then be informed that all the Jews who were removed from Lodz were killed most brutally; they were tortured, then burned in fire. Be well. If you survive, avenge our blood.

Carved on the wall of the synagogue in Kovel, signed by David Elster, September 15, 1942.

A chill passes through us ... here come our murderers, dressed up ... their filthy hands adorned in white gloves, they herd us two-by-two ... tender-hearted brothers and sisters ... O how hard it is to part from this beautiful world forever ... let no one who remains alive ever forget—Jewish boys and girls from our Jewish street, innocent of any wrongdoing. Wreak vengeance on our murderers.

The will of the members of "Dror": signed by Sheindel Schwartz, Leah Fish, Rachel Fogelman, and David Aisenberg. These words were written on the wall of the Kovel synagogue in which the Jews were concentrated before being taken to be killed.

Greetings to our comrades from a group of *halutzim* about to die. We remained faithful to our cause to the end. Avenge our blood that is spilled.

Part of a will written by a woman of Kovel, to her husband; carved on the synagogue wall.

Reuben Atlas, this is to inform you that here, in this place, your wife Gina and your son Imosz were murdered. Our child cried bitterly; he did not want to die. Go forth to battle and avenge the blood of your wife and your only son. We die for no crime whatever.

Gina Atlas

The will of a young woman, written on the same synagogue wall.

I am a daughter of Israel, twenty years old. O how lovely is the world about us! Why should they destroy us when everything within me desires and yearns for life. Have my last minutes really arrived? Vengeance! Come and avenge me, whoever reads this last request of mine.

These lines, written in chalk on a small board, were found by one of the Jews brought in by the Nazis to clear the streets of the Warsaw Ghetto after the Uprising. The charred board was found next to the bodies of a Jewish couple.

Fellow Jews, when you find us, bury my dear wife and me according to our Jewish faith. I request that you say Kaddish three times—for my little eight-year-old son, for my devoted wife, and for me. We lived, we loved each other, we fought, and believed in the God of Israel.

Berl Tomshelski

This note was written to the Blozhever Rebbe by a Polish Jew just before going to his death. The recipient survived the war and read it at a meeting in New York, reported in the Morgen Journal, *January 14, 1946.*

Dear Rebbe:

I write you these lines a few minutes before I go to sanctify God's name. Soon they come to take me to the ovens. I beg you, dear rebbe, if God saves you from this, then for heaven's sake, perpetuate my name and my wife's name. If you are in Eretz Yisrael, please drive a stone into the holy ground in our names; and if you come to America, please write a Torah scroll in our memory.

The Chief Rabbi of Grodzisk

Since ancient times Jewish sources have described the period leading to the coming of the Messiah as characterized by "birth pangs." The travail of childbirth was seen as analogous to the tribulations and agonies which would precede the birth of the new era. The rabbi of Grodzisk referred to this oft-expressed belief in his exhortation to several thousand of his fellow Jews as he and they were led to the gas chambers. The event was reported to the late Chief Rabbi Isaac Herzog during his tour of Displaced Persons camps in Italy.

Brothers and sisters! One of our sages in talmudic times said in his days: "Let him come, but let me not see him" [*Sanhedrin* 98b], That is to say, let the Messiah come, so long as I don't have to see him. That sage did not want to witness the great agonies with which Israel would be afflicted preceding the coming of the redeemer. However, he may have allowed himself to make such a request because in his days the time of redemption was still very distant. But now, at the hour when we stand on the threshold of the redemption proper, now as we wash and purify with our blood the path of the redeemer, at the time we purify with our ashes, like the ashes of the Red Heifer, the people of Israel, to render it worthy of greeting the Messiah of righteousness, now we are forbidden to speak thus. On the contrary, we are obliged to see ourselves as fortunate that it fell to our lot to blaze a path for the redeemer and to accept with love our binding upon the alter of the sanctification of God's revered name. Come, then, my fellow Jews, and let us recite joyfully "Shema Yisrael."

With song on their lips they approached and entered the gas chambers.

On the Walls of Bialystok Prison

On the walls of Cell 81 in the infamous Bialystok prison one sees many names inscribed and a number of still-decipherable messages in familiar Yiddish script. Here many Jews spent their last hours before death. These are the surviving traces of their tragic fate.

Berkowicz, Grodno, was killed here, July 15, 1944, seven o'clock in the morning. Convey greetings in Moscow to Kilgin Samuel Georgevitch.

Isaac Kulbin was killed here July 15, 1944, for the Jewish people. Take revenge!

Born in Bielsk-Podliaski in 1921. The whole family was killed in the prison. The last Jew—Henekh Hoffman. I go to my death with head high. I greet my comrades, the brothers Okon and Posnanskin. Avenge me. They tortured me. I betrayed no one. Avenge us.

Avenge us! This is written by Berl Hirshenboim of Grodno. Twenty Jews from Bialystok and Grodno are spending their last night here. We are living through our last minutes. We await our death. Today is one month. 15/7/44

Berl Schatzman. I sit manacled in chains and await death. August 1944.

The following letter was received by the Blozhever Rebbe, who survived the war. It was written on a Sabbath eve, in winter 1942.

My dear rabbi, Reb Israel Shapiro, may you flourish:

They have surrounded the Burstin Factory in which 800 Jews work, and they are going to annihilate us. They are still undecided whether to shoot us here in Lemberg or take us to Bergen-Belsen to gas us.... I must hurry because the order has already come to strip. They're going to shoot us here.

My sister's children are with the Christian, Voshilevski, in Greiding [Latvia]. So I ask you to devote your efforts to take them from there and deliver them into Jewish hands. Whatever happens happens, but let them remain Jews. My wife, Shevah bat Hannah, they shot yesterday.

I hope that after my death I will be able to approach your holy ancestors and convey greetings from you and to intercede on your behalf for long life.

Your servant,
Arieh ben Leah Korn

Shulamit Rabinovitch

These letters were written by Shulamit Rabinovitch and her husband from the Kovno Ghetto. They were grandchildren of Rabbi Yitzhak Elchanan Spektor and devoted communal workers in Kovno before and during the war. The letters were addressed to their sons in the United States. We stand in awe of the ethical sensitivity of this couple: The wife takes pride in the fact that her husband did not take advantage of his position to show favoritism to the members of his own family. We also note the date as D-Day.

June 6, 1944

My dear, fortunate sons!

We sense the end is near. It will not be long before they finish us off. On one hand it is good, on the other hand very bad, to die right now. Good that we have lived to see the end come; and bad to die now, a moment before the redemption.

Actually it is not difficult for me to die, or for Papa either. What is very hard, infinitely hard, is the fact that your young brother Shmuel will die when we do. And he is such a wonderful boy. Even under the most brutal conditions he developed into a fine human being; perhaps with less formal education, but with so much humane feeling and refinement, that it would be truly worthwhile for him to remain alive. How few of those who suffered this treatment retained the human image! The struggle for existence is hard and everyone wants to live, to save himself; the law of the jungle is dominant: "Save yourself if you can."

But you may be very proud of your father. He is among those who never took advantage of his public office, never put Shmuel or me ahead of the other sufferers for whom he was responsible. How we wish you could have some knowledge about these past three painful years. I hope that some will survive and that you will receive some word about our sufferings and our dying. It is now in its fourth year and the end is approaching. It didn't really pay for us to hold out and suffer so long and then not to survive. Were *they* the righteous ones (if there is such a thing), those who were first to go? For years we learned so much, suffered so much. We could teach others so very much, and it is too bad that it all comes to nothing, along with us.

Were we to be rescued, we could dry up the oceans, and demonstrate with how little a person can get along! If I could only bequeath you the ability to get along with little and the ability to do everything for yourself, then you, being free, could never be unhappy.

I have already written you several letters with various dates and have left them for you at a number of locations. I doubt, however, whether you will receive them.

Our greatest consolation and good fortune is that you are not here. But, dear children, don't take foolish things to heart. Be happy, contented people; be good human beings and loyal sons of your oppressed nation. Never abandon your land or your people. Fight for freedom and social justice. Be just and honest; and under normal conditions this is so easy! We speak of you very often, and you are our consolation. Whenever Muka gets very depressed, he says: "Mama, how I'd like to see Amos and Nioma again."

There is still a remnant left here of your friends, boys as well as girls. They mention you often with affection and with ungrudging envy. Know how to appreciate your good fortune and use it not for yourselves alone but for others both near and distant. Lighten the life of your grandfather, grandmother, aunts, and uncles who have also survived. And don't mourn for us with tears and words, but rather with deeds. We were not useless here; in any way we could we tried to make things easier for those around us. I am leaving the world with almost a clear conscience. I lived my life. I have no complaints to anyone. It is a matter of fate; I believe in *beshert*, that things are destined. But why Muka? That is our greatest sorrow. I regret that I cannot communicate to you everything we have experienced. You will probably know something; but whatever you will ever hear and know, the reality is a thousand times more horrible and more painful. Words don't exist to tell it; no colors exist with which to represent it.

I hope you are under the influence of your grandfather, grandmother, and Aunt Jennie. Obey them and be good people. Too young you have become orphans. But better to be orphans there than to be with father and mother here. I kiss you very warmly. Kiss and greet all those near to me, whoever may be there. After all, I know nothing about anyone, just as no one knows about us. We have been buried alive here for three years now.

Your mother

Shulamit Rabinovitch's Husband

This letter, also dated June 6, 1944, was written by the husband of Shulamit Rabinovitch, and accompanied her letter to their children in the United States.

June 6, 1944

Dear and beloved sons:

I reproved your mother, telling her that her letter to you was transformed into a will. I don't know at all how much longer we are destined to be tormented; our fate lies in wait for us. But even a life of suffering is life, and we constantly wonder at how much a human being can bear.

Perhaps these lines will come into your hands by some unbelievable chance. If so, we want you to know that during the summer of 1944 your parents were still alive, thinking often of you, and completely devoid of hope of ever receiving any message from you.

Materially speaking this past year has not been the worst. Also, in my position I have seen and have been saturated by so much anguish and have borne so much sorrow that one becomes hardened, and one wonders how it was possible to live through it all.

Even more, one is in awe over the will to live and the power of resistance of the surviving remnant present here.

Meanwhile we have beautiful summer days. Through the window we can see the greening of the little garden, tended by Youngest Son. The roads are sandy here; who knows whether we will end our days here or be forced to relocate farther still.

Be well and strong.

The God of Abraham, Isaac, and Jacob shield and protect you.

Part Three

Wills from the Land of Israel

The Land of Israel is multifaceted; it presents us its many faces, evolved out of its unique history and as the result of its special relationship to the People of Israel.

Over the centuries and to the present moment its people have come to it for many reasons and have responded to it variously. Some came to be buried in the holy ground on which walked the patriarchs and prophets; many came to build the Land, to live on it and to be up-built by it; some built philanthropic bridges to it from afar, then came to forge personal links with it; many came to pioneer and to build a just society based on Jewish values; and many have been there always, manning the barricades of Torah, seen as the first line of defense for the Holy Land and its People. Many came in this century to live in peace, but were impelled to fight in defense of the Land and the People of Israel, some to die for it, in distant lands.

The ethical wills in this section reflect the diversity of meaning Israel the Land has had for the Jews and how they have responded to its influence and its call.

Elijah David Rabinovitz (Teomim)

Rabbi Elijah David Rabinovitz (1843–1905) was appointed as the first Ashkenazic chief rabbi of Jerusalem in 1900, a post he filled brilliantly but briefly, until 1905. Among the changes he wrought was the institution of a system of official inspection services for supervising the weights and measures used by local merchants. We note in his *tzava'ah* the intense introspection and the preoccupation with improvement of personal traits which are both typical of the true *ba'al musar* (moralist), and his scrupulous care in the performance of the mezuzah and tefillin observances.

All my life I have despised conceit. From earliest childhood I have felt revulsion for a person in whom I detected signs of arrogant pride. It seems to me that there is in my heart not the least bit of arrogance. Although I often see clearly what my few skills and positive attributes are, I thank God that I am not moved to pride over them.

Love of money never found a place in my heart. Still, I cannot claim purity of heart to the extent of *despising* money; I have not yet attained to that trait. But to love money—no.

So also have I always disliked personal glory, and I always feel wretched when people honor me. Especially is this so when I am given honor by those greater and better than I ... always have I received more honor than I deserve. Nor can I dissuade people from doing this since, as set forth in the Talmud [Jerusalem Talmud, Tractate *Shevi'it*, end], doing so causes them to attribute the trait of *modesty* to me as well! So what am I to do? These precious traits are an inheritance from my revered father and teacher, of blessed memory.

So also has truth been a lamp unto my feet, and I have hated falsehood, despising it exceedingly. I never covered up the faults of loved ones or of my relatives whenever it was contrary to the truth, nor will I take liberties with the truth, even inwardly perverting strict truth; nor make excuses improperly when something turns out wrong, denying responsibility for an outcome. These latent characteristics are also bequeathed me by my father, of blessed memory. And though the term "modest" was fitting and proper for *him*, in whom the trait of modesty was truly present, since he had much of which to be proud, not so is the case with me, who am but "dregs of the wine ..." [Jerusalem Talmud, Tractate *Ma'asrot* III, 50d] for of what value am I and my deeds. I recognize in my little worth and very limited knowledge that I have nothing whatever to boast of, so the trait of modesty does not apply at all; simply and literally stated, I am and possess nothing. But this I can say with certainty: that source of all evil, that foremost of impure traits—*arrogance*—is something I have despised to the ultimate degree, even the slightest hint of it. It is the root of all transgressions, the major ones and the minor ones alike, among human beings. Whoever has the slightest trace of it cannot remain free of guilt. I thank God that it has not found a place in my heart until now; may the Almighty protect me from it for the remainder of my life.

Love for the sacred Torah and for those who study it, especially for the greatest of these scholars and for the truly God-fearing, is rooted in my heart and soul. To this day I yearn to stand and minister to those great, thoroughly pious geniuses, simply to serve them as a servant ministers to his master. To my regret I have not yet been privileged to do this. Where I am known this is denied me, and elsewhere the opportunity has not been present. I always keep before my mind's eye the sayings of our holy sages, "Let your fellow's honor be as dear to you as your own" [*Avot* 2:15], and "whoever recognizes that his fellow excels him even in one thing is obliged to pay him homage" [*Avot* 6:3]. I am therefore careful in treating others with respect, especially anyone who is my superior in something, for the sages have imposed an obligation upon us to honor such individuals.

Because of my habit to avoid honors, I have been retiring and socially withdrawn. I have not shown my writings and religious compositions to any but a very small number of my closest friends. This was in order to avoid experiencing conceit from seeing many writings in print. On the front page of every one of my compositions I have written the aphorism of Rabbi Yohanan ben Zakkai, "If you have learned much Torah, do not credit yourself for it" [*Avot* 2:9].

I have always exercised care in honoring those greater and older than I, in not writing to them "Dear friend," as if imposing myself upon them by virtue of the correspondence.

From my earliest days I have been careful to set aside a tithe of all profits that came my way. In the observance of timely recitation of the *Shema* I have been scrupulous since my earliest youth; and it is now about twenty years since I have become accustomed to recite the *Shema* just before sunrise, in fulfillment of the view of a number of ancient sages who specify that the morning recitation of the *Shema* is before sunrise.

Regarding public worship, I have been very careful, with God's help. Sometimes it necessitated great effort to assemble ten for a quorum, and to this day when I must pray alone I feel as if I haven't prayed at all!

For the past several decades I have trained myself to wear small tefillin all day, especially when, en route, I am away from my studies. In such cases I take comfort in the words of the sage in the *Mekhilta*, "Donning the tefillin is considered equivalent to studying Torah." For the past several years I have developed the habit of wearing several different pair of tefillin every day, because of the risk that a single pair may be ritually imperfect; with several pair this risk is eliminated.

All my life I have never been slow to perform deeds of personal service to others; my hands are not tied to prevent my gathering alms for the poor, and my feet are not chained to prevent my going from door to door for charitable donations.

Many are the sufferings and travails that have overtaken me, may you be spared such troubles, and these have aged me before my time. But nothing brings me to tears so quickly as when I remember Jerusalem, our holy city and house of glory, the exile of God's Presence, the exile of Torah and of Israel, the memories of which cause my eyes to flood with tears.

Before I undertook rabbinical duties all my thoughts were tied to matters of Torah. Even in conversation with people my mind was on Torah. It has been a favorite saying of mine that this is the literal meaning of the verse "Thou shalt meditate on it day and night" [Josh. 1:8].

For many years now I follow the practice of observing the commandment of mezuzah in every detail. Thus whenever I rent a new flat (in which mezuzah observance is not by biblical but by rabbinic injunction, according to most authorities) I purchase one room from the owner, for cash, for a specified period in a way that it belongs to me fully by Torah law. In this way I am able to afix the mezuzah immediately, while a renter is obligated only after thirty days. One thing is certain: dwelling in one's own house obligates a mezuzah from the first hour, according to the Torah.

With anything owned by another I always exercise great care; and I avoided coveting another's possession. I have been guided by the interpretation of the *Ehen Ha'ezer* on this negative commandment, namely, that the property of another is simply unattainable under any circumstances, and is repugnant to me like the flesh of pig and other forbidden things.

Whenever I preached in public, on the Sabbath before Passover and on the Sabbath of Return, I always announced beforehand, "I am prepared to observe the commandment 'Thou shalt surely rebuke thy neighbor....' [Lev. 19:17]. May it be God's will that my words be well ordered and well received in the service of the Almighty, and that I not miss the mark by offending anyone, God forbid." With God's help I have always been careful in this regard in every possible way. May He also preserve me in the days ahead for good.

Theodor Herzl

Theodor Herzl (1860–1904), founder of the World Zionist Organization and acclaimed father of modern political Zionism, was born in Budapest. His background was in the spirit of the German-Jewish Enlightenment. Herzl earned a doctorate in law and worked for a time in the courts in Vienna before embarking on a writing career in 1885. During the next few years he published half a dozen books and many plays, most of which were staged in Germany and Austria to public acclaim. Contrary to popular belief, Herzl was aware of and involved in the Jewish question long before the Dreyfuss Affair. His drama *Das Neue Ghetto* was written and presented in order to stimulate public discussion of the problem of anti-Semitism. It was the attitude of the French public during the Dreyfuss trial, which Herzl covered for the *Vienna Freie Presse*, that brought him to a crystallization of his ideas about a territory of their own for Jews. Herzl sacrificed years of his life as well as a successful writing career for the Zionist ideal.

It is fitting to prepare for the day of death. One cannot speak in flowery language.

What I have meant for Jews, future days will tell better than the general public in my own time. My primary estate consists of diary entries about my activities in Jewish affairs. They comprise, to date, four books, a portion of which are being kept at father's and the remainder with me. I shall perhaps place them in a more secure place. These memoirs shall be published immediately following my death.

For the purpose of publishing them, for the style editing, etc., a committee shall be appointed.

To this committee, the Austrian Zionist Federation shall appoint two members; the guardian of my children shall appoint a literary adviser who shall be, if possible, from among my circle of friends.

A contract is to be signed with a proper publishing house for the publication of the writings in German and English. The contractual-legal aspects entailed in this rests upon the guardian of my children.

It will be desirable, perhaps, to publish as well a collection of my Zionist articles and addresses.

The conditions for this shall be the same as for the publication of my memoirs.

Similarly, I suggest seeking a publisher for the rest of my writings. I believe that all my plays should be published in one volume.

My favorite play is *The Ghetto*. Also, the fragment *Marriage Comedy* which I began writing in Wiesbaden shall be included in the collection; furthermore, incorporate the notes to serve as a curiosity for creative artists. One volume shall contain the feuilletons and the articles which I wrote from Paris to the *Neue Freie Presse* and which have never been assembled in a book.

The rest of my feuilletons, which have not yet been gathered into a book, will fill several volumes.

My name will grow after my death; I therefore believe that a publisher will be found for all my writings.

I know today, as I have known every single minute since I began my writing career, that I wielded my pen as an honest man.

Never did I sell my pen, never did I utilize it for base or obscene purposes, not even for social reasons.

It is permitted to publish this last testament.

Even after my death no one will gainsay my words.

Officially recorded in the district court of the state, at Wahring, July 4, 1904.

Edmond James de Rothschild

A scion of the famous banking family in France, Edmond de Rothschild (1845–1934) became involved in active support of the *Yishuv*, the Jewish community in Palestine, during the Russian pogroms of the 1880s. Because of his strong desire for anonymity, he was, in the early days, referred to as *Hanadiv Hayadu'a*, the "Well-Known Benefactor." His support took many forms: he gave direct support to developing colonies, underwrote long-term agricultural experiments by experts sent from France, and purchased large tracts of land later transferred to the ownership of the Jewish authorities in Palestine. The settlement of Binyamina was named in his honor. The following is from a statement of his credo delivered at the Great Synagogue in Tel Aviv on May 17, 1925, on his final visit to Palestine. The framed text is hung on the east wall of the synagogue.

To the Rock of Israel I lift up my heart and thank Him with all my soul for His kindness to me, for the privilege of beholding at my advanced age this wondrous sight, the vision of Israel restored. When I call to memory the past, about fifty years ago when I first began my work, when I recall the appearance of the land, strewn with stones, full of thorn and thistle, its inhabitants struggling to produce meager kernels from the poor soil, it is as though I were in a dream. It never occurred to me that *all* Jews would be gathered in Eretz Yisrael; today, too, this remains an impossibility. What was in my heart was the establishment of a center, one that is as significant as possible, for the enhancement of the spirit of Judaism and its exalted Torah and its noble culture; and that this center would exert a beneficial influence upon the condition of Jews in all the countries of the world.

They used to say to me, "You are building on sand!" Now, here is the sand and, in the words of the psalmist, it has become a cornerstone[1] in the rebuilding of Israel. The fields are cultivated, the numerous vineyards and orchards are like oases in the desert—all giving testimony to the energy and endurance of the Jewish people.

The fact that the great powers accepted the [Balfour] Declaration, and that the League of Nations approved it as well, seems like the realization of the prophecy which sustained the spirit of our ancestors throughout the many centuries of anguish and travail. Now, after two thousand years, the utterances of the prophets are being fulfilled before our eyes: "Surely the isles shall wait for me, the ships of Tarshish first, to bring thy sons from afar" [Isa. 60:9]. Happy are we to live in a blessed time as this when we may add, "Certainly, this is the day that we have looked for; we have found, we have seen it" [Lam. 2:16].

Long ago, when I visited the settlements for the first time, I was impressed by the Hebrew studies in the schools. After several years I was happy to observe that Hebrew had become a living tongue. Jews who came from various lands could communicate in one language; and this language served also as a link between the past and present and also as a bond with the ideals of the forefathers.

Basing myself on what I have done in Eretz Yisrael, I wish to tell how, in my opinion, the National Home ought to develop so that it not founder on shoals born of false hopes, and how to clear away the stumbling-blocks which may cause you to trip if you stray from the course.

First, you must be concerned about intensifying and enlarging the ideal of the National Home in every possible way and to work with all your might for its fruition. Its blossoming will help all the inhabitants of the land. You must continue to live, as heretofore, in the best relations with your neighbors and thereby be true to the principles transmitted to us by our ancestors: "Love thy neighbor as thyself" [Lev. 19:18].

The Jewish people in their land cannot exist by virtue of physical energies alone, without a connection to our noble past and to our tradition. What can a small group of Jews in a tiny corner of the world do against the storms that uproot even the mighty powers of the world. You cannot survive even a small gale; you would be like a wind-blown straw, like a fleeting cloud.

In all that you try to do—both in your daily work and in your exalted tasks—you must follow the ideals of Judaism, act in accord with its clear guidelines, toward that moral perfection that is the essence of our faith. An eternal Law of the highest spirituality, this is the Law the Israelites received two thousand years ago at a time when all surrounding peoples were barbaric, steeped in their abominable practices. These are the ideals that preserved the Jewish people, living and enduring, maintained its strength and courage these thousands of years.

The Tablets of the Covenant which Moses received at Mount Sinai, and whose remembrance we celebrate a few days hence on the festival of Shavuot, have remained to this day the basis of all civilization. While Israelites wandered in the desert, the Ark of the Covenant went before them constantly, and in it were the tablets of stone, more desirable than pure gold; for on them were engraved the sacred principles guiding them in the ways of faith in the unity of God and His spirituality—this at a time when all others sought to appease their deities according to their cruel practices. The sanctity of the family, founded upon reverence for parents, is the foundation of all society, and without which all is chaos and disorder. The relationship between man and his fellow is based on the admonition: "What is hateful to thee do not do unto thy fellow" [*Sabbath* 31a].

… If you continue to maintain this tradition, you too will be enabled to fulfill a noble role in the world, the role that so befits the descendants of the patriarchs, the offspring of those who heard the voices of the prophets. As you merit by your conduct, so will the nations honor you. Live your lives with generosity, with exalted thought and deed, for the betterment of mankind and for peace among nations.

Educate your children by the precepts which our fathers bequeathed us, which preserved our people and brought us to this day. Be faithful to your past and labor to perfect the world under the Kingdom of Heaven. The lamp which our ancestors conveyed to us will not pass away nor be lost over the generations. In this way will the Homeland flourish even though it remain small. In this way will the People of Israel live to fulfill its noble mission. It will take its place among the great nations, and the building blocks which it raises up in Eretz Yisrael will be strong and endure forever.

I have reached advanced age—to those years which, according to Ecclesiastes, "I have no pleasure in them" [Eccles. 12:1]. I have fulfilled my duty, "Because man goeth to his long home" [Eccles. 12:5]—and my eldest son, James, who is of one mind with me, will further my work and will devote himself to the enterprise which I have begun.

May God protect the National Home in Eretz Yisrael!

Abraham Isaac Kook

Rabbi Kook (1865–1935) was the first Ashkenazic chief rabbi in modern Eretz Yisrael. He was a preeminent talmudic scholar and a prolific writer from an early age. His writings vibrate to a deep mystical chord and are permeated by a profound love of mankind. It is said of him that his main concern was the redemption of the Jewish people and of all mankind. Rabbi Kook was a leading spokesman of religious Zionism. After serving as rabbi in several Lithuanian cities, he came to Palestine in 1904 to be rabbi in Jaffa. After World War I he became rabbi of Jerusalem and in 1921 he was elected chief rabbi of Eretz Yisrael. He wrote the following will in 1919 when stricken with serious illness.

By the grace of God, Iyar 21, 5679 (1919), between the hours of nine and ten in the morning.

My hope is that God, in His mercy, will grant me a complete healing, among the other sick persons of His people Israel, and that in His abundant kindnesses He will enable me to return to Him in love. Especially do I pray that He enable me to mend whatever wrong I may have committed, whether in man's relationship to God or man's relationship to man, and that He grace me with the opportunity to repay my debts.

To my great regret I do not remember all my debts in detail. But I hope that God will bestir me and remind me of them all, and that He will help me to repay them. Some of those that have come to my mind I wrote down in a small notebook with a white cover, where there will also be found some poems. Some pages that were torn off from this notebook are with Zevi Yehuda [his son], may he be granted life, and some debts are also recorded there.

Most of the books in my apartment here do not belong to me. May God help me to return them to their owners. In my house in Jaffa too there are also many books that belong to others. May God enable me to clarify everything and to set everything in order.

May it be God's will to inspire whomever I may have pained or offended to forgive me with a full forgiveness. As for me, I surely forgive all. On the contrary, I regard as a good every pain and humiliation to which I was subjected. May it be God's will that no one suffer retribution on account of me, and may God bestow on all members of the fellowship of Israel only good and mercy.

O Lord, help me and heal me in Your abundant mercies, and strengthen me with Your help. Help Your holy people, and hasten the light of Your deliverance and establish Your holiness in all the worlds. Amen.

Resigned, yet anticipating Your help,
Abraham Isaac Hakohen Kook

My gold watch and chain is a gift of dear Shlesinger, may his memory be for a blessing, and I have some scruples about the gift. May God enable me to straighten it out properly, in accordance with the precepts of our holy Torah.

Ben Zion Meir Hai Uziel

Rabbi Uziel (1880–1953) was "Rishon LeZion," Sephardic chief rabbi of Eretz Yisrael. He was distinguished for his wisdom and for his efforts at reconciling all classes and elements of society and was universally beloved and respected. He was the author of a noteworthy volume of responsa, *Mishpetei Uziel*. The following testament was written when he knew he had only two or three days to live following the amputation of a limb.

In my role, I constantly kept before me as a lamp unto my feet these aims: to disseminate Torah among the students; to love the Torah and its commandments, the land of Israel and its sanctity; absolute love for every man and woman of Israel, for the entire peoplehood of Israel, and for the God of Israel; to implant peace among all men and women of Israel, in its body and soul, its speech and action, its thoughts and meditations, its progress and exploits, at home and abroad, in town and city, to bring true peace into the household of Israel and its family, among the entire congregation of Israel in all its classes and factions, and between Israel and their Father in heaven. These latter two are actually one, since both emanate from one source, and that is *the Torah* of the living God, King of the universe, King of Israel and its holiness, who gave the Torah of Truth to His people; all whose ways are pleasantness and all whose paths are peace.

These two aims have been the ideal and the purpose of my life, and by them have I directed my path; and this prayer was on my lips each day: "Guide me by Thy counsel, lead me in Thy way, establish peace and truth among all Thy people Israel, to love and sanctify Thy name."

Certain it is that I have not succeeded even in the smallest measure to fulfill these goals which I set as my life's goal, but this I know—and the Almighty Who knows all secret things, knows—and all Israel knows that this was my intention and my prayer.

And now, as I take leave of you, my brethren and sisters, my teachers and mentors, all the House of Israel, to be gathered unto my fathers reposing in Eden, I thank you from the depths of my heart, collectively and individually, for honoring me in my lifetime beyond what my deeds and wisdom deserve, for the pleasantness with which you surrounded me by granting me a generous and substantial income with which to support myself and raise my family, may God preserve them, Amen.

I herewith ask your forgiveness and full pardon for any sins or offenses, slights or affronts I may have committed against any group or individual and failed to conciliate during my lifetime; if so, know and believe that it was unintentional. For the honor and wishes of every Jewish man and woman are the most precious and beloved to me of all public groups. But it is possible that as a mortal human being I may have caused someone, by accidental word or deed, some hurt or financial injury, and I hereby entreat you and say, forgive me and permit my soul to rest in peace.

Set aside all causes of separation and dispute from our midst and from our land, and establish in their stead all the elements for peace and unity, that our encampment may be pure, sanctified, fortified, and integrated, like a fortified barricade, against whom no destructive or vengeful force can be effectual. May God, Who maintains harmony in His celestial heights, cause peace for us and bless us according to His word by Moses His prophet:

> The Lord your God has multiplied you, and behold, you are this day as the stars of the heaven for multitude. The Lord God of your fathers make you a thousand times as many as you are, and bless you as He promised you…. The Lord will give strength to His people, the Lord will bless His people with peace…. And may the offering of Judah and Jerusalem be pleasant to the Lord as in the days of yore and years of old. [Deut. 1:10, 11; Ps. 29:11; Mal. 3:4]

Now I, your brother, take leave of you for life eternal, with blessings for peace, for the world's redemption with the establishment of the throne of the Davidian House, and for the rebuilding of God's sanctuary in Jerusalem, City of Holiness.

Alter Ya'akov Sahrai

Rabbi Alter Ya'akov Sahrai (1874–1937) was born in Poland where in his youth be studied under the Grand Rabbi Yehiel Ostrowski. He was an ardent Zionist and played an active role in the Mizrahi movement in its early stages of development. He settled in Eretz Yisrael in 1910, and served as communal secretary in Jerusalem for a number of years. He was a strong proponent of Jewish self-defense, and in his will he urges his children to defend those who cannot do so for themselves.

Written in Tel Aviv, Tamuz 13, 5693 [1933]

Praise and thanks do I give to the Creator of all and Master of the world for the soul He implanted and maintained within me, in His great kindness, all the years of my life. I did not expect that my frail body would endure to reach this age, but despite the many emotional crises, the physical infirmities, accidents, misfortunes, and the anguish of parenthood that I experienced, I survived, and by His will reached this point.

The days of my life have been days of sorrow and pain and not always have I been forbearing.

For forty years I have stood in the ranks of those laboring for the rebirth of our people and its land; and now, too, facing the end of my life, I maintain this view with all my might, and acknowledge the call to service incumbent upon every Jew who is loyal to his people, its Torah, and its land.

I address my children: I pray you, my dear ones, to remember that you are Jews, members of the Jewish nation, set apart from other nations and distinguished from them by virtue only of its Torah, that "Torah which Moses commanded us," and expounded by our sages in each generation.

A person who writes his will sees death before his eyes, whether it come now or after a time; and at this important time I say to you that the words of the Torah and of its expounders, the prophets and the sages of the Talmud, they are the guides who lead us to Divine Providence. Devote yourselves to constructive labors, to the task of physically rebuilding our land. It would be well if you affiliated with

Mizrahi, Hapoel Hamizrahi, or a similar group. Do not withdraw from any constructive work, particularly protecting the lives and property of the people of Israel in the Land of Israel. On the contrary, take your stand where those who are weaker and of a faint-hearted temperament are incapable of standing.

Meir Dizengoff

Meir Dizengoff (1861–1937) was the first mayor of Tel Aviv. He was born in Bessarabia where he was active in the Hovevei Zion movement, and he attended the early Zionist Congresses where he was strongly opposed to the Uganda Plan. In 1905 Dizengoff settled in Jaffa where he became a founder of the Ahuzat Bayit Company whose aim it was to establish a modern Jewish quarter near Jaffa. In 1921 the new quarter became the city of Tel Aviv and Dizengoff its first mayor, a post he held until his death except for the years 1925–1928. Before leaving for a rest cure in Jerusalem, he wrote a testament for publication upon his death. Shortly thereafter, on the day he died, the press carried the full text, portions of which appear here.

Tel Aviv, July 12, 1936

I should like my death to be by Divine Kiss. Is it not written that every man can be like Moses our teacher, and if he died thus, why not I? As a child, I imagined it in a plain and simple way: When Moses and the Israelites reached Mount Nebo, the Almighty Himself, in all His glory, came down to the mountain, called Moses to Him, and kissed him; and in that moment his soul fled. Later, after learning from my revered teachers that God has no bodily form or substance, I imagined the matter of death by Divine Kiss differently: On the summit of the mountain, from which one can see Jerusalem, the Dead Sea, and the land of the Jordan, God revealed Himself to Moses and said to him, "'Enough, my servant Moses, you have accomplished much: You led the Israelites from Egypt, carried them through the wilderness, gave them the Torah, and brought them to the threshold of the Promised Land which I swore to give to them and their descendants as an eternal inheritance. Here is the land, a pleasant land, spread out before you; view it from the mountaintop, because your duty on earth is done. Ascend!' And Moses died; and no man knoweth the place of his sepulchre until this day" [Deut. 34:6]. This was death by Divine Kiss.

Viewed thus, many deaths may be seen as being by Divine Kiss. The last minutes in the life of Chief Rabbi Abraham Isaac Kook, of blessed memory, for example. As his expiration came near, his rabbinic comrades ringed his bed and prayed aloud, repeating the supreme declaration of every believing Jew, "Hear O Israel, the Lord our God, the Lord is One!" The dying rabbi responded to them in an ever-weakening voice, until at last, on the word "One" his soul fled. Now this was dying by Divine Kiss—because Harav Kook died calmly and contented, as one who had achieved the objectives of his lifetime. About such a person one may say, "The righteous live by their faith" (Hab. 2:4), and in their faith they die.

When I think about my own dying, the thought does not arouse in me any feeling of sorrow, morbidity, or sadness because this entire process of putting off one and putting on another aspect of existence is natural and normal. The time has come to conclude all the affairs of my life, my mundane activities; and I stand at the threshold of a new period and of a new world, far beyond me, on the other side of Awareness. The roles I have filled during my lifetime are satisfying, in that I did not spend my years for naught, and in that all my communal endeavors were for the benefit of my people and for the good of our beloved land.

I visualize my last day [on earth] as follows: After my bier will walk the children of Tel Aviv—those angels, those cherubs whom I loved so much all my days. In solid ranks, with heads held high, they follow behind my bier. And I can hear these youngsters' voices as they cry, "Don't leave us, dear grandfather; we love you dearly!"

Behind the children march the stalwart youth groups before whom are open unlimited opportunities in the tasks of liberty and redemption, and who live in an environment of dreams and idealistic strivings. I have always considered myself a friend to this younger generation and there has existed between us always a close spiritual bond. Whenever anyone asked me my age, I would reply, "I don't know precisely the number of years I have lived, but I feel ready for any daring, fantastic initiative, so long as it is worthwhile and leads to an ultimate goal." These youth will inherit our place and will lead us to the realization of our national strivings. It should be no wonder then that these youth accompany me to my final rest and that I rejoice within me over the fact; because even when I am on the other side of Awareness I shall maintain contact with these daring youth.

Next comes a large contingent of women who take part in the funeral. These are the mothers who gave birth to the young generation and who guard the chain of tradition linking the forefathers and their children....

When they lower my body into the cold, damp grave and cover the bier with layers of earth, it seems to me that as a consequence of the great demonstration of the funeral procession, rays of light will break forth to penetrate the clumps of earth and illuminate the new journey on which I am bound, and to tell me that my death is not forced upon me but rather is by Divine Kiss.

Yitzhak Ben Nehemia Margalit

Yitzhak Margolis (1870?–1937), a scion of a distinguished hasidic family in Russia, was an active Zionist leader and organizer before, during, and after World War I. He was highly respected for his learning and acknowledged as a motivating influence in awakening a nationalist spirit among his contemporaries. It was his belief that Zionism and the Jewish Homeland could assure Jewish existence, a view which his hasidic contemporaries considered heretical. In 1921, he settled with his family in Palestine, where he died sixteen years later. The testament which he wrote to his son is sprinkled with biblical and talmudic allusions and reveals the fervor of his religious faith as well as his lifelong Zionist zeal. It is written in the cover of a prayer book which he presented to his son.

Nehemia, my darling son!

Come and I will show thee the place where heaven and earth kiss.[1] I know where this wondrous place is; it is very close to us—it is the synagogue of our people.

There, my son, is "the ladder set on the ground, with its top reaching to the heavens ..." [Gen. 28:12] and the soul of all our generations ascend and descend on it. There we hear, too, the vibrations of generations yet to come.

Take these five small volumes, my son. They are the prayer books for the weekdays, for our festivals and holy days. Here, in these volumes and in this place your forefathers, giants of spirit and humaneness, poured forth their hearts. When you open this wondrous book before you, you feel as though their presence encircles you, watches over you and hears your whispered prayers....

I know, my son, I know well how indifferent is the attitude toward the synagogue among many, especially among the youth. This results mainly from lack of understanding and from insensitivity. This condition has caused and will yet cause immeasurable harm to our rootedness in the Land of our Fathers.

But blindness is not forever! The time is coming—and it is not far off—when the House of Prayer will again occupy its rightful place in our people's revival and become a cornerstone in the rebuilding of our people and our land.

My son, my beloved son! Do not absent yourself from this House, the House of the God of your fathers. There will their noble spirits rest upon you. There will you imbibe the spirit of the festivals and be animated by their joy, whose absence is so keenly felt here in our land.

My blessings upon you for the new year. May the Almighty be gracious unto thee, my son,[2] who art called by the name of my fathers.[3] May you grow old and established in the Land,[4] you, your children and your children's children.

These are the words of your father who loves you with love profound.

Yitzhak ben Nehemia Halevi [Margalit]
Rosh Hashana Eve, 5689 [September 14, 1928] Tel Aviv

Naftali Swiatitsky

The will of Naftali Swiatitsky is arresting on two counts: first, it describes the regrets of an aged father over a sin of omission committed many years earlier against one of his children and steps taken to amend the wrong; and second, it calls for the wronged son to return to Eretz Yisrael in order to claim his patrimony. Between the lines of this unusual will, ostensibly dealing with material bequests alone, we read a fuller story of a father seeking to reunite a son with his family and, simultaneously, with his brethren in the Jewish Homeland. Naftali Swiatitsky came to Petakh Tikva, "Mother of the Colonies," from Russia during the past century as one of the early pioneers. He was born in 1849 and died in Petakh Tikva in 1949.

Petakh Tikva
October 25, 1945
Heshvan 18, 5706

Because no one knows the exact time of his death and I am now already up in years when "I have no pleasure in them" [Eccles. 12:1]; being now ninety-five years of age, although I am still alert in my senses and I can walk with a cane on my own feet,

and since I have no tangibles or valuables or real estate to leave my children after me, since whatever I had from my labors during my years on earth I have already distributed among my children and I have no more to bequeath them,

now, before I go and am no more, and while I am still on my feet, normal in sense and limb, a certain realization picks at my mind like a mosquito, namely, that toward one of my sons—Mr. Gershon Swiatitsky, now forty years in America, in the city of Chicago, and who is called George Sweet—I have not properly fulfilled the duty of a father to his son.

This son left my home in Petakh Tikva forty years ago, and when he left he borrowed a sum of fifty or more francs, the coin of the realm at that time. This sum I have not been repaid by him till now, and in the meantime I have divided my properties among my three other children, while to my son Gershon Swiatitsky, who resides in the United States and is called George Sweet, I gave nothing because he was "out of sight, out of mind," as the saying goes.

Now, as I stand at the sunset of my life, I cannot forgive myself for the injustice with which I treated my son Gershon who is in America; and inasmuch as I myself own nothing today, neither movable nor real property, and can therefore bequeath him nothing whatever of my own, I have made a careful computation of the assets which I distributed earlier among my other children and divided it into four parts. The results indicate that I gave of Gershon's (called George) share to my other children in the following amounts: (1) To my son David, I gave 150 pounds; to my son Arieh, 150 pounds; to my daughter Mrs. Shifra Zimirovsky, 420 pounds, all appraised in terms of money values current at that time in Eretz Yisrael. By all rights it comes out that Gershon Swiatitsky (George Sweet) is owed 750 pounds from the properties that I gave my children during my lifetime.

It remains only for me to address my above-named two sons and daughter and to convey this as a final request. [I do this] in order that I may depart this world of vanities with the feeling that I have done my duty toward all four of my children and that I may not be ashamed, when I stand before the heavenly tribunal, over the unwarranted discrimination which I directed against my above-named son, George (whom I have not seen for forty years and whom I doubt I shall ever see again during my lifetime), in dividing what little I had in my power to give my heirs. I therefore instruct my three above-named children, David, Arieh, and Shifra, as a deed of final reverence for a parent, to consider themselves duty-bound to pay their brother Gershon Swiatitsky, known as George Sweet, whenever their brother comes to Eretz Yisrael, the amounts I have set, in cash, immediately upon his arrival in Eretz Yisrael. Let this be done immediately upon his arrival without hesitation, vacillation, or bargaining whatever. This is my last request of my children who received my property years ago, whose value has increased many-fold since then, and I instruct them to fulfill my request exactly as in this will.

I trust that my children will carry out this request faithfully and precisely so that I will not be ashamed of them when I come before the Judge on high, before Whom are revealed the ways of all men and Who repays men according to their deeds [Jer. 17:10].

I have no other requests of my children. I pray they may attain long life, to ripe old age in joy; and may the Almighty grant them strength and wealth many times over what I was able to give them of my hard work over many years, and may they derive much pleasure from their own offspring.

The text of this will I sign in the presence of the chief rabbinate of Petakh Tikva and its environs, in the office of the chief rabbi of Petakh Tikva, Rabbi Reuven Katz, and I deposit in their care for safekeeping the original of this document with the requests that at my demise the above be brought to the attention of my children, to fulfill all the above; and a copy of this will be given to each of my four children so they may be informed exactly what the final request of my life is.

Not an elaborate funeral nor a beautiful tombstone, no pomp or honor—this I leave to the judgment of my children alone. I have only the one request which I have detailed above, simple and unambiguous, which I ask them to fulfill exactly, and I hope they will do so. Then I shall truly be able to rest in peace when my time comes; then shall I be an advocate on their behalf in the next world. All this have I set forth above. It is the sole request I make of my children.

Hannah Senesh

Hannah Senesh (1921–1944) immigrated to Palestine from her native Hungary just before the outbreak of World War II. She volunteered for the parachute corps and was dropped behind Nazi lines to work with partisan forces. She was captured by the Nazis, and after months of imprisonment and torture was executed in 1944. In addition to a legacy of heroism, Hannah Senesh left a collection of poems and a personal journal that reveal a gifted, sensitive spirit. She wrote this letter in December 1943, and arranged to have it given to her brother upon his arrival in Palestine should she fail to return from her mission. As it happened, he arrived the day before her departure. He was able to read the letter, then return it to her for security reasons.

Haifa
December 25, 1943

Darling George!

Sometimes one writes letters one does not intend sending. Letters one must write without asking oneself, "I wonder whether this will ever reach its destination."

Day after tomorrow I am starting something new. Perhaps it's madness. Perhaps it's fantastic. Perhaps it is dangerous. Perhaps one in a hundred—or one in a thousand—pays with his life. Perhaps with less than his life, perhaps with more. Don't ask questions. You'll eventually know what it's about.

George, I must explain something to you. I must exonerate myself. I must prepare myself for that moment when you arrive inside the frontiers of the Land, waiting for that moment when, after six years, we will meet again, and you will ask, "Where is she?" and they'll abruptly answer, "She's not here."

I wonder, will you understand? I wonder, will you believe that it is more than a childish wish for adventure, more than youthful romanticism that attracted me? I wonder, will you feel that I could not do otherwise, that this was something I had to do?

There are events without which one's life becomes unimportant, a worthless toy; and there are times when one is commanded to do something, even at the price of one's life.

I'm afraid, George, that feelings turn into empty phrases even though they are so impassioned before they turn into words. I don't know whether you'll sense the doubt, the conflicts, and after every struggle the renewed decision.

It is difficult because I am alone. If I had someone with whom I could talk freely, uninhibitedly—if only the entire burden were not mine, if only I could talk to you. If there is anyone who would understand me, I think you would be that one. But who knows ... six years is a long time.

But enough about myself. Perhaps I have already said too much. I would like to tell you a few things about the new life, the new home, as I see them. I don't want to influence you. You'll see for yourself what the country is. But I want to tell you how I see it.

First of all—I love it. I love its hundred faces, its hundred climates, its many-faceted life. I love the old and the new in it; I love it because it is ours. No, not ours, but because we can make ourselves believe it is ours.

And I respect it. Not everything. I respect the people who believe in something, respect their idealistic struggle with the daily realities. I respect those who don't live just for the moment, or for money. And I think there are more such people here than anywhere else on earth. And finally, I think that this is the only solution for us, and for this reason I don't doubt its future, though I think it will be very difficult and combative.

As far as the kibbutz is concerned, I don't think it is perfect, and it will probably pass through many phases. But in today's circumstances it best suits our aims, and is the closest to our concept of a way of life—about this I have absolutely no doubt.

We have need of one thing: people who are brave and without prejudices, who are not robots, who want to think for themselves and not accept outmoded ideas. It is easy to place laws in the hands of man, to tell him to live by them. It is more difficult to follow those laws. But most difficult of all is to impose laws upon oneself, while being constantly self-analytical and self-vigilant. I think this is the highest form of law enforcement, and at the same time the only just form. And this form of law can only build a new, contented life.

I often ask myself what the fate of the kibbutz will be when the magic and novelty of construction and creation wear off, when the struggle for existence assumes reality and—according to plan—becomes an organized, abundant communal life. What will the incentive of the people be, what will fill their lives? I don't know the answer. But that day is so far in the future that it is best to think of existing matters.

Don't think I see everything through rose-colored glasses. My faith is a subjective matter, and not the result of outer conditions. I see the difficulties clearly, both inside and out. But I see the good side, and above all, as I said before, I think this is the only way.

I did not write about something that constantly preoccupies my thoughts: Mother. I can't.

Enough of this letter. I hope you will never receive it. But if you do, only after we have met.

And if it should be otherwise, George dear, I embrace you with everlasting love.

Your sister

P.S. I wrote the letter at the beginning of the parachute training course.

Noam Grossman

The months between November 1947 when the U.N. resolution for partition had been achieved and May 15, 1948, the date of the establishment of the State of Israel, were fraught with danger for the *Yishuv*, the Jewish settlement in Palestine. The defense of the *Yishuv* was organized and carried out clandestinely and was poorly armed due to prevailing regulations of the British Mandate authority. Some pitched battles were fought and many Arab ambushes were repelled by self-sacrificing young men and women. Noam Grossman was one of these. His will, written January 12, 1948, was delivered inside a small envelope on which was written "To be opened only after I die."

This will of mine is written hurriedly without the opportunity for a farewell, even in a letter:

1. Bury me in Nahlat Yitzhak, Tel Aviv.
2. No need to write anything about me in the paper.
3. With my salary and any insurance my family receives—set up a fund for buying guns for the Irgun.
4. Return all my personal belongings to my family.
5. Do not eulogize me; I did my duty!

Avraham Kreizman

Chicago-born Avraham Kreizman came to Eretz Yisrael in 1921. Avraham fell in the War of Independence, alone, hurling hand grenades to protect the withdrawal of his friends. He left a wife and two young daughters. Here, three days before his death, he writes to his wife.

I know: When I die, for you I shall continue to live. No one will take me from your faithful and tender heart. But if you meet a comrade who understands your sorrow, and you love him a bit and your life brings forth a new life and a son is born to you—give him and let him carry my name and let him be my continuation.

And if it comes to pass that he does not understand—leave him without pain and let the child be our son alone....

And when it comes to pass that a new settlement is built here, come and plant poppies in this place; they grow so beautifully here and thrive so well! And let this be the place of my grave....

And perhaps you will err and your flowers will not be planted on my grave but on that of one of my comrades nearby. Well ... another wife will think of her husband as she plants flowers on mine.

No one will be overlooked. Because we lie close to each other in this spot and there is no space here to divide a man and his friends....

Eldad Pan

Eldad Pan was killed in Israel's War of Independence at the age of twenty, a veteran of many battles. The translation from the original Hebrew is by Sidney Greenberg.

Lately I have been thinking about what the goal of life should be. At best, man's life is short. His life may be kind or harsh, easy or difficult, but the time passes before he realizes it. An old person wants to live no less than a young person. The years of life do not satisfy the hunger for life. What then shall we do during this time?

We can reach either of two conclusions. The first is that since life is so short we should enjoy it as much as possible. The second is that precisely because life is short and no one can completely enjoy it (for we die with half our desire unsatisfied) [Eccles. *Rabba* 1:2], therefore we should dedicate life to a sacred and worthy goal, to sacrifice it for something which will be valued above life. At times the first feeling is stronger and at others the second one. Of late, however, I think that the second feeling is dominant. It seems that I am slowly coming to the conclusion that life by itself is worth little unless it serves something greater than itself.

Dvora Waysman

Dvora Waysman is a distinguished writer in Israel who contributes articles and studies to the English language Jewish press in many countries. She and her family were *olim*, settlers in modern Israel. The problems of migrating to a new land are many and, with young children, intensified. In her ethical will she speaks eloquently and poetically of her deep love for Israel and of her everlasting joy at her family's becoming part of the Land and its people.

As I write this, I am sitting on my Jerusalem balcony, looking through a tracery of pine trees at the view along Rehov Ruppin. I can see the Knesset, the Israel Museum, and the Shrine of the Book—that architectural marvel resembling a woman's tilted breast, that houses the Dead Sea Scrolls.

I am at an age where I should write a will, but the disposition of my material possessions would take just a few lines. They do not amount to much ... had we stayed in Australia where you—my four children—were born, they would be much more. I hope you won't blame me for this.

For now you are Israelis, and I have different things to leave you. I hope you will understand that they are more valuable than money in the bank, stocks and bonds, and plots of land, for no one can ever take them away from you.

I am leaving you the fragrance of a Jerusalem morning ... unforgettable perfume of thyme, sage, and rosemary that wafts down from the Judean hills. The heartbreaking sunsets that give way to Jerusalem at night ... splashes of gold on black velvet darkness. The feel of Jerusalem stone, ancient and mellow, in the buildings that surround you. The piquant taste of humus, tehina, felafel—foods we never knew about before we came here to live.

I am leaving you an extended family—the whole house of Israel. They are your people. They will celebrate with you in joy, grieve with you in sorrow. You will argue with them, criticize them, and sometimes reject them (that's the way it is with families!). But underneath you will be proud of them and love them. More important, when you need them—they will be there!

I am leaving you the faith of your forefathers. Here, no one will ever laugh at your beliefs, call you "Jew" as an insult. You, my sons, can wear *kippot* and tzitzit if you so wish; you, my daughters, can modestly cover your hair after marriage if that is what you decide. No one will ridicule you. You can be as religious or as secular as you wish, knowing it is based on your own convictions, and not because of what the "goyim" might say. You have your heritage ... written with the blood of your people through countless generations. Guard it well and cherish it—it is priceless!

I am leaving you pride. Hold your head high. This is your country, your birthright. Try to do your share to enhance its image. It may call for sacrifice, but it will be worth it. Your children, their children, and all who come after, will thank you for it.

I am leaving you memories. Some are sad ... the early struggles to adapt to a new country, a new language, a new culture. But remember, too, the triumphs ... the feeling of achievement when you were accepted, when "they" became "us." That is worth more than silver trophies and gold medals. You did it alone—you "made" it.

And so, my children, I have only one last bequest. I leave you my love and my blessing. I hope you will never again need to say: "Next year in Jerusalem." You are already there—how rich you are!

Part Four

Wills of Modern and Contemporary American Jews

In this section we read some of the wills that document how parents have tried to convey the tradition to children growing up in America. The New World has been a place of hope for Jews, a synonym for opportunity. But life in America has also been a challenge, for American life offers choices. Some of the options threaten to supplant tradition and others tend to weaken the links between the generations.

It is not surprising that these American wills differ from the traditional ones; time and place have altered even the language in which they are written. The traditional values are not emphasized in these pages as often as in the earlier wills. Instead, the urgency here underlies exhortations to group survival and to family fidelity.

But these ethical wills share with those of all the ages two common characteristics: One is optimistic hope for the individual and collective future. The other is a palpable seriousness; for the prospect of death, even the dim awareness of its ultimate reality, imbues one's thoughts with an edge of gravity.

Nissen Sheinberg

Nissen Sheinberg (1833–1920) came to the United States in his mature years at the turn of the century. A learned, patriarchal Jew, he instructs his family in traditional matters. A portion of his will, however, records the extraordinary events surrounding the return of a niece to the family. This was written in Yiddish, in 1918; the translation is somewhat abridged.

Listen, all my children, to what I desire of you, and I hope you will observe my requests. Man does not live forever, and he does not know the exact time when he ends his journey on this earth. As he may not be able to speak during his final days, I decided on this plan while, thank God, my mind is still clear.

First, I beg you not to allow me to die in a hospital. Also, when I am placed on the floor, light the candles both at my head and at my feet.[1] Let the candles bum until I am taken from the house. Also, I request that you not allow me to be buried in a coffin but in the bare earth. They may say this can't be done, but they buried Mordecai Zoleniker, Eli Anise's father-in-law, this way. I have some earth from the Holy Land which should be sprinkled on my face and heart and some on the ground, so that its holiness may enter the body.[2] Sprinkle some also on the Sacred Covenant [circumcision]. Please, if you would, my children, find me a grave such that I may have for a neighbor one who was a Sabbath observer.

Send a note to the rabbi in Yalowka and ask him, in my behalf, if he would say the Kaddish for me the entire year. I know it is hard for you to keep up the Kaddish but I ask that you do as much as you can, personally, at least at the evening services, even though you will engage someone to do it. You are, after all, my flesh and blood so your Kaddish is preferred.

Also, let me ask you, dear children, perhaps I may forget at the end to say *viddui*[3] and some praise to God; if so, for Heaven's sake, remind me and don't think this will frighten me.

Another thing I wish to ask of you; Do not go to a salon [rented hall] for a big celebration the way it was done in Russia among the non-Jews, but go straight to the house (after the funeral).[4] As you have been obedient to me during my lifetime, so will you surely carry out these requests.

I request all my children to sit shivah[5] all seven days and to hold prayers with a minyan.[6] When you rise from mourning, live in harmony ever after. God, Himself, loves peace, and He will bless you with peace.

My dear daughters and daughter-in-law: As you know, we Jews are required to remove *halla*[7] from the dough when we bake. Here, in America, nearly everyone buys baked bread. Since this is an obligation that rests on women, make certain to take *halla* from the bought bread. For this may the Almighty bless you.

I am actually quite embarrassed that I have lived, thanks to God, more than eighty-five years, raised four children, but have left no material inheritance. But you well know that I did not spend it on drinking nor lose it at cards. Had I not come to America, then something would have remained. However, may God reward you for your good treatment of me. I do have a few books. But as you know, neither you nor your children have the time to look into them. So I would like to give them to places where they will be used. I have the *Menorat Ha-maor* and *Hovot Ha-Levavot* in Yiddish. Give these to the old age home; there are people there who occasionally look into a text. Present the Midrash volumes to the Krinker Synagogue because they don't have these.

When you give the books away, inscribe my name in each volume, that such and such person donated them. So perhaps someone will see it and remember me. Inscribe my name and the name of my father, of blessed memory, Yehuda Binyomin ben Zevi. Also, I request that on the holidays when yizkor is recited you not forget your grandfather and your grandmother, Sheine Leah bat Gedaliah, of blessed memory.

I want to tell you when my date of birth is: My mother, of blessed memory, told me I was born in the month of Heshvan, in the year 5594 [October or November 1833] in Yalowka.

This is the sum total of what I request of you. Be well, my beloved children. Do what I have written here, and may the Almighty, praised be His Name, provide you with all that is good, just as you have done for me.

From me, your friend and father who bids you farewell until the time of Redemption by the Almighty, praised be His Name.

Nissen ben Yehuda Binyomin Sheinberg

The following section of Nissen Sheinberg's testament appears to have been written in the same year. In it he recounts details of his strenuous efforts to restore his niece's daughter to her family.

I, Nissen, son of Yehuda Binyomin Sheinberg, come from Russia, Grodno Province, from the Bialystok region. I have already, thank God, played my way through this foolish world[8] and am well beyond the age to which the sages in the *Ethics of the Fathers* refer as "… the age of eighty, rare old age" [5:24].

The following did not happen during my years here in America. In Bialystok, I had a niece, a sister's daughter, who had a husband. They had a child together, but they didn't get along, so they separated and she took the child. My children sent her passage and she came to Chicago with the child. As she wanted to earn a living, she sent the child to a Jewish Home and paid a dollar and a half [a week] to the Home for her care.

As it happened, the child's mother died when she was only twenty-four years old and the child remained in the Home. My children wanted to take the child to raise but, instead, they gave her to a childless couple. They told us we would never get the child or know where she is.

I couldn't rest easy about the child. I couldn't get an answer from anyone. I couldn't speak English; I was a greenhorn, so I didn't know what to do. This way seven years passed and I got no help, until God helped me. I asked to see the Russian Consul.

I went to see him and he spoke to me in Russian. He listened to everything I told him from start to finish. He gave me his card and asked me to write out exactly when the mother came to America, when she gave the child to the Home, the name of the Home and who received her there. I wrote everything out and sent it to him.

About two months later, a woman from the Home, a Mrs. Davis, came and asked for me. She asked,

"Are you looking for a child, Ida Friedman?"

I answered,

"Yes, I have been looking for her."

She said to me,

"What do you need her for? She has a good home and a good life. She goes to school and her mother has taken her in as her own child."

I answered her,

"All that is fine, but I want to see her."

"Maybe you can come to our offices to see her there."

I said that I could come to their offices and we arranged a day. Two days later I received a letter to come downtown somewhere, on the eleventh floor, for a trial. I didn't know what sort of trial this was; and all because I reported to the Consul about the child!

When I arrived, Mrs. Mandel was already there, the one who had received the child originally from the mother's hands. Also Mrs. Simon was there, who had come to see me. Now she told me to leave the child with the present mother who would sign over a large sum of money to her. But I maintained that I want to see her.

They postponed the case for two weeks. Two weeks later there was another postponement. Finally, the woman who had the child and the child were both there and they called the case to trial. The judge asked if she wanted the girl, and asked some questions about the past. He told her she must take good care of her and asked the child if she wants to remain with the woman. He called me forward and asked me what my request is. I had written down the names of all my children and I stated,

"This child has neither father nor mother of her own. She is staying with strangers. Perhaps this woman will fall ill, or the child herself, and won't know where to turn. So I want to record the family name so she'll know who her real family is."

The judge accepted this from me.

When the hearing was over, I asked whether I could ever come to see her. They did not deny this request. Then I said to the child:

"Ida, I want to give you a little present."

She said that she would like a little locket. I went and bought a locket for her and engraved her name and my name and the date on it. I called the office to say that I wanted to give the child the gift.

They told me to bring the gift to the office. This I did, but did not see the child or hear about what was happening to her. Time passed and the girl was sixteen. Now, three months ago, the same Mrs. Simon, the director of the Home called to say that if we wanted to see the girl she would bring her to us. So she brought her but still did not reveal her whereabouts and instructed the girl not to tell.

Later the woman asked my daughter,

"If they would give her up, would you take her?"

My daughter replied immediately,

"With both hands I would accept her!"

She said she would let us know.

More time passed. Now the girl, herself, called my daughter saying she was coming over. She came alone now without the woman, and began to tell us about where and how she lives … and now that we knew where she was, we took her to live with us….

The child grew up and married. Now in her nineties, she and her children and their children reside in the Midwest, well established and recognized in their community. Nissen Sheinberg's other descendants are a large family active in their far-flung communities, including Alaska. The family gathers together periodically, young and old, to maintain the family connections and the traditions.

Emil Greenberg

Emil Greenberg's will contains a rare combination of literary style of high quality with fervent devotion to the Jewish heritage and its continuity. After a brief introduction to ethical wills, the writer lucidly sets forth his "legacy of intangibles."

Dated, this 59th birthday,
the 15th day of February, 1965

The ancient Hebrew tradition of an ethical will, "a legacy of intangibles" as characterized by Stephen Vincent Benet, has regrettably fallen into disuse. I presume that it is a matter of values. The monies and properties, the tangible assets we bequeath, have solid, corporeal, material value and in these hurtling times what are the real values of *Pirke Avot*, the ethics of our fathers?

Nevertheless an anachronistic but stubbornly persisting insight and foresight impel me to give, devise, and bequeath unto my progeny and perhaps to their progeny the conscious presence of a sense of ethics, a continuity and tradition of a way of life.

So here we take inventory of precept instead of property, of concern instead of cash, of love in lieu of legacy. I am humbly grateful that this inventory includes such great contributions from your family forebears.

It is no smugness that evaluates the unassuming goodness of my mother and the twinkling kindliness of my father. But the inheritance they left was more than pervading goodness; they handed down a great hunger, a hunger for knowing, for inquiring, for helping, a many-faceted hunger. I earnestly believe they handed down to their sons their encompassing concern for everyone in every station of life, augmented by the opportunities afforded by that education in the professions for which they strove so indomitably. Complete financial disaster was just an obstacle, never a deterrent.

So the family tradition of love for learning which an unschooled mother had inculcated so well, I would that I could too.

It is also in our Hebrew tradition, the choice of a people who chose the book instead of the brand, the Torah, not terror. But even learning can become sophistry. It would be the greatest of ironies if the ceaseless search for knowledge were to find its goal in submergence under the smothering quicksand of conversion and conformity. The threat of obliteration is urgently real and deadly.

When you wonder why you are and should remain Jews throughout the generations, always remember as your heritage, millennia-old, the unbroken continuity and tradition literally paid for in blood and torture, pogrom and Bergen-Belsen. It isn't just an unbroken chain, it is a lifeline. However, you cannot just feel it, you must also know it; study it and you must share identity with every Jew who ever suffered and died for *kiddush ha-Shem*.

Lives are not always grand nor are they epic. We interweave vignettes of small-talk, little gestures, minor favors, and family folkways so that we do not live alone within our solitary selves. No people are all bad or all good. When you degrade or derogate others, your own stature is correspondingly lessened.

Seek graciousness. It is the lubrication of civilized life; it makes the essential harshness and ruthlessness and crudity of Truth easier to live with, when it cannot be solely lived for. However, you should also remember that graciousness is a way *to* life, but not by itself a way *of* life.

Here your Hebrew heritage becomes manifest. Other civilizations—the Sumerian, the Chaldean, the Babylonian, the Egyptian, the Hellenic, the Roman—were cultured and grandiose, hedonistic and amoral. It was the ethical gadfly of your irritant, uncompromising Hebrew ancestor prophets which gave high purpose and meaningfulness to Civilization and its cultures.

In our present fabulous era of wondrous change and achievement each little ego becomes literally overwhelmed. Without fundamental guidelines and basic roots in a family heritage, each of us, in the words of Clarence Darrow, "is not the captain of his soul and the master of his fate, he is just a hapless deckhand on a rudderless raft aimlessly adrift in a limitless sea."

If I can bequeath something of my concept of mores and aspirations, distilled of its inevitable portion of baseness and frailty, so that my children and their issue may partake in some measure of high hope and heritage, to that degree a wisp, a whisper of immortality becomes mine, and yours.

Yitschak Kelman

Rabbi Yitschak Kelman was born in Galicia in 1867. He was descended from a long line of scholars and rabbis, and he continued the family tradition. After serving as rabbi in several Eastern European communities and in Vienna, he came to America to serve as rabbi in Jamaica, Queens, at the invitation of countrymen who had settled there. Despite the suffering he and his family experienced in Europe, he remained a kind and warm person and earned the affection of his people by his piety, learning, devotion to the Law, and his many deeds of loving-kindness. Because of his fairness and love of peace, he was often called on to arbitrate disputes. Although he did not write for publication, his studies, sermons, and notes have been gathered by his family and published in a volume, *Moreshet Avot*, from which this will is taken and translated. Rabbi Kelman died in 1933.

These are my instructions as to what is to be done for me in my time of illness and from the time of my death until after the burial. Since a person is not always in full possession of his faculties then, I set these requests down now:

1. People should visit frequently so that when the final time comes there will be a minyan present.
2. I should be reminded to recite the confessional, and before this to give charity in accordance with my means.
3. I should be reminded to repent and to recite *Adon Olam* and *Yigdal* for they contain the thirteen essential principles of faith which a person must believe.
4. The book *Shevet Musar* should be brought, or Reb Feival Sfard of Zlotnick should be asked to bring the fourteenth section of *Sde Hemed* in which the text of the declaration of intention is found. A minyan of pious and observant Jews should be brought into the room so that I may recite the declaration in their presence.
5. Then I should be given the book *Ma'avar Yabok* and together with the quorum of ten Jews let me recite what is written there.
6. If it is known that I am on bad terms with anyone, I should be reminded of this so that I can forgive him. And if it is known that anyone is on bad terms with me, he should be requested to forgive

me. I ask that it be announced in the synagogue that I forgive any and everyone who may have aggravated me and that I ask any and everyone whom I may have aggravated to please forgive me.

7. Let ten pious and observant Jews say Psalms on my behalf and let a prayer for my recovery be recited with my name and the name of my mother, and let charity on my behalf be given to the fund that is named for Rabbi Meir Ba'al Hanes in the Holy Land, and let that charity be placed in the charity box of that fund promptly. If funds are available let them be distributed to poor scholars and to ordinary poor Jews, and if money is not available then let the best clothes or the watch or books be sold and the money given to charity, both before and after my going. It is best to do these things in the morning after the prayers, for this is a time of mercy and a favorable moment.

8. Before the prayers and the giving of the charity one of the ten should say a word of instruction to the people reminding them that they should realize and repent, and asking them to learn a lesson from what is happening. He should ask them to pray for me, both in this world and after my departure, that no harm should come to me.

9. The Holy Presence is with the sick. Therefore my family should be reminded to keep the sickroom and the house clean and pure as if a king were coming. And I too should be kept clean. This is a part of human dignity, so that those who come to visit the sick should not feel any discomfort, as it is written: "Let your camp be holy for the Lord is in your midst" (Deut. 23:15). Let there be a fresh sheet and a fresh garment regularly.

10. You should be very careful to see to it that I do not neglect any commandment which a well person is required to fulfill. For example, when I am given food to eat or water to drink, I should be reminded to say the appropriate blessing, and I should be reminded to wash before I say the blessing, as it is written: "I will wash my hands in cleanliness" (Pss. 26:6, 73:13).

At the Time of Death

The sages have taught that it is a good deed to be present at the time of death, and that this takes precedence even over prayer. Therefore there ought to be many people present at such a time so that they can divide into two groups, one to pray, the other to stand by the sick person's side. They should say Psalms and study Mishnah and do those things that are prescribed in the *Ma'avar Yabok*. (My copy can be found in the section of my library where the booklets are kept.)

The soul is pleased when relatives are nearby at the time of death, but only if they do not wail. Therefore only those men who know they will not break down should be there. Women should not be allowed in for it is their nature to weep uncontrollably.

The children should be kept away from the time of dying until the time to say Kaddish at the grave....

Since a person is not always in full possession of his faculties at the end there is the danger that he may deny his faith. Therefore it is important that at this time he say: "Hear O Israel, the Lord our God, the Lord is One," and take upon himself the yoke of the kingdom of heaven.

In case that I am not lucid at the end I hereby authorize my closest friends to recite the declaration of intent for me, and I hereby declare this authorization to be noncancellable. The text can be found on page 12 of the *Ma'avar Yabok*. It begins with the phrase: "My brothers, my friends, and my teachers."

When the Soul Separates from the Body

If possible let me be attended by those who have purified themselves in the mikvah that day....

Let there be no eulogies for me, but if someone knows something good that I have done they may mention it. And let no one say anything derogatory for it is surely forbidden to speak badly of the dead.

Before the purification and the washing let charity be given in an amount equal to the numerical value of my name, and again when my body is put into the coffin let this be done again.

Let this be the contents of the announcement that appears in the newspaper after my death:

> On such and such a day, in the week of such and such Torah portion, on such and such day of the month, Rabbi Isaac, the son of Mirel, who was once rabbi in Wizniowczyk and for one year in Podhorvyze and then here in Jamaica, in America, departed this life. His friends and his students, wherever they

may be, are requested to study Mishnah for the first month, and especially for the first week, and to say that they do this for his sake, and let them make mention of any good quality of his to which they can testify such as loving-kindnesses that I did for many people.

Whatever rituals are performed out of respect to the living may be done after me, but let there not be any praise that is not true, for this is a great detriment to the soul.

Immediately after the week of mourning let a tombstone be erected, or at least by the end of the first thirty days, for according to the *Zohar*, the soul yearns for the body and craves to at least know where it rests.

1. Even though I have said above that I want no eulogy, if there are any rabbis present at the funeral they may say a few short words of comfort to the mourners and teach those present a lesson in how to live if they wish, but if so please let them not be too long.
2. Let there be only pious observant Jews who put my body in the grave. I ask that they break the bottom of the coffin so that the body rests directly on the earth. This is what I did for my father, my teacher, may his soul be in heaven.
3. I ask that the washing be done in the mikvah of my dear friend, Reb Avraham Reizman, but only if my death should occur on a weekday. But if it should be on the eve of the Sabbath, especially if it is in winter when the days are very short, then let the washing be done as quickly and simply as possible so as not to lead, God forbid, to a desecration of the Sabbath....
4. After the burial let charity be given to the poor once again in accordance with the numerical value of my name.
5. Let services be held all during the week of shivah in the room in which my soul expires and let a light be kept lit there all during that week. After services let several chapters of Psalms be said. If the people wish they may study a chapter of Mishnah every day. Each chapter should begin with a letter of my name.

I ask that a bit of earth from the Land of Israel be put into my grave. You will find the earth in a package which is in my dresser.

And know, my children, that you should show very great reverence for my helpmate. By doing this you will fulfill a double commandment—honoring her, and honoring me through honoring her. For it was she who kept me in health, for I was always a sickly person, and she kept me from sin as well. Therefore do not be ungrateful and do not aggravate her in any way in her old age. Show her reverence, please, just as I did for my mother, after the death of my father. I adorned her with glory and honor until her dying day. This is in keeping with the teaching of Rabbi Judah the Prince, whose last words at the time of his death were: "Be careful of the honor of your mother." I know that it is enough to ask this of you just once....

Bernard L. Levinthal

Head of the Orthodox rabbinate in Philadelphia, Rabbi Levinthal (1865–1952) was among the founders of the Union of Orthodox Rabbis of the United States and Canada and of the Mizrahi Organization of America. European-born Rabbi Levinthal had profound admiration for the American way of life and was deeply proud of the biblical roots of democracy. A son, Judge Louis E. Levinthal, told how his father used to take the family on Sabbath walks to Independence Hall and point out the biblical verse from the Book of Leviticus inscribed on the Liberty Bell.

> My help is from the Lord,
> Creator of heaven and earth.

To my sons—long life be theirs:

I request of you, my dear sons, to strengthen yourselves and be punctilious in the retention and the observance of the commands of our holy Torah. Now in the matter of observing the law and commandments and living up to the mitzvot in practice, all of us, of course, continue to be bound by the oath taken at the foot of Mount Sinai. What I say here therefore refers more particularly to such matters as require special care, namely, that you be watchful and solicitous in public and communal affairs so as not to cause, God forbid, the profanation of God's name and His Torah. Now in these matters there are degrees, so that personality has a chance to express itself.[1] Therefore please be very careful not to profane my name and the name of our fathers and the name of our family. Be careful not to participate in and waste your efforts on movements which are not to the advantage of traditional Torah, or on activities which go counter to efforts which I—with the help of God, blessed be His name—have made and to achievements for the strengthening of Torah and observance which I have nurtured and fostered with a sense of dedication rising from the very depths of my soul and for which I have sacrificed my very life. Each one of you should try, in accordance with his powers, to strengthen Traditional Judaism in this land of our habitation, and you will thereby merit participation in the life of the Torah in our Holy Land.

I am certain that my sons will—with God's favor—be careful to observe, during the days of mourning for me, everything which Jews accept as proper in the observance of the commandment to honor one's father after his term of life has ended. They must be careful indeed not to commit even the slightest transgression in connection with this. Every day of mourning for me they shall study a portion of the Bible, Mishnah, and Halakhah in whatever language they understand; and every day they shall give charity for my soul's elevation.

If, whenever my Creator, blessed be His name, wills it, my passing from this life occurs in our country, here in America, they shall bury me in the grave which I have fixed for myself here. I do not ask to be carried to the Holy Land, out of respect for the rabbis who preceded me and especially out of respect for my father-in-law, the Gaon, blessed be his memory, as well as out of respect for the pious and righteous laymen, peace be upon them, whose honored resting place is here and who worked together with me in all manner of sacred causes. If, however, my departure from life occurs, God forbid, outside of our country, I request that my sons carry me to the Holy Land; and I command my sons—long life be theirs—that in such a case they carry also the remains of the wife of my youth, peace be upon her, to the Holy Land in accordance with the condition which I made at the time of her burial.

I request that no adjectives be inscribed on my tombstone, other than "The well-known rabbi who labored at his sacred task so and so many years." I request also that those who eulogize me refrain from multiplying their praises of my learning and fear of God, but that they shall speak of my labor at my sacred task and of my activities and achievements in realizing the commandments of the Torah—perhaps this will be, with God's help, of my encouragement to others, and so add to my merits as well.

At the time of the funeral, and also during the period of eulogizing, the elder among the rabbis present—long life be his—shall three times, in my name, make announcement of my request for forgiveness by all those whom I may have caused, God forbid, some financial loss either as the result of an error in teaching or in judicial decision; as well as by those whom I may have pained by words uttered or otherwise harmed, knowingly or unknowingly. He shall ask that all these persons forgive me. I, for my part, forgive those who angered me or ever caused me shame or financial loss; I do so in the hope that they too will forgive me.

I request my sons—long life be theirs—to come together, if at all possible, on the day of my yahrzeit and discuss practical and spiritual matters concerning the realization of my requests in this my testament, as well as to heighten the sentiments of affection and brotherliness among themselves.

Also my sons—long life be theirs—shall at all times stand at one another's side in an hour of need, God forbid. They shall support a needy brother with good advice as well as with practical aid. This matter is an obligation and takes precedence over all other charities; for so our sages, may their memory be for a blessing, said: whichever (of the following) expressions precedes the other in the Bible takes precedence also in observance: "To thy brother; to thy poor; and to the needy in the land." ...

To my daughter's son-in-law, the rabbi, the Gaon, Rabbi Samuel Belkin—long life be his—I advise that he make his Torah—the Torah of truth, the Torah of instruction and judgment—his wholehearted occupation. He will thus be a branch of our family, a family of rabbis, teachers, and leaders in Israel for many generations. And I have faith in God—blessed be His name—that his learning and his fear of God will stand by him, so that, with God's help, he will be a source of pride and glory and honor to us all.

David De Sola Pool

Rabbi David De Sola Pool (1885–1970) was head of New York's Sephardic synagogue, Shearith Israel, the oldest synagogue in the United States. London-born Rabbi Pool was brought to New York in 1907 to lead Shearith Israel, and he held that position until his retirement in 1956. He wrote several books, including *An Old Faith in the New World: Portrait of Shearith Israel, 1654–1954*. His many communal endeavors included his serving as president of the American Jewish Historical Society, representing the United States as delegate to the NATO Atlantic Congress in London in 1959, and as founder and a director of the Jewish Education Committee of New York.

The end of the matter, all having been heard: revere God and keep His commandments; for this is the whole man.
—Ecclesiastes 12:13

Whensoever death shall come, it will find me unafraid. I pray that it may find me ready. I have ever tried so to live that I might be prepared to meet my God. I love life and the exquisite gifts of work, of play, of joy, of chastening, of light, of laughter, and most of all, of love that it has brought me. I am, and have always been, deeply grateful for the abundance of life with which I have been blessed. Life has been inexpressibly sweet to me. Yet, come death when it may, I yield up life as gladly, as gratefully, as I have accepted its gift for the while ... it would be selfish to ask for more. All my life long I have been blessed with the gifts of love, far, far beyond my deserving. I have tried, haltingly, inadequately, but sincerely ... to repay through service some of the debt I owe to life for its profuse bounty toward me. I gave three years (the happiest of my life because the richest in service) to the Holy Land. I have tried at all times, and for all who called upon me, rich as well as poor, gentile as well as Jew, to give service through such poor gifts as my physical strength, my mental power, and my spiritual resources enabled me to offer. I have tried so to do. More than that I cannot say, for I know that often, pitifully often, I have failed through weakness and inadequacy—physical, mental, and spiritual. Yet the stimulus and the joy of trying have been mine.

From anyone toward whom I have failed in human kindness I ask forgiveness. I do not feel, and I never have felt, any unkindness or malice in my heart toward anyone. Where I have failed, it has been through my insufficiency, never through ill-will.

But I would not leave with you who care to hear, and even perchance to cherish, a message from me any emphasis on failure. Though in tangible achievement I have not done what perhaps I dreamed of doing and what the world may rightly have expected me to achieve, the very living of my life has been supremely successful. There has been no day in which my heart has not leaped with gratitude to God for the joy of life and its fulfillment in the perfect love that has been given to me both as a child and in every moment of my sacred married life. There has yet never dawned the day when I have not been able to give thanks unto God for His goodness, and the day of death shall be but one more such day.

Therefore I would not have my death darken the life of anyone. Life to me has always been joy with humor and laughter and happiness. I would have it so, and I have tried to make it so for all others with whom my lot has been cast. I have tried to comfort others in their sorrow and to show them the sunshine of life's path. So if any would remember me, let my name be mentioned with a smile, with brightness, with humor, with happy memory, with wholesome gladness. Pain not my memory with tears or regrets, but let my spirit live among you after death as it has on earth, with joyousness. I would have the children of the religious school of my congregation gladdened on the Sunday nearest its anniversary or, should that be in the summer, then I would have some other children's lives made sweeter on that day, and at all times I would have my wife and children and those who have been the sweetest blessings in my life recall me with a smile as they think of how much heartwarming love they gave to me.

I can never even begin to express my thanks to all whose goodness, whose forbearance, and whose friendship have made my life so wondrous an adventure. May God bless you all for the blessings you have given to me. I have had all and more than man could dare ask for—a life that has known no want, a life of wide and varied interests, with music, travel, humor, work, opportunities of spiritual service. But most of all I have had friendship and kindness from everyone, and a perfect, exquisite love from my life's partner.

Many waters cannot quench love
Rivers cannot drown it....

To those I have loved my message is contained in Eleanor Graham's sonnet:

It is not for myself that I fear death....
Hear then my infinite conceit; I fear
That those I love, who love me too, may heap
Small portions of their lives upon my bier.
Would there be tears and I not here to bring
A cause for living laughter?
Would there be darkness and pain, and I not here to sing
Return of day? Oh, take this from me—
Promise that when I'm one with all the after
You still will greet each newborn day with laughter.

To all I would sum up what I have tried to be in the deep wisdom of the ancient words: "The end of it, when all has been heard, is revere God and keep His commandments, for this is the whole of man."
  So,

I rest my spirit in His hand,
Asleep, awake by Him I'm stayed.
God with me still, in life, in death,
I face my future unafraid.

Sholom Aleichem

Sholom Aleichem (1859–1916), the pen name of Solomon Rahinowitz, requires no introduction to readers of Yiddish, or any of the many languages into which his works have been translated. What is not widely known is the fact that Sholom Aleichem spent his last years in New York, where he died in 1916, mourned by 150,000 people, young and old, who lined the streets at his funeral. His will was read into the Congressional Record, and published in the *New York Times*, which called it one of the great ethical wills in history.

To be opened and published on the day of my death:

New York, 11 Tishre, 5675 (September 19, 1915)

Today a great misfortune has befallen my family: my elder son, Misha (Michael Rabinowitz) has died and taken with him into the grave a part of my own life. It remains for me now to redraw my will … which consists of ten points:

1. Wherever I may die, let me be buried not among the rich and famous, but among plain Jewish people, the workers, the common folk, so that my tombstone may honor the simple graves around me, and the simple graves honor mine, even as the plain people honored their folk writer in his lifetime.
2. No titles or eulogies are to be engraved on my tombstone, except the name Sholom Aleichem on one side and the Yiddish inscription, herein enclosed, on the other.
3. Let there be no arguments or debates among my colleagues who may wish to memorialize me by erecting a monument in New York. I shall not be able to rest peacefully in my grave if my friends engage in such nonsense. The best monument for me will be if my books are read, and if there should be among our affluent people a patron of literature who will publish and distribute my works in Yiddish or in other languages, thus enabling the public to read me and my family to live in dignity. If I haven't earned this in my lifetime, perhaps I may earn it after my death.

I depart from the world with complete confidence that the public will not abandon my orphans.

4. At my grave, and throughout the whole year, and then every year on. the anniversary of my death, my remaining son and my sons-in-law, if they are so inclined, should say Kaddish for me. And if they do not wish to do this, or if it is against their religious convictions, they may fulfill their obligation to me by assembling together with my daughters and grandchildren and good friends to read this testament, and also to select one of my stories, one of the really merry ones, and read it aloud in whatever language they understand best, and let my name rather be remembered by them with laughter than not at all.

5. My children and children's children can have whatever beliefs or convictions they will. But I beg of them to guard their Jewish heritage. If any of them reject their origins to join a different faith, then that is a sign they have detached themselves from my will "and they shall have no portion and inheritance among their brethren."

6. (Here Sholom Aleichem apportions the royalties from his books and plays among his family, and for his two granddaughters' marriage dowry).

7. From the incomes mentioned in the above paragraph, a sum shall be set aside for a foundation for Jewish authors (writing in Yiddish and Hebrew) of: 5% up to 5000 rubles a year; 10% if more than 5000 rubles. Should such a foundation exist at that time in the United States or in Europe, let this contribution be given annually to it.... But if such a foundation should not exist, or if one should be established that would not meet my wishes as set forth in this paragraph, then the money shall be distributed to needy writers by my heirs directly, as they may agree among themselves.

8. (He speaks here of a stone to be placed over Misha's grave in Copenhagen, where he died, Kaddish said for him, and money given to the poor).

9. (He asks that his works be not sold in perpetuity and arranges for his family to have a permanent income from them).

10. My last wish for my successors and my prayer to my children: Take good care of your mother, beautify her old age, sweeten

her bitter life, heal her broken heart; do not weep for me—on the contrary, remember me with joy; and the main thing— live together in peace, bear no hatred for each other, help one another in bad times, think on occasion of other members of the family, pity the poor, and when circumstances permit, pay my debts, if there be any. Children, bear with honor my hard-earned Jewish name and may God in Heaven sustain you ever. Amen.

Sholom Ben Menahem Nahum Rabinowitz,
Sholom Aleichem

Appended to the will is his epitaph, written by him in Yiddish, like the text of the will, and engraved on his tombstone in the Workmen's Circle plot in Mt. Carmel Cemetery in Brooklyn, New York:

Here lies a plain and simple Jew
Who wrote in plain and simple prose;
Wrote humor for the common folk
To help them to forget their woes.

He scoffed at life and mocked the world,
At all its foibles he poked fun,
The world went on its merry way,
And left him stricken and undone.

And while his grateful readers laughed,
Forgetting troubles of their own,
Midst their applause—God only knows—
He wept in secret and alone.

Mordkhe Schaechter

A contemporary American ethical will written in flawless Yiddish is a rarity. Professor Mordkhe Schaecter (1927–2007), renowned scholar and authority on the Yiddish language, addresses two wills to his wife and children, respectively. Both wills partake of the strong, conscientious zeal for Jewish continuity, ethical standards, and social justice which has characterized the best in Yiddish life and culture.

My beloved Charne,

You know what I want to say to you but still I want to review it.

See that the children grow up to be good Jews and decent human beings. Bring them up in the same way as though I would be present. Guide them to undertake Jewish activities, as in Yiddish theatre. Speak to them in Yiddish, provide them with Yiddish books and periodicals for their reading. Once a month let them visit with my family.

If you should wish to re-marry, do so with my good wishes for happiness. But see that our children not become estranged from me.

With love,
Mordkhe

March 30, 1963

Beloved Sureh-Ruchele, Dobbe-Gitele,
Frimet-Eydele, and Yosl-Binyumele,

I want to ask you and you and you to follow the ways of your father and mother, just as *they* walked in the paths of their fathers and mothers:

To love—not just with words but actually with deeds—the Jewish people, the Jewish language and the Jewish way of life.

To speak Yiddish among yourselves and with Jews who know Yiddish.

To have no fear of being in the minority; avoid doing as others do for conformist reasons.

To conduct yourselves Jewishly—observe Jewish customs, celebrate Shabbos and festivals, marry in the Jewish manner.

To be faithful to the Jewish people.

To stand up for the weak, the oppressed and the beaten.

To be plain, honest, trustworthy and punctual.

To live for not self only; to remember we are part of a large family—the Jewish people—and of a larger family still—the human race.

Not to wait for someone else to do what is right, but begin yourself, as though the whole world is on your shoulders, as it were; as if the task were waiting for you to perform it.

Not to discriminate between poor and rich, between white and non-white, between educated and uneducated, between Jew and non-Jew (but, for God's sake, do not marry a non-Jew by birth and religious belief, unless converted according to our prescribed ritual.)

In summary, be a true human being and a good Jew!

May 5, 1979

Dora Chazin

When Dora Chazin was forty-two, desperately ill, and fearing imminent death, she wrote seven letters in rhymed Yiddish poetry, one to each of her six children and to her husband Cantor Hirsch L. Chazin, with instructions that the letters were not to be opened until her death. Happily, she recovered and lived for twenty-five more years. On the last day of shivah the letters were read. The following letter was written to her youngest son, Pinchos, then age eight, now an eminent rabbi.

February 11, 1923

My little son, my precious Pinchos,
Your loving mother feels she wants to say
Something to you in verse
To carry deep within your heart, forever.

Beloved child, I see before me now
The seriousness of my state;
Still, I do not question the Almighty....

You are too little now to understand my writing
Nor will you much remember of
The mother's love I've given you.

I beseech God with tearful plea
To grant me yet the privilege
Of beholding with my eyes your becoming
A man excelling in all worthy things....

When you become Bar Mitzvah, please Almighty God,
I hope that nothing will deter you, ever,
From *davening* the daily round of prayer
As I, your loving mother, am asking you to do.

For if, my child, you will it,
You'll find the time for it,
By developing a proper pattern
Of lying down to sleep on time,

And waking up at measured hours.

When one is good *and* keeps the rituals, my child,
Then is one beloved by everyone and everywhere.

My blessings I bestow upon you now
    For one hundred twenty years of life and great
        fulfillment; and
    May it be true of you (and I have thought about
        this, O so long):
    "Find favor in the eyes of God and man," in joy
        and full contentment.

With these lines I take my leave of you;
With anguish pressing on my heart
I penned these lines, beloved child,
To be for you a remembrance everlasting.

Your mother,
Dora Chazin

William Schulder

William Schulder (1879–1949) was a successful businessman in New York recognized for his nobility of character, love of learning and lifelong philanthropy. He was devoted to the practices of Judaism—a Sabbath observing man all his life—and was well-learned both in Torah and secular learning. He was brought to the United States from Lisensk, now Poland, at the age of one by his parents, and was reared and lived in New York all his life. His father, Avraham Schulder, was a founder of the Solomon Kluger Yeshiva, and William in turn was a founder of the Yeshiva Torah Vo-Daas. In keeping with his character, William Schulder shunned the honors which organizations and institutions sought to bestow on him. His brief ethical will reflects his belief that reverence for God and love of man are inseparable.

With the help of God
March 28, 1932 Monday, Torah portion *Shemini* 5692

To my dear children,

You know how hard I worked and tried my utmost to give you the best I could afford in food, shelter and education, to lead an honest, clean and respectable life. Therefore, I plead with you to uphold my wishes as follows:

1. Be strict Sabbath observers. Your homes to be strictly kosher and otherwise uphold the Jewish religion and traditions.
2. Honor, respect and take care of your mother as long as she lives as she is your best friend in the world.
3. Be honorable in your dealings, commercially and socially.
4. Be respectful to all—never consider yourself greater than the next man.
5. Try your best not to insult anyone.
6. Talk and treat everyone as kindly as possible.
7. Keep together, a family, with one another.
8. Pass all this along to your children and see that they are brought up as Orthodox, honorable and respectable Jews.

This being fatherly advice I hope you will follow these rules and God will help you.

Your dear father William Schulder

P.S. I hope you will keep this letter and read it once in a while but at least on the day of my yahrzeit.

Give a copy to each child.

Hayim Greenberg

Hayim Greenberg (1889–1953) was born in Bessarabia. In his youth he moved to Odessa and came into contact with Hayim Nahman Bialik and Menahem Mendel Ussishkin, the moving forces of the revival of Hebrew letters and culture. Hayim Greenberg emerged as a leading Zionist orator and as a writer on Jewish themes as well as on world literature and philosophy. From 1924 to the end of this life he lived in the United States. He was editor of the journal *Farn Folk* until 1934, then of the Labor Zionist monthly the *Jewish Frontier*.

Written in New York, April 18, 1949

The monument on my grave shall be plain, of utmost simplicity, and not a thing should be inscribed on it besides this: "Here lies Hayim Greenberg (day, month, and year)." Do not note the date of my birth: for various reasons my documents were altered several times ... and I myself do not know the precise date.

I hope that there will be no speeches at my funeral. A religious-poetic service will be sufficient. One or two psalms can be read or sung (Pss. 103, 23, 42), a chapter from Job (28)—in the original, in Yiddish, or in English—and if a suitable singer can be found, a song by Lermontov, dear to my wife and me since childhood, could be sung: "*Vichozhu odin ya na dorogu....*" ["I Go Out Alone upon the Road ..."]. If the facilities available do not prevent it, the well-known March by Chopin could be played at the end.

There are a number of men and women who brought their spiritual illumination into my own life. I hereby send to each and every one of them my profound blessing. Doubtless, there are also men and women whom I have offended and caused anguish. Of them I ask forgiveness. I erred not out of love of sin; I am guilty out of human weakness and caused hurt without any intention of hurting.

Rafael L. Savitzky

On business stationery, in beautiful Yiddish script, Rafael Savitzky of New York detailed for his children a series of vital instructions: the purpose of a *tzava'ah*, admonition on specific values of Judaism, burial instructions, and a detailed list of obligations and pledges to be paid. Thus his will contains all the elements of a traditional Jewish ethical will.

My beloved and devoted children, both males and females:

Inasmuch as I am not well and God alone knows whether I will ever arise from my sickbed, and who knows whether we will be able to talk during the final moments; and since it is a mitzvah to instruct children before death, as it is related in the holy Torah, that God says [Gen. 18:19], "For I have known him, to the end that he may command his children and his household after him, that they may keep the way of the Lord...." And we find concerning King David, of blessed memory [1 Kings 2:2–3], "And he charged Solomon his son saying: 'I go the way of all the earth; be thou strong therefore, and show thyself a man; and keep the charge of the Lord thy God, to walk in His ways, to keep His statutes, and His commandments, and His ordinances and His testimonies, according to that which is written in the law of Moses, that thou mayest prosper in all that thou doest, and whithersoever thou turnest thyself.'" I had written many things, many points, in a previous will, the things a father says to his children; but the times have changed. Mama, of blessed memory, passed away; part of my own self also died with her. And you, my children, also went through a great deal. One who has no faith in God is not aided by that fact.

Therefore, my children, I come now to add to my testament that under all circumstances and at all times you must have trust in God. Only by having faith in God will you be able to overcome everything in the future. Children, now your true friends will be of help to you; having no mother, no father, you must always remain united; in the words of King David, "How good and how pleasant it is for brethren to dwell together in unity." In joy and in sorrow alike, brothers and sisters should stay close together—in word and deed, with a loan, with comfort and advice. You must know: "Have we not one father? Did not one God create us?" I hope that as I have been a good father to you during my lifetime, so shall I intercede in your behalf in every way.

Further, when Mama, of blessed memory, died, the Burial Society promised that I would be interred next to her, and they opened the grave lower down. I therefore request that no change be made and that our Bet Aaron Burial Society will carry this out in detail. Two weeks ago when they were here I spoke with Yudel Cohen, David Shapiro, Lezer Sosner, and Gershon Lezer Zareike. So I asked them and they promised me because they remembered what we had talked about.

Further, my daughters, remember that in America the women are the saintly souls. They hold the keys to the hearts of the men. They are the keys to the children, the keys of kashrut. Therefore, beloved daughters of mine, observe Judaism, your kosher homes, and the upbringing of the children in God's ways and in respectable ways. Then it will be well with you now and in the time to come.

Following are my obligations:

Rabbi Mareminsk	$100.00
Yaffe	300.00
Gershon (or Gershman)	200.00
Biber	50.00
Yeshivas Tiferes Yerushalayim, contribution	50.00
Chevra Tzemach Tzedek	50.00
Rifas (?)	18.00
Plumber	17.00
Meir Yona	13.00
Yerme Lavin	14.00
Meir Bloom	17.00
Chevra Bnei Aharon	15.00
Poilishe Folk Division	80.00
Yitzhok Elchonon	25.00
Torah Voda'as	25.00
Hayyim Berlin	25.00

If you fulfill my requests, God will fulfill your requests; I, your father, who writes this in full awareness and with clear mind.

Rafael L. Savitzky
[signature in Hebrew]

Monday, the week of Toldos, Heshvan 29, 5692
November 9 (in the general calendar), 1931

Samuel Lipsitz

The following will of a New England businessman, handwritten on sheets of business stationery, is remarkable for its clarity and insight. It is the more noteworthy because its author points the finger of reproof at himself for possible annoyances under the pressures of daily work alongside members of his family.

October 16, 1950
January 2, 1951

Dear Children:

Somewhere among these papers is a will made out by a lawyer. Its purpose *is to dispose of any material* things which I may possess at the time of my departure from this world to the unknown adventure beyond.

I hope its terms will cause no ill will among you. It seemed sensible when I made it. After all, it refers only to material things which we enjoy only temporarily.

I am more concerned with having you inherit something that is vastly more important.

There must be a purpose in the creation of man. Because I believe that (as I hope you will some day, for without it life becomes meaningless), I hope you will live right.

Live together in harmony! Carry no ill will toward each other. Bethink of the family. Help each other in case of need. Honor and care for your mother. Make her old age happy, as far as in your power. She deserves these things from you. It was your mother who always reproached me that I was not concerned enough about my children. She always insisted that we give them more. She would never visit a grandchild without a gift. I often felt she was too devoted a mother. Prove she was wise by being worthy of her devotion.

Carry your Jewish heritage with dignity. Though you may discard trivial ritual things, never discard your basic Jewish faith. You cannot live out your years happily without it.

Coming to the synagogue for Kaddish will reacquaint you with the old prayers and you may find comfort in them as I did when your grandfather died in 1923. I was then thirty-two years old.

Being together daily in business has its disadvantage as far as a father wanting to be noble in the eyes of his children. The aggravations and the heavy pressure in our business cause friction and annoyance with one another. Maybe we said things at such times that in calm retrospect we are sorry for. I was as guilty of these things as anyone. I hope such things will not stand out in your memory of me. I must have done some worthwhile things that left good impressions and nice thoughts with you. Please recall these, or anything you feel worth carrying on, on the occasion of my yahrzeit. I leave with happy thoughts, because as your mother and I often said, "God has been good to us. Our children are all good, and married to good mates. Their lives can go on without us just as well. They will meet none who can speak ill of their parents."

I have enjoyed a loving and appreciative wife. She always praised and told me how capable I was. Then I had to live up to her expectations. Any worthwhile thing I ever did was due to her urging and her faith in me.

So don't mourn for me. I have enjoyed my life. Carry on from here, using the many blessing which you have (and I didn't have at your age) with wisdom and consecration to your family and mankind.

You can serve your family best by serving mankind also.

Remember me affectionately as your father.

Shmuel ben Shalom
[Signature in Hebrew]

Sadie S. Kulakofsky

Sadie Kulakofsky (1892–1978), of Omaha, Nebraska, was a woman who possessed strong convictions, fine leadership qualities and great energy. Her Zionist zeal led her to devote herself to the Hadassah Medical Organization and to Bonds for Israel. Her efforts were significant in Hadassah's coming to the Mountain Plains region when it did, and she served in various offices including that of National Vice President. She was a strong advocate of social justice and an early champion of equal rights. Mayor of Jerusalem, Teddy Kollek, when meeting her son years after she had been active in Jewish life, remembered her as "one of the most important people who came from Omaha," reflecting the interesting fact that a disproportionate number of American Jewish leaders hailed from Omaha.

Above the material things bequeathed to all of you both in the Last Will and Testament and in a little book, I hope I shall have given all of you something which is more precious than gold and jewels.

I hope and pray that during the years we have had together I have given you a love of our faith, a trust in God, from whom all blessings flow, a devotion to righteousness to justice and to peace—all of which one will find as the principles of Judaism, and the basis of civilization.

These are the jewels, more precious than rubies which I hope will make your lives rich in all that is worthwhile for many years to come as I think they have made mine.

May God shower you with his blessings and may you share your blessings with others.

God bless all of you,
Your Mother,
Sadie S. Kulakofsky

April 24, 1953

Sidney Rabinowitz

Sidney Robins (né Rabinowitz) was working in the advertising department of R. H. Macy's store when he joined the United States Army during World War II. On April 26, 1943, in Tunisia, knowing he was going to the front, he wrote a letter to his dear ones. It was to be sent to them only if he died in action. Three days later, at hill 609, he was mortally wounded. As he lay dying, he plucked his "last letter" from his pocket; it was found tightly clutched in his hand when his body was recovered. He was 21 years of age. What a pity!

Dear Pa, and Adele:

This is my last letter to you. I am keeping it in my pocket, and if I should be killed, I hope somebody will mail it to you.

Ever since I arrived in North Africa, I have been moving closer to the front. I finally got here yesterday, Easter Sunday.

We have just been told that we are moving up to the front lines in a few hours. Tonight or tomorrow morning I will be attacking the Germans. In case something happens to me, I want you both to know how I feel now.

I'm not scared or frightened. I feel tense, but I suppose that is to be expected. If I get shot, I would rather be killed than horribly wounded.

I'm only worried about how sad you would be if I get killed. But I hope you will also be proud that your son gave his life for the greatest cause in the world—that men might be free.

Pa, if I caused you heartaches and disappointments, I'm sorry. You'll never know how much I have always loved you, and how much more I love you now. Please take care of your health, for my sake.

Adele, whatever good qualities I may have, I owe to you. You were always kind and helpful, and you understood me better than anyone else did. I'm proud to call you "Mother." I leave you all my love.

To both of you, I want to say that you were the best parents in the world and I love you both. I hope God will take good care of you.

There is so much I wanted to say to you when I see you again; about how I was going to take care of you in the future and how I would make you proud of me.

Well, you will have something to be proud of anyway.

Do you remember, before I became a soldier, how I used to say that I wanted to do something to help make the world better?

Now I have the chance. If I die, at least I will know that I died to make the world a better place to live in.

I'll die, not as a hero, but as an ordinary young man who did all he could to help overcome the forces of evil.

I don't have time to write a letter to anyone else. So please give my love to Midge and Ben, Ralph and his family, Willie and the Rosenbergs, and all our friends and relatives. But most of all, give my love to Bobby and Larry. Please don't let them forget their uncle. I've always been so proud of them and I like to feel that they were proud of me, too. I hope they grow up in a peaceful world and become fine men.

God bless you both. I'll always love you,
Your Devoted Son,
Sidney

Samuel Furash

On February 3, 1944, Corporal Samuel Furash sent a letter to his baby daughter, who was not yet a year old. This young noncom, born in 1922 in Washington, D.C., was stationed in England; World War II was raging. Furash, a graduate of a Jewish high school, had already spent some time at a teachers' college. He was a political radical who hoped that his daughter would grow up to help build a world where all men and women would be free. He wrote movingly and eloquently. For many of us today, it is a sad letter, given the state of the world.

My dearest Toby:

Probably by the time you receive this, you will have reached your first birthday; and by the time you will be able to read and understand it we will be together as father and daughter, living through the days being missed now. Then again, there is always the possibility that never shall we know the relationship which is so deserving of us, but that possibility is quite remote. However, whatever the future holds in store for us, now is the time for us to get acquainted. As difficult as it may be, your mother's words to me through letters are descriptive enough to offer a realization of your habits, characteristics, personality, and other traits of you in different stages of your young life, [but] the scene still remains incomplete, of course, because we are still strangers to each other. However, Toby darling, I'm speaking to you now, because the words I say are my sincere beliefs and always will be, and some day you, too, shall share these thoughts with your mother and me.

You were born into a world which was experiencing the second stage of the "dark ages," a world filled with turmoil, suffering and grief, and a civilization on the verge of destruction and total chaos. By this statement you might easily assume that the responsibility for all this lies upon the shoulders of all mankind; and you would be right! I do not mean by this, that man is evil; to the contrary, man is good, *but* he has been lax and smug and because of this has allowed his basic principle of life, freedom, to be snatched from his hands by the long, murderous talons of fascistic tyranny through the rule of a small group of individuals. At this moment, this group of men have not succeeded in their attempts in this nation and a few others, but even though the people of these nations are in an all-out war against fascists and the principles of fascism, these men are still in important positions in our own set-up of government. And that is where you come in Toby, dear. You see, though we are fighting a war now, which we will undoubtedly win, the victory alone will not bring about the complete and happy change in our way of life. No! The struggle will then only begin and you and your generation will be the spearhead and main body of our fighting forces. We have begun the drive; you will finish it! Our victory will destroy tyranny; yours will establish freedom, freedom in every sense of the word; and that job constitutes the renovation of our whole system of society. Your mother and I are the fighters of the present; you are the builders of the future.

You are lucky, Toby, because your life will be full of love. It can be no other way; you see, you were born out of love. Never has there been a more perfect relationship than your mother's and mine, for when we are together, we are united as one individual, laughing as one, crying as one, thinking as one. We are melody, harmony and rhythm, together with courage, forming the most stirring symphony of love. Your mother is the "zenith" of kindness and understanding, and you originated within her, and will learn from her now; you will be the same. You are under the watchful and loving eyes of four grandparents who cherish you as their own child; and you have a father who as yet has offered you nothing materially, only a little help in the assurance of your free future.

You shall benefit by your parents' tutelage, and soon will be aiding us in the education of your younger brothers and sisters, for there will be more, and we shall be more than a family for we have a foundation which is stronger than the very earth that holds us, the belief in truth, righteousness, and the right of all men to live and work happily in a society of social and economic equality, and to receive all the fruits of his labors. You shall believe as strongly as we, and shall fight to achieve such a glorious goal. The things I am trying to say are difficult, but you will understand later, for you will read the works of the great poets and authors, listen to the music of great composers, and their words and melodies shall fill your heart and mind with the understanding and spirit to carry on in the battle for freedom.

Though my body be miles away, my heart is with you and I remain forever your father, whose heart is filled with love for you and your mother. You are the nearest stars in my heaven and each night I sing out my love and best wishes.

Cpl. Samuel Furash

Harold Katz

On March 30, 1945, Corporal Harold Katz, a youngster from the Bronx, was cited for bravery in action. After two of his comrades had been wounded in an attack on the German town of Attweilmann, this medical technician exposed himself to enemy fire, gave first aid to his comrades, and was himself seriously wounded. Although unable to move his legs, he pushed the other wounded soldiers to safety. Later, he was killed in action. A letter found on his person was sent to his mother. This is what he wrote.

Dear Mom,

I realize that this is a war and that men will be killed winning it and since I am included in these I know there is a possibility of my not coming back.

If you receive this letter it will be because that possibility has come true. I am writing this letter now while I have the chance, in the hope that it will ease the weight of the sad news, in that it will make you better understand my viewpoint on the matter.

Mom, I want you to know that I asked for a combat assignment. I did so for several reasons. One is that I had certain ideals within my own mind, for which I had often argued verbally. I didn't feel right to sit safe, far behind the lines, while men were risking their lives for principles which I would fight for only with my lips. I felt that I also must be willing to risk my life in the fight for the freedom of speech and thought I was using and hoped to use in the future.

Another reason … is the fact that I am Jewish. I felt again, it wasn't right for me to be safe behind the lines, while others were risking their lives, with one of their goals the principle of no race prejudice.

I knew this meant fighting for me and my family because if Hitler won, my family—you, Rolly and Pop—would certainly suffer more than the families of other soldiers who died in the fight.

I felt that I must risk my life, on that point, so that I could earn the right for my family to live in peace and free from race prejudices. I didn't think it right to stand by and let others fight for things which would benefit me. I asked for combat for the above reasons.

Those are the feelings I had inside me, Mom, and I could not push them aside. I felt if I did not face them, I was not a man of true good character.

I hope you realize exactly what I am trying to tell you Mom, I want you very much to be more proud than sorry. I don't want you to think of it as losing a son for no good reason, but rather as sacrificing a son so that all of mankind could live in a peaceful and free world.

Madeline Medoff

Madeline Medoff (1915–1965) came to the United States at the age of six with her parents, from Hungary. After graduating Cooper Union Institute of Technology with an engineering degree, the first woman to do so, she went on to a successful career which included editorship of *Consumer Reports* and lifelong advocacy of the public interest. Her spiritual odyssey was equally interesting: Until well into adulthood, Madeline Medoff maintained a firm scientific view of life. In her later years, however, when she discovered fuller, rich meaning in Judaism, she added a strong dimension of spirituality to her life and outlook. Her openness to new ideas and experiences is also revealed in her learning to paint. During the illness which led to her death in 1965, despite extreme discomfort, she finished a remarkable four-part painting titled "Creation" which hangs in a hall at Temple Israel, in Long Beach, California.

I Leave Behind Me Life

I do not fear death.
Its approach leaves me with regrets,
Regrets
Not for things I have missed seeing or doing or
    experiencing;
What difference these—
In death I cannot have them with me.

No ...
My regrets
Are for the memories I will not have left
With those I love, whom I must leave behind.
Have I missed giving warmth to my loved ones
    when they needed it
In favor of some selfish whim?
Have I deprived them of some cherished
    memories
By my refusal to admit them to my heart?
Were the trifling matters for which I scolded them

and nagged them so important
As to give them pain both then and later—
Later, when I can no longer add
A balance of more love to sweeten the taste of the
     bitterness I sowed?

I do not fear death ...
Not for me
But for them.
They are the me that is left behind.
They are my stake in eternity
And they matter, more than ever,
When they are the only future that remains.
Their destiny is set;
Whether they will or not
They carry something of me in their lives
And in their children's
And in the children beyond.
For I have touched them!
My self has made its impression on theirs.
To the degree that I have shaped them
Have I shaped them well?
Have I so designed them
That they can live well with themselves?
Will my faith in them
Have touched them so,
That they will go where they must with
     confidence?

Have I let them glimpse
That the world is big
And growing hour by hour;
That there is no greater joy than to explore it—
To view its past—
To lift even the merest corner of its future.
To look it squarely in the face,
Whether with joy or horror,
But with unfilmed gaze.

Have I passed on to them the joy
Of a deed of human decency?
Of what satisfaction there is
In doing good—
Not without gain,
For there is measureless return
For even minute acts of consideration,
Especially *for* those done unheralded.

Then there is obligation,
Not in the common sense,
The sense of paying one's debts
Or saying thanks for favors done,
But in a broader view.
A view that involves all mankind, that reckons as
    obligation
The duty to do kindnesses unasked
Or at least unrequired,
To do it willingly and gladly
And without *keeping* score.

Will they know love?
Not passion—love.
The kind that does not ask
Nor care about reward.
The kind that seeks only to give to the loved one,
The kind that has its satisfaction
    in a look of momentary joy
That is relaxed and free of question,
Of rivalry, of jealousy, of fear;
That can keep its vigor,
Over the years and over the miles.
The kind that gives and asks without
    the insult of questioning.
This is true love,
Much more so than the kind where passion flames
And burns itself out
Leaving ashes, or at best
A not-too-bitter memory.

Do they know that I love them
Not from duty or some awkward sense
    of conventional piety
But because they are so close to me
They are me—
And when I am no more
They are more me than ever.

Have I taught them these
And many, many things,
The things of elemental beauty
That give joy
Far, far more real
Than the contrived, man-made amusements
That insult the mind, the ear, the eye.

Have I taught them the joy of work,
The satisfaction of working well,
The special pride of accomplishment
    in a task well mastered
Into which one puts more
Than the minimum essentials for completion;
Into which one puts a little of one's self,
And from which one derives
Far, far more than one has funnelled in.
I have waited until now
To speak of Faith and God
For this I cannot teach them.
This they must learn for themselves.
My kind of faith will not be theirs, exactly,
Nor would I wish it to be
Mine serves me well—
It was not handed me
But grew from years of searching and not finding,
Then searching more.
For me it is good
With it I am comfortable.
It is rich
And as I search it more, grows richer.

Faith, like God, has oneness
But there is no one Faith,
No one God
That can serve all.
Each must find his own,
Must search and find it.

It is a quest worthwhile,
More than any that I know.
For its fulfillment is peace
And lack of fear;
And understanding,
And the capacity
To live with one's self and others
And, if necessary, to die.
No, I do not fear death
For I leave behind me
Life.

Allen Hofrichter

On a day between Yom Kippur 1973 and August 21, 1974, the day of his death, Allen Hofrichter wrote the following will. In the brief space of less than two typewritten pages he says much and implies even more about himself, his beliefs and expectations. He is a realist about the world, but does not rail against it as, in recognizing human imperfection, he observes, "Gratitude is the Mayfly of all virtues ... life is too crowded to observe the ordinary amenities."

I have requested my children not to engage the services of a rabbi. He never knew me and his eulogy cannot be anything but erratic and traditionally fulsome. Nor in his peroration will the few interlarded Hebrew phrases that few can understand be an "open sesame" to heaven.

Credit Sybil and me with this one indisputable fact: that no one, from Sybil's family or mine, has ever been turned away when they came to us for assistance. When we had no funds, we even pawned our insurance; but in no case has anyone had his request denied. The pity of it is that no one of the score or more we have helped has been interested enough to inquire how Sybil and I are faring.

Nor do I fault them for this. Gratitude is the Mayfly of all virtues, and in this hectic world, life is too crowded to observe the ordinary amenities.

We have adhered to the biblical injunction, and in our contributions to others we have more than tithed ourselves.

After the Yom Kippur War we received a warm and most gratifying letter from Hadassah of which the following is a quote:

> You will be interested to know that the wing at the Hadassah Hospital that bears your name was the most crowded with wounded soldiers almost shattered by the fighting in this recent war. The orthopedic surgeons were operating around the clock, and after the recovery room, the patients were then sent to the Orthopedic section—The Hofrichter Wing.

I have tried to be a good father. How successful I have been, only my two children know. But this I am sure they must realize, that no sacrifice on my part was too great, no amount of thought and effort was too much for me to assure their comfort, peace, and happiness.

They repaid me generously. Our grandchildren, Richard and Michael, and those blessed chattering angels whom I adore, Lisa, Sharon, and Evie, have brightened my declining years.

What can I say about Sybil, my wife these many years. Sybil of the low, gentle voice, the ready laugh, and the soft, ministering hands. For forty-odd years we can honestly say that we have never gone to bed angry with each other. Not a day ever passed without an overt attempt to show our affection for each other; whatever our moods, we were as one.

She extolled my triumphs, belittled my failures, and in her eyes I possessed all virtues and no faults. She was the better part of me, a gentler, more forgiving part.

When our family was younger and we lived in Suffern and Sybil lit the candles ushering in the Sabbath, the world outside our door was nonexistent, an ineffable peace entered our house, and Sybil's presence filled the room like a benediction on all of us.

Her handicap? She disavowed it and laughed more in one day than most women laugh in a month. We were as one. Nothing could come between us to mar our joy in each other.

By this time I am sure Sybil's nose is pink and her eyes are welling with tears. Don't cry, Sybil. I'm at peace at last. No aches, no pains, and happily, no doctors or hospitals. You've given me a good life, and I am grateful. I hope there is a heaven and that I will be admitted there so that I may continue to love you as I have on earth.

To my children, I need not foreswear you to love and cherish your mother, to guard and protect and shield her from any hurts this ugly world may direct at her. Be good to her. She amply deserves your devotion, and please, please do not let her feel alone and lonely.

To all who are here, be well and stay well and may your remaining years be as full of happiness, joy, and peace as mine have been.

Bless you all.

Jennie Stein Berman

Jennie Berman was brought to America from Lithuania by her family, which settled in Ohio. Following her marriage she lived in Chicago until the end of her life. Her children and grandchildren remember her as fully observant of Jewish tradition, but very progressive and modern in outlook. A granddaughter recalls her "dressing like a princess for the Sabbath." Sam, for whom she is concerned, is a bachelor brother. The date of this letter is 1956.

To all my children:

This is your mother's last wish. After I am gone, you should always be together and well and happy; and of what is left in money I want you to *share* and *share alike*. Florence, Alvin, Julius, Lester, if it is only one dollar you should each get a fourth of it. That is my last wish. And if I go before Sam, you should all see to it that he has a place to sleep with something to eat at all times. Please. Then I can rest in peace. That is my last wish, that you all be well and happy. And I give you all my

Blessing and Love
Mother
This is my last wish.

Leonard Ratner

The following note was found among the papers of Leonard Ratner following his death in the mid-1970s. An immigrant to the United States, the writer attained exceptional success and was a noted philanthropist. He expresses his desire that his children and grandchildren emulate the charitable deeds of his deceased wife, their mother and grandmother.

To my Family ... and Grandchildren

This is my last letter and when you will read it, I will only be memory.

I don't think that I have to write you much as, thank God, you are educated and smart enough to understand that this world is not easy. I am sure you will endure it and will continue to follow in the footsteps of mother, as she was one of the greatest women who ever lived.

The luckiest thing for me was meeting your mother, and she to some extent was responsible for many of the successes in our life as she was not only looking for herself but what can be done for the family and others. To some extent she copied our grandparents. I am sure you will continue the kind of life and keep close with all our families and try to do as much as you can for each other.

Don't forget your seats at the Park Synagogue.

Stay well and keep up your good work.

Your Father, Grandfather

Harold

I address myself to my children—to all of our household. My father died at the age of 83 and I have a premonition that in this, my 83rd year, I too will be called to my final resting place....

My deep concern is for your mother. What will become of her if I should be the first? She is so dependent on me. I pray to God and ask Him to prolong her sister's life so that they may spend the rest of their lives together. By that I mean that Fanny should move in with Mom.

... All my life I have tried to help others without expecting anything in return—and now I make a simple request—call Mom if possible every day—visit her once a week—dine with her once a week—call her and tell her what you want for dinner—make her laugh, have the children call, and visit her once in a while. When she is away, write to her frequently. Do it not as an obligation but because I know you really love her and want to make her happy.

Forgive me if I hurt you by suggesting this—I mean well—I am very proud of you and love you all dearly. I am grateful for the many blessings He has showered upon us one and all. In fact I feel that we have received more than our share of *naches* [parental pleasure].

And now I must make a confession. For the past few months I have gradually developed a hate for money and what it does to people. I honestly feel that if one reaches the stage where he has provided fully for his family and himself, the balance does not belong to him. It is a lend-lease from the Almighty to distribute to charity. If I survive I will try to spend the rest of my life seeking out avenues of worthwhile charities, preferably in Israel.

Mother and I lived modestly. I never succeeded in convincing her to buy a mink coat. She always felt that was showing off. I lived the same way. If we lived luxuriously we could never have helped the families for most of our married life.

You have now reached the stage where you can broaden your philanthropy and in larger amounts. I hope and pray that my and your children will follow the same pattern. The children should have begun long ago. Teach them to put aside from their allowance and from any money they earn for charity. Do it now.

Above all—be forever vigilant for those in need and don't wait until they ask you—that is humiliating.

One last request—when the time comes for my last journey, I would like Mother's and my casket facing each other—she on my right side—all it needs is to place the caskets at an angle, like this:

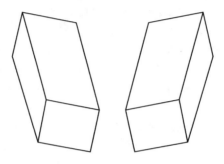

Fare Well

Randee Rosenberg Friedman

Randee Friedman, a Jewish music resource specialist, resides in San Diego with her family. She is the founder of a company called Sounds Write Productions (now part of URJ Books and Music), which commissions and produces Jewish music. In her ethical will, the writer reveals deep commitment to values and practices of Judaism and concern for its continuity in the lives of her descendants. Advice is offered about some of the important observances and about coping with possible intermarriages.

To my beloved children and grandchildren, inheritors of the planet earth (may it be God's will), I share the following thoughts:

I. On the Subject of *Hachnasat Orchim* (Welcoming the Stranger)

As technology advances and mass communication and transportation bring people from all walks of life in closer contact with one another, welcome the stranger in your midst.

    A. Remember that your ancestors were strangers in a strange land so open your hearts and homes.

    B. If the travelers are inclined toward Judaism, show them the ways of our people.

        1. Instruct them in the teachings of Torah and the rituals and ceremonies of our faith.

        2. Share with them the emotional and spiritual connections that flow from Judaism and enrich your lives.

II. On the Subject of Rabbis and Temples

No matter which branches of Judaism remain in your time, there will still be a need for you to affiliate with like minds and souls, so find your style of congregation and embrace it.

    A. Choose a rabbi with empathy, compassion and a sense of humor—remember she or he is a spiritual leader, not a performer.

    B. Choose a Temple for the community of people within its doors, not for its exterior facade.

III. On the Subject of Intermarriage

With new peoples from all over the globe assimilating into your culture intermarriage will be inevitable.

   A. Remember the covenant that God made with Abraham, Sarah and your people Israel.

      1. If you choose to marry a non-Jew, keep your religion and share it with your mate.

      2. Of utmost importance, raise your children within Judaism for they are the seeds of survival for a great nation.

   B. If you need help adjusting to new situations like this, seek out Jewish communal agencies or institutions where Jews are employed who can be of help.

      1. Jews have a long history of helping one another in times of need.

      2. Follow the principle of *Sh'lom Bayit*—make your household a peaceful haven in the midst of a complicated and often stressful environment.

IV. On the Subject of *Tzedakah*

Follow the precept that *tzedakah* is for us a form of justice, not charity alone.

   A. Be generous with your portion in life without expecting or needing recognition.

      1. There is always someone who can benefit from your love and kindness.

      2. Neither silver nor gold are of use in the world beyond, so allocate your resources while you live.

   B. It has never been without cost to be Jewish—pay for your freedom by supporting Jewish institutions.

V. On the Subject of Israel

May it be at peace throughout your lifetimes and forevermore.

   A. Return to the land of our mothers and fathers at least once.

      1. You will then know who you are and from where you came.

      2. Study the land and people for they are the source of our history and our liturgy.

B. Accept the turmoil within Israel's borders—whether fighting with the Arabs or disagreeing among themselves.
   1. Do not judge your Israeli brothers and sisters harshly—try to view their life situations through their eyes.
   2. Whether or not you become Zionists, support Israel by any avenues available to you.

VI. On the Subject of Mitzvot. *Mitzvah goreret mitzvah*— one good deed leads to another one.

A. With every passing year, discover new mitzvot and do them.
   1. Be responsible members of the world community by helping others learn to help themselves.
   2. Your generous acts of kindness will be returned to you with even greater strength and intensity.
B. Live your lives as positive role models for equality and justice, mercy and compassion, truth and righteousness.

VII. On the Subject of Torah and God

In your words and your deeds remember the wisdom of these two ancient thoughts.
A. *Talmud Torah K'neged Kulam*—the study of Torah is above all else.
B. *Shema Yisrael Adonai Eloheinu Adonai Echad*—Hear O Israel, Adonai is our God, Adonai is One.

My life is filled with blessings—I am nurtured by the love and support of my dear husband, friend and soulmate. My children give me delightful moments of happiness and pride. Friends and relatives enrich my days with positive interactions. My work in Jewish music inspires, challenges and satisfies me deeply. All these things I wish for you, and more. Every day, no matter where I am, I think about being a Jew, and feel blessed to be part of such an incredible people. I hope that you too will share this sense of belonging that is the foundation of our existence.

And to this may you say: Amen

Rosie Rosenzweig

The number of ethical wills written by women in the modern period is far greater than by women in earlier periods. This is in keeping with other, ongoing, salutary social developments. What is equally noteworthy is the observation that in their ethical wills women more often than men draw upon psychological insights to personalize their hopes and counsel. Rosie Rosenzweig is a contemporary wife and mother residing on the East coast. In addressing her children she individualizes her hopes for them on the basis of strengths and inclinations they possess. This emphasis, whether conscious or unconscious on the part of the writer, is reminiscent of the mode of the patriarchal blessings in Genesis 49 and in Deuteronomy 33.

This will, and the one that follows, was written at a workshop on ethical wills that was conducted at her synagogue Beth El of Sudbury Massachusetts, as a way of preparing for Yom Kippur.

7/25/79
5 Tishre 5740

My dear family:

It seems appropriate that I just mailed a proof of a correction on my father's tombstone to the monument people. I was concerned … with the correct manner of recording his good name. He was a *Kohen*, of the priestly class, and it had to be so recorded.

So is my link to you, not of words on dead stone, nor nitpicking, but of the good way to keep a good name, as a member of the family you came from, the family you'll spawn and the tribe from whose roots you flower.

Shakespeare did say "A rose by any other name still smells as sweet" (I know I had to remember that during my days on the printing press), but so it is with character from which emanates the good name … you can be in rags, in a poor state, a misunderstood laborer, a misunderstood professional … but your good character will earn you your way. It goes without saying you'll work hard toward your chosen goal by education, by working at occupations up the ladder, etc., but it is the uses of your intelligence as you would use it to build character that I would address now.

If there is a pleasure in acquiring knowledge, there is greater pleasure in applying it.

But what knowledge is useful to the end of building character?

I wish for you the joys of understanding the knowledge of our tradition to its deepest soul. I guarantee it will resonate in your heart at times of deepest trouble and soundest joy. There is a mellowness I would wish for you in your later years, that I now am just beginning to perceive.

For instance, take the commandment "Thou shalt have no other Gods before you." If the name of God, "Yehovah," means the future tense of "to be," then you as His reflection should also always be becoming ... working for a future image of yourself, a better self of more enduring character. You take *teshuvah* [repentance] seriously, you change, you redeem your life, you take Yom Kippur seriously ... and when you do this which is your tradition and your best selves, I live for you, my living heritage, my ever-bearing fruits.

I urge you to understand your roots, as they are in you as archetypes and beg you not to deny [them]. The Torah teaches logic, values, and history. For example, if you pass your enemy in trouble you are bidden to help him as you can and go on your way. Logically the seeds of a better future are here. Rabbi Jacob is quoted in *Sayings of the Fathers* (4:21) that this life is like a waiting room before the bigger banquet. Logically one should always be in preparation. This not only refers to afterlife but to your passages in life from decade to decade.

So many words I've written and so many generalizations. What about specifics:

I would like you to know my writings and keep them ... however little of significance or insignificance I've produced. I want my grandchildren to know the fancies of my mind. That is who I am and all of substance I can give them. I leave three notebooks full of experiences with the weekly Torah Service. If nothing else, pass these on. This is my most important life through the decades. Keep family records, of our history, our events. It is a pleasure I want you to have. The only stability in a drifting society is the fabric of our family. Know who are its members and of what character.

It would be nice to always keep the house in some form.

Elizabeth, I wish for your happiness and stability. That your feelings fly toward the dream of fulfillment but still be balanced by your keen intelligence, is what I hope for you. I hope you remember our times of understanding, and wherever I am I will send whatever healing is possible. I trust the mountain-guide sense in you to go to peaks I'll never see. Be there for me.

Benjamin, I wish that your keen intellectual nature be rounded by that intuition that comes from the artist in you. At thirteen your insight into the *Akedah* was remarkable. May that become more cultivated as you grow older. I live for you in the applause of that day, that brightened your face, and the applause now for such continued adventurous and original trailblazing.

Rachel, my youngest, who has my name and my old place in the family, the youngest, I want to leave you only my best qualities and not my worst. Listen to the still, small voice of the best in yourself, regardless of what the people around you feel. Be swayed only by wisdom, and not the momentary emotions of others.

Sandy, should you outlive me, I release you to the memories of those happinesses that endured and survive me. I know you will forget all else. I urge you to hold on to your visions but ground them in reality. We will meet again as no quantum in the universe dies but is attracted to others for whom it has charge. If I have outlived you I go to meet you now.

Remember, please, to talk to one another on the anniversary of my death, and forgive me for my transgressions against you. Of all other dealings, the commonsense mitzvot, the good values, the way to deal with people and each other, I need leave you no further instructions. You have been rigorously schooled by me, and I assume you will know how to put my body to rest....

Live out your lives wisely, well, and with few regrets.

Your loving mother

William Joseph Adelson

William Joseph Adelson, a contemporary father and husband, was a member of that same study group at Congregation Beth El of Sudbury, Massachusetts, that prepared for Yom Kippur by writing ethical wills. He is a pediatrician and an allergist whose interests include painting, sculpture, and photography. He and his wife are the craftsmen who made the Eternal Light in their synagogue.

5 Tishre 5740

My Dearest Family:

In the busy and often structured pace of our lives there have rarely been times to stand back and reflect upon the big and important things. Our attention has usually been taken by practical details. I want to tell you about what I consider really important.

I was fortunate in time and place. I was born in the America of challenge and opportunity because my parents succeeded in the struggle to get here. I was spared the danger and tragedy of pogroms, of the Holocaust, of major war, of starvation and human misery. I was free to strive and to achieve—to set my goals high and to realize their fruition.

I have always been an optimist. I have never really regretted any of the choices I have made—although I could have lived and been happy with other choices.

I have been blessed with a happy and understanding first marriage and with a happy and sharing second one. I cannot leave you the example of lifelong steadfastness. Let me instead leave you the example of compassion and flexibility. When an old relationship became lost, both your mother and I were honest and insightful enough to recognize this—to make the break, releasing one another and leaving one another free to find new happiness.

Life is imperfect—yet in its living lies ever-renewed excitement.

I have been privileged to watch each of you grow up and move out into the world. I have enjoyed watching your interests and skills develop. I have offered you what I had to share, but have not been disappointed when you have each said, "No thanks—I will find my own thing and do it." I have been pleased that each of you has taken pride in doing what you do well. Quality has its own rewards. Yet flexibility is also important. It is important to be able to let something go if it doesn't prove to be as important or necessary or satisfying as you had thought. You are not enslaved by the rigidity of your aspirations.

I have enjoyed watching you share things with one another. Next to your own husbands or wives and children, the closest affinities you can have will be with one another. You know one another's weaknesses as well as strengths. You have generally supported one another. You have helped one another. I don't ever remember telling you to do that. Chalk that one up as an undeserved bonus for me.

I have felt it important to have you establish your own priorities. I have respected those priorities.

I have tried to set an example for you in active participation in the Jewish and secular communities. I have always felt the importance of sharing in these dimensions. You are young and I cannot tell whether you will be so inclined. It would please me if you found some of the same enthusiasm and excitement in the Jewish tradition that I have. (Or if not in that, I hope you will participate actively in some spiritual tradition.) It is a dimension of spirit that can bring great meaning and intensity to your lives.

I hope you will also enjoy musical, artistic, and intellectual interests. One can live without these aspects, but they enormously enhance the quality of life. I hope you will always feel close to nature—aware of the many subtleties and miracles that unfold constantly around us and in harmony with these cycles. I hope you will share some of these deep gratifications and awarenesses with your spouses and children, and that you will have the maturity to not expect them to necessarily accept your sharing or see things as you do.

I hope you will continue to have intense interests—although these may change. Disappointments may be more painful, but achievements are more gratifying.

I hope you will have compassion for your brothers and sisters—both Jews and non-Jews. That you will ever strive to help those who need the help—that you will ever speak out against injustice and bigotry—that you will never become smug and complacent because you *have* when others *have not.* All people deserve the feeling of respect and realization in their lives. I hope you can help many attain it.

To my beloved Paula—you stepped into such a big job. It has been hard for you to catch up with the complicated life of the family. You have done wonderfully in understanding my needs and pressures. It has been hard for you, coming from differing family background, to cope with assertive, grown children. You have really tried to grow and extend yourself.

You have accommodated yourself to a hard and demanding pace. I hope you will have enjoyed the race of our lives together as much as I have enjoyed sharing it with you.

When I am gone—all of the things I possess will have no further meaning to me. Although I have not left you all objects of great value, I hope you will want some of the things I have created and that we have accumulated over the years. I would be pleased to have you share these things among you—taking those that please each of you or have special meaning for you. Be magnanimous if more than one of you want a particular thing.

More than material possessions, I hope I will have left each of you:

> an optimistic spirit
> a fervor and enthusiasm for life
> a sensitivity to nature and esthetics
> a closeness and regard for one another
> a sense of responsibility and concern for others
> and a sense of worthwhileness about your selves.

I wish your life may be as good and satisfying as mine has been, and thank each of you for having contributed to it.

Lovingly,
Dad and Bill

Hayyim and Esther Kieval

The following selection is taken from a contemporary ethical will written by a father, in Albany, New York, in his name and in the name of his wife. It is written in the form of a letter from both parents. Rabbi Kieval was the spiritual leader of Temple Israel in Albany, New York, and the author of a commentary on the High Holiday Prayerbook. Esther, his wife, was a seminary graduate and a community leader. Rabbi Kieval passed away in 1991 and Esther passed away in 2010.

In addition to making out the usual last will and testament and the usual financial and family arrangements, it has always been a beautiful Jewish tradition to leave to one's beloved children what is called an Ethical Will or *tzava'ah*. You will remember that the first fathers of our people, Avraham, Yitzhak, and Ya'akov, gave blessings and other guidance to their children upon which they might draw when their parents were no longer with them in life. Your dear mother and I, of course, hope and pray that we shall be with you to help and guide you for many, many years; but at the same time if (God forbid) we should not be able to fulfill this deep desire, we wanted to have some thoughts with you at this time on what we consider to be the most important things in our life.

First and foremost, we want you to know that we have had a very happy life so far and that we are full of thanksgiving and gratitude to God for all our blessings. Even if (God forbid) we would have to say goodbye today, we would not feel that we have been cheated by life or forgotten by God. Life is a previous gift from a Power greater than ourselves and beyond ourselves. One must be thankful always for as much or as little as he or she receives from the Divine Source of life. It is the deepest wish of your parents that you will not only grow up to be healthy in body and mind and that you will lack nothing in the way of material needs, but that you will also continue to live according to the ideals and values which your parents have cherished all our lives and which have given us so much happiness.

It would be foolish for us to command you in these matters. You must and you will, of course, live your own lives. We only hope and

150

pray that, as your parents and teachers, we have succeeded in filling your heart with a love and reverence for the Torah, for the Jewish people and its religious way of life, and above all for God. God unites parents and their children even when they are far apart from one another, even when one generation is in the land of the living and the other is in the world of Eternity. The Universe is one, and in the mind of God there is no difference certainly between the living and the dead, nor can there be any difference in the care and concern which God gives to all the creatures.

Of the many blessings which Mother and I have enjoyed in our lives so far, we tend to forget the great privilege of being Americans and all the precious freedoms and opportunities that go with it. Though Mother was born in a foreign country and I in this land, we have both loved the United States equally, and tried at all times to be loyal and contributing citizens. This too we pray will be your way all your lives. It is sometimes difficult for people to see how it is possible to love America with all their heart and soul, and also to love the Jewish people and the Holy Land of our people "with all your heart and with all your soul and with all your might." But when one has enough love, one can manage to love many people and many things that deserve love, without conflict. Mother and I have never felt any such conflict and we are confident that you will also find the way to do this.

We ask you to forgive us all the angry moments we have shown you and pardon whatever pain, sadness, or shame we may ever have caused you. Let all these less-than-happy memories be illuminated by the endless and bottomless love which we have always had for you. You have given us so much joy, so much pride, so much *nachat* [parental pleasure], that I would not know how to begin to describe it. I wish I had the time and the words to write separately (for Mother and myself) to each of you, each in his or her own language according to his or her understanding. But, somehow, we hope that you will know what we are trying to say.

No matter what may happen, know and believe that Mother and Daddy will always love you, always be with you, always be united with you through God, who is the loving Father of us all. I shall end this letter to you, dear children, with all our love and kisses. Try to remember us and always love each other.

Nitzah Marsha Jospe

Some ethical wills are written in an hour or a day, others over longer periods. Some are written in prime health, others in the grip of infirmities of age or disease. Nitzah Marsha Jospe (1947–1980), young Denver wife and mother, felt impelled to record her thoughts and feelings during the closing months of her struggle with the ravaging illness that claimed her before her thirty-third birthday. In a magnificent eulogy, her husband incorporated selections from her notebook and diary, culminating with a letter to her children. Brief excerpts from the eulogy provide continuity and a frame for the ethical will of a remarkable, courageous woman.

25 Adar 5740
March 13, 1980

We all knew, as did Nitzah, that this time would come, but that knowledge could still not prepare us for the final loss. I have some thoughts I'd like to share with you, but more important, I'd like to share with you some of Nitzah's thoughts as well.

At no time did Nitzah delude herself about herself or her condition. She faced her disease realistically, and with remarkable equanimity. On the day we left Israel, the *Jerusalem Post* ran an article about a journalist we had met a few times and with whom Nitzah had discussed, with her typical frank honesty, her disease and our cancer self-help program. The article, while not mentioning Nitzah by name, mentioned a program this journalist was planning with a woman "dying of cancer." Some of our family and friends begged me to keep it from Nitzah, to spare her feelings from this rather blunt reference. But, perhaps inevitably, Nitzah saw a copy of the paper with the article on the plane back to America. When I told her of the concern of our family and friends for her feelings, she wrote down her own reaction to the article and to their desire to shield her from its brutal reference to her. She wrote:

> Your concern continues to astound me because I don't
> know how I deserve it, but I certainly don't want you to

be overprotective. I had to laugh that anyone would think I would be upset by the *Jerusalem Post* article. The subject is one that I talked about with her [i.e., the journalist]—it's no surprise to me that the doctors do not have a cure for my disease and consider it terminal. The whole purpose of the course Raphi and I have gone through was to deal with all possibilities, including death and dying, and this is far from the first time the subject has occurred to me or been openly discussed by me. There are lots of things I'm very emotional about, but this article was certainly not one of them. Thank you for trying to protect me, but it was totally unnecessary.

During the last few months of her life, Nitzah kept a diary, and I would like to share with you a few of her thoughts. She always offered to let me read her diary, so I don't think she would mind my reading some selections to you.

Tuesday, 8 Kislev 5740, November 27, 1979
Our session tonight was on death and dying—very appropriate for me this week and very good. It's better to think about it and sort it out than push it away. I'm even supposed to write my own obituary, and I think I can.

After we returned from Israel, where Nitzah was incredibly energetic, full of life and joy, she seemed to recognize that she would not be able to continue much longer, and her tone changed somewhat.

Saturday night, 17 Tevet 5740, January 5, 1980
For my obituary, I've always imagined age 33. It's the magic number. If I were to make it to 34, I think I could make it to 120. But somehow May seems very far away…. I think I have to try harder to live up to what I said when I first got sick—if this does not kill me, there is no need to let it occupy my time and thoughts; and if it does, then it shouldn't be allowed to interfere with the time that's left. I do hope it will be good time, not bad.

Her last entry starts with thoughts of our youngest, Tamar:

Sunday, Rosh Hodesh Adar 5740, February 17, 1980
She's a good girl, and is learning all kinds of English sentences, and I've tried to spend as much time with her as she
wanted. But I'm afraid she won't remember me. I'm not even
sure what Ilan at 4½ will remember—not much I'm sure; and
Deena at 7½ may remember some harsh things because for
her it has been pretty negative lately, and I'll try to make
things better when I go back, but I find I'm very tired.... I
feel sometimes I could go on forever, and at other times that
I wish the end would come....

Most important, to our children: If you cannot understand me now,
perhaps you will read and understand these words when you are
older. Your Ima's greatest frustration was the realization that you
might not remember her at all, or that you might remember her only
as she was sick, and not always able to express to you properly her
love for you. Your Ima wanted very much for you to know her love
for you. Since she knew that she might not be able to say this to you
at the end, and since you may only understand this when you are
older, she wrote a letter to the three of you. This is your Ima's last
letter to you, which she gave to me:

I can't really tell you what I want for you, because even now
I don't know what I want for myself. What is important is to
make each day good, and not to say "tomorrow" or "in the
future it will be better." Happiness is a goal, but not something we must have every moment. That is not life.

I want you to be good Jews. It's something I've always been
proud of.... I would like to be able to help you and enjoy
you, just as my parents did with me. Since that is not possible, I want you to know how much I love you. I wish you
had more memories of me to help you know me.

Sometimes the memories are better than the reality.

The saddest part is leaving you and not knowing how you
will develop. I would like to think you will be good, honest
people, who have enough self-esteem and self-worth to stand
up for yourselves, and not be afraid to say what you think.

Don't think anyone else is better than you are. You are as good as anyone. Every person is special, and so is each of you; not just to me, but to yourselves.

You, of course, want your own things from your own life, but parents can't help having dreams for their children.

You mustn't be bound by what I would like for you. I expect you to go your own way as good people, the best way you know how.

These were your Ima's parting words to you, her *tzava'ah*, her ethical will and instructions to guide you as you grow up.

William Lewis Abramowitz

New York-born William Lewis Abramowitz (1914–1972) was a prominent scientist and industrial leader of Swampscott, Massachusetts. He was a leader in his synagogue, in the work of Weizmann Institute, and in behalf of numerous other worthy causes. The product of a traditional Jewish family, be maintained a lifelong devotion to Jewish learning and to its advancement.

Jerusalem, 1963

Dearest Lee, Susan, Gail, Kenneth, and Ava,

Weep not and dry your tears. At least in my behalf. The years that God has allotted to me have been good, and I have no *tayneh* [complaint] to our Maker. Death is the final state of all human beings, and a few years more or less do not matter. I have drunk fully of the cup of life, and a few remaining drops left unsipped will cause me no grief or regrets. If there is one thing I ask, it is that I may be permitted to see all my children happily married; if not, I'll be watching from somewhere anyway. Marriage is the fulfillment of life, and I have been blessed with a jewel of a wife and four wonderful children whose love has sustained me during those times that try a man's soul and has nourished me during times of *simhah* [joy].

To my wife: Your love has been to me beyond measure. Remember what has been and weep not. Time is a wondrous healer even as you and I have recovered from but not forgotten the loss of our son and our parents. You are too much of a woman to live alone, and the children will mature and go their own way. Look for a man you can respect and love and know that I only want you to be happy.

To my children: In material things I have seen to it that you will not want. These are the least important things, although the lawyer has prepared a megillah to safeguard them. Remember to be Jews, and the rest will follow as day follows night. Our religion is not ritual but a way of life. To us as Jews, life is its own *raison d'être*, its own self-justification; we await neither heaven nor hell. Ritual is only a tool to remind us who we are and of the divine commandments. Jews do not lie, steal, nor bear false witness—*past nisht*, as our parents used to say—such things are simply unbecoming for a Jew. Take care of one another, and in honoring your mother, honor yourselves. I know the love she has lavished on you without thought of self.

Marry within your faith, not to please me, but so that you may be happy, not because gentiles are inferior—they are not—but because marriage is complex enough without the complicating variables of different viewpoints. You are the bearers of a proud tradition of four thousand years. Do not let the torch drop in your generation.

Never turn away from anyone who comes to you for help. We Jews have seen more suffering than any other people; therefore we should care more. That which you give away, whether of money or of yourselves, is your only permanent possession.

To my son: I mention you first, not because I love you more, but because you will now be the head of the family. The girls may call this sexism, but I hope they will forgive me. Don't fail your sisters or your mother. Their tears are my tears. Money is only a tool and not an end in itself. Your grandfather taught me that a man should earn his money till the age of forty, enjoy it till fifty, and then give it away, that a man who dies rich is a failure as a human being. I say this because I know that your abilities will make you a wealthy man materially. But my real desire is that you be rich in heart and soul....

Don't forget Israel. You can be a builder of the homeland for the remnants of our people. There is no conflict between your obligation as a citizen of our country and your concern for Israel. On the contrary, a good Jew is a better American.

To my daughters: You are warmblooded. Jewish girls keep themselves clean, not because sex is dirty—it is not—but because the love you will bring your husbands should not be sullied by experimentation or dalliance. It has always been the Jewish mother who has preserved our people. I shall be content if you follow in the path of your mother.

To all of you: Let your word be your bond! Those mistakes that I regret most keenly are the times when I let human weakness forget this. I know it is hard to learn from the experiences of others, especially of parents, but if there is one thing I beg you to take to heart, it is this.

Say Kaddish *after* me, not *for* me. Kaddish is the unique Jewish link that binds the generations of Israel. The grave doesn't hear the Kaddish, *but the speaker does*, and the words will echo in your heart. The only immortality I seek is that my children and my children's children be good Jews, and thereby good people.

God bless you and keep you. I love you.

Your father

Marcia Lawson

The writer of this ethical will is involved in Jewish communal endeavor at the highest level, in Chicago. A notable feature of this will is the fact that, in spite of her own powerful commitment to Judaism and its creative continuity and enhancement, this mother does not admonish her children. Rather, she presents ideals and a spiritual ambiance for their earnest consideration.

My Dear Children:

Tradition warns us that one of the signs of a false prophet is his claim to foretell the future. How much care should we ordinary beings then take in refraining from glib statements regarding what will be in the days to come.

Therefore, I cannot say in what way your lives will differ from the path my life has taken. All I can recount here are my hopes, dreams, and desires for spiritually rich, rewarding and productive lives for you both and for the families you will raise in your turn.

My life was shaped by crashing waves of history: mass emigrations of desperate people, economic depression, war, the decimation of our people, the rebirth of Israel, and the unverbalized response of my family to these momentous occurrences. They were not considered topics to discuss with children, opinions were not asked for, no overt teaching came forth, only background murmur of adult conversations, a sense of uneasiness, of time rushing too quickly forward yet creeping incredibly slowly.

Your life is being formed amidst quieter events on the stage of history. Yet a much more verbal coming-to-grips with the meaning of these events is demanded of you. You must consciously determine how you will internalize them, how you will make the past as well as the present an integral part of yourselves as Jews within the human family.

We, your elders, solicit your perceptions. Perhaps we are too intense and do not leave you time for unfettered dreaming and childish selfishness.

My Jewish identity began as pride in belonging to what seemed an "interesting" and "different" people. Sociologically speaking, I found us a treasure trove of unplumbed depths. At the same time I shared in Toynbee's misconception of us as "fossils." The inchoate feelings of Jewish affirmation which demanded expression by marriage in the devastated, conquered Germany were many years later to lead us to Massada for your Bar Mitzva, Freddy and, God willing, the same for your celebration of Bat Mitzva, Dina.

I have attempted to give you a more "normal" Jewish life by living the Jewish calendar as part of our daily life. I hope this steadiness along with the continuous study of our people's history, the shared memories of the Jewish past from biblical times through the rabbinic tradition into the middle ages, Hassidic lore, the Haskalah and the Zionist idea will give you a meaningful understanding of our group personality. Certainly, you will be able to bring a measure of spontaneity and authenticity to your own homes that I was unable to reproduce.

You were not born into the world at large, but into a certain family and at a certain time. I would wish for you comfort, love, an "at homeness" in this family which shares a common historic experience. But I also wish you always a yearning and a seeking for something more for yourselves and the generations to come after you. These generations go back beyond Sinai to a lone wanderer, our father Abraham, and continues into the future. It endures so long as this unbroken chain of generations continues to struggle toward an end beyond itself, to be of value to others, to dare to be a partner with that power that causes us to struggle for justice, peace, love and beauty.

In conclusion my dears, care for and protect each other's wellbeing and share in each other's joys and be an emotional support in times of difficulty.

Your Mother

Sam Levenson

Sam Levenson (1911–1980) was raised and educated in New York. He taught in New York City high schools for fifteen years before making a successful career as a humorist. He became a beloved, nationally known personality through his books and appearances on radio and television; he had his own program, the "Sam Levenson Show," on Columbia Broadcasting System television. The major focus of his humor was the family—raising children and growing up in an urban environment. Some of his writings appear in textbooks on urban sociology. It has been said of his humor that it was of a special kind: it sought laughter at nobody's expense. This is his "Ethical Will and Testament to His Grandchildren, and to Children Everywhere."

I leave you my unpaid debts. They are my greatest assets. Everything I own—I owe:

1. To America I owe a debt for the opportunity it gave me to be free and to be me.
2. To my parents I owe America. They gave it to me and I leave it to you. Take good care of it.
3. To the biblical tradition I owe the belief that man does not live by bread alone, nor does he live alone at all. This is also the democratic tradition. Preserve it.
4. To the six million of my people and to the thirty million other humans who died because of man's inhumanity to man, I owe a vow that it must never happen again.
5. I leave you not everything I never had, but everything I had in my lifetime: a good family, respect for learning, compassion for my fellowman, and some four-letter words for all occasions: words like "help," "give," "care," "feel," and "love."

Love, my dear grandchildren, is easier to recommend than to define. I can tell you only that like those who came before you, you will surely know when love ain't; you will also know when mercy ain't and brotherhood ain't.

The millennium will come when all the "ain'ts" shall have become "ises" and all the "ises" shall be for all, even for those you don't like.

Finally, I leave you the years I should like to have lived so that I might possibly see whether *your* generation will bring more love and peace to the world than ours did. I not only hope you will. I pray that you will.

Grandpa Sam Levenson

Richard J. Israel

The four letters which follow are not, strictly speaking, ethical wills. They are included in this collection because each of them, in sequence, touches on themes parents consider landmarks in the lives of their children, hence their own. The writer of these letters, Rabbi Richard J. Israel, was Bnai Brith Hillel Director of the New England Region. He addressed the first letter to his unborn daughter, Alisa, in May, 1961, as he waited outside the delivery room for her arrival. The second was written eighteen years later as Alisa prepared to leave home for college the first time. The third was written on the eve of Alisa's marriage; and the fourth as Alisa awaited the birth of her first child.

To my (as yet) unborn child:

It is late. Though expectant fathers are supposed to be nervous, I am more restless than worried and wish you would already arrive.

Observing the children of friends, it is my impression that it may be some time before I will once again have the opportunity to address you in an much quiet as I have available this evening. Since talking to you at this time in the waiting room would merely raise questions in the nurse's mind about my potential competence as a stable parent, I shall commit this address to writing, to deliver it at some presently unknown and undesignated time.

I am full of expectations for you. Not about your sex. I don't have the least interest in whether you are a girl or a boy. Five or six children from now, if the law of average treats us shabbily, I might have some feelings about the question, but I don't now.

There are other matters that seem far more significant. It is, for example, very important to me that you be fun, not so that you should keep me amused, though I wouldn't mind that, but, more significantly, that you should be joyful. It appears that whatever you turn out to be, you are likely to be named after my father, who was an Isaac ("Yitzhak," from "laughter"), so that somehow your name will have to do with laughter or happiness, and that seems right. I do not commend earnestness to you as your chief virtue.

That does not mean that I don't want you to care about others. I want that very much. May you be able to be either kind or angry for others' sakes. You will know which is appropriate when the time comes. Even more, may you be willing from time to time to risk doing something that may turn out to be foolish, for the sake of a wise concern.

Tonight I am particularly conscious of our responsibilities to make the world a better place, since it is with mixed feelings of guilt and relief that I am now sitting in the hospital rather than driving to Montgomery, Alabama, with Bill Coffin and John Maguire (they drove off without me) in pursuit of what seems like a very important cause. (Someday, if you like, I'll tell you about them and what their adventure turned out to be.)

I write all this to warn both of us that I shall try not to live out my deficiencies through you but at the same time that I do not plan to abandon all goals and aspirations for you just because they happen to be mine, too. One goal that I think I shall not give up is that I want you to be clearly and irrevocably Jewish. I do not know if my way will be your way, but your way must be a real way, and a serious way. I won't give an inch on that one. It is perhaps a sign of our (or at least my) time that I am already taking a defensive posture on this issue. Perhaps for you being Jewish will be an easy and relaxed thing, not the struggle and effort it has been for me, but I don't feel compelled to wish you an easy time of it. Valuable things usually cost quite a bit. Perhaps part of your struggle will be with me.

I want you to be happy, caring, and Jewish. How am I going to get you to be any of them—ah, now the anxiety begins. I don't have the vaguest notion of what it means to be a parent or how one goes about the task. Doing what comes naturally is clearly no panacea. People have been doing that for years, and we can see what the results have been. But then what alternatives have I but to promise you that I will try hard and hope that you won't have to pay too much for my on-the-job training. If you try to forgive my mistakes, I'll try to forgive yours. We are both going to make them—lots.

But, alas, my noble sentiments are rapidly leaving me as I am slowly becoming engulfed by the desire to sleep and my impatience for you, or at least for Dr. Friedman, to appear with joyous tidings.

The Almighty is clearly helping me to practice parenting even before your arrival. I am not sure that I am grateful for His concern in this area at this moment. In any event, my wishes for you and the Messiah are the same at this moment. May you both come speedily.

With love of unknown and untested quality,
Your expectant father

September 4, 1979

Dear Alisa:

It is eighteen years now since I wrote you from the waiting room of the New Haven Hospital. Though we have communicated by letter from time to time over the years, this seems like the right occasion to resume that earlier correspondence. The last time I wrote, you were an abstract idea. This time I am writing to a very concrete you. In a few hours, I am going to take you off to college. I don't know about you, but I certainly don't feel old enough for this sort of thing. I am not sure which of us is more nervous, though we probably are not worried about the same things.

I should imagine that you are worried about losing old friends and making new ones, about how you are going to do in your classes, whether it is really difficult to survive in big, bad old New York City, and the distant, but not distant enough question about what you will do with your life four years from now.

I am worried about the same matters but some additional ones as well. (At the time of the last letter, I thought I was worrying more than you.) In addition to worrying about you, I am worried about myself, worrying about my failings, worried about whether I have adequately prepared you for what is to come.

The Talmud says that a father must teach his children three things: Torah, a worldly occupation, and how to swim. It is presumed that with skills in these three areas, you can manage anywhere. You are certainly a splendid swimmer, far better than one who is as ill coordinated as I am had a right to expect. I am very pleased about your cooking and catering abilities. They are formidable and will always give you an occupation if you want one, whatever else happens in your life. Whether it is a skill you will use or only store away in your head doesn't matter. I have always been grateful to my grandfather for teaching me to bind books. I doubt if I am ever going to bind books for a living, but it is comforting to believe that I could if I really had to.

I don't think that I have taught you enough Torah. When I was growing up, Judaism for me was mostly something I found in books. For you and your other three siblings, I wanted it to be more immediate, the sounds you heard, the food you ate, as natural as breathing. As a result, though you know a lot of pieces of the tradition, certainly much more than I knew at you age, I don't know if you have the right set of connections, the ideas that make it all hang together. I wanted you to be both traditional and modern at the same time, and I am not sure that I have given you the tools. I am also concerned about the extent to which I have tried to glue onto you my kind of Jewishness and what that might be doing to your soul.

I think I should try harder to realize that we are different people. Of late, I have taken to counseling parents that they have no more right to take credit for their children's success than they are obligated to blame themselves for their children's failures. The most casual glance at your brothers and sisters makes it clear that kids raised in the same home turn out to be very different people in ways that can hardly be accounted for by position in the family. It may be biology, it may be *mazel* (luck), or even will that has made each of you unique.

That is what I believe in my head. In my gut, however, I and the other parents to whom I dispense this wisdom feel great personal satisfaction from their children's triumphs and great shame from their failure. I secretly say of you: Look what I did (hooray)! or Look what I did (sigh). For both of us, part of the process of our growing up is learning to separate out some of these issues.

I feel comfortable with your political sensibilities, particularly that you have them but also insofar as they incline in the same direction as mine. Then I say to myself, What right have I to be happy about such a thing? They are, after all, your sensibilities, or if they aren't they have no meaning. But on the other hand, didn't I help give them to you? Do I deserve no credit? How do I give you standards as a parent while at the same time view you with at least as much non-judgemental compassion that I would want to extend to any other independent adult? I don't yet know.

You haven't made it any easier, either. Whenever I give you the no-adult-privileges-without-adult-responsibilities speech, you always respond by telling me that you are neither an adult nor a child but are something in between. That is true, but also an easy dodge. We are both rather muddled about this issue, and I am aware of no way out except to be aware of it.

You turned out to be named properly. You are certainly a joy and a ray of sunshine for everyone who knows you. But when I expressed the wish that you would be that way those eighteen years ago, I forgot that the energy that gives people like you, especially, good cheer would from time to time be quite depleted. It is reassuring, however, how much better in control of your gloom you are than you once were.

We have had a special closeness, you and I, perhaps because you were a first child or perhaps because so many of our best and worst qualities and even our styles of dealing with the world are so similar. Perhaps it is because of the way we seem to sweep up after each other. It is more than likely that your mother will have a bird tomorrow upon seeing the state in which you will almost inevitably leave your room. To me, it seems the most natural state of affairs in the world that you should be going to visit Eva in the hospital, and if everything doesn't get done, so be it. On the other hand, you should be clear that people like us need people like her to keep our worlds ordered, and our "flexibility" is most often sustained at small cost to her, by her sense of orderliness, resist it though we may.

I do not think I am much better a parent now than I was eighteen years ago when you were born. I have learned much less along the way than I should have supposed. I have far less insight into how I think you should raise our grandchildren than I would have suspected. What I have learned is that as complex and exhausting as I thought raising children would be, I greatly underestimated the measure of effort and time that would be required. I am now more tolerant of other people's styles of child rearing because I have discovered how much more confusing, exhausting, and sometimes even desperate a task parenting is than I imagined. I certainly no longer believe that if you are sincere, everything works out nicely. But though we have had moments together that have been painful, I can honestly say I do not regret any of them. I have come to view even those hard times as part of what it is all about.

And so, Alisa, may you go in peace and come in peace. May you always be both our child and your own independent person even though it will never be very neat. May you find your path to Torah. May you succeed with hard things. Whatever you do in this world, may you do it well, for then you will remain *aliza* ("happy" in Hebrew, pun intended).

With a love that has been well seasoned
Your satisfied father
Richard Israel

June 18, 1985

Dear Alisa and Harold:

I should like to address you this day of your marriage with great love, respect and not a little anxiety.

On two important occasions in the past ... when you were about to be born and when you were about to go to college, I have written letters to you, Alisa, that were a sort of cross between a classical ethical will and what might be described as a parental position paper. This seems like a significant enough event for the third in the series, though this time, the letter does not go to you alone Alisa, but, rather, to the two of you.

It goes to both of you because my relation to Alisa is no longer unmediated. Though you Alisa are no less my daughter now than you ever were, you are a daughter whose new primary relationship will be to you, Harold, her husband. That suggests that the areas in which it is permissible for me to nag are now greatly restricted, indeed, *almost* entirely eliminated. Now that your home, Alisa is elsewhere and that this house in which you grew up and where you will always be welcome, has become a place to visit, a storage warehouse (though it should be noted for only a finite period of time) and a laundromat that doesn't charge quarters.

That is a very hard thing to think about, much less say, particularly inasmuch as I don't feel ready for you to be my married daughter. It is not that I want to discourage you from getting married. Certainly not! I have been a very active encourager. We all know that. It is just that I have an un-reasonable wish that first you should know as much about what it means to be married, as in retrospect, I now wish I had known those many years ago. I want you to know how wonderful it is and how hard and how many things you can do wrong and what are the comforts you can expect and how to muddle through when the comfort season is a little lean. You clearly ought not get married without knowing these things ... and alas, neither should I have, nor should anyone else who also can't be told and who has to make those discoveries alone.

It doesn't much help me that I understand perfectly well that my concerns are just part of the inevitable war between the generations in which parents always find their children not quite prepared for whatever their children believe themselves to be ready. Whether the question is, who holds the cereal spoon, when it is appropriate to begin using the family car, or when to have babies, parents and children are only rarely on the same time-table. I shall do my best to make my peace with your current innocence in the reassuring knowledge that in the first place you are probably less innocent than I was when I married and second, you, like the rest of us, will get older.

As you spend years getting to know one another, you will learn that one of the more curious features of the human personality is how close virtues are to deficiencies. It is likely that you both cook too well for either of your long term good. Alisa, wherever you are, there is a party but parties sometimes take up quite a bit of space. Also, your extraordinary ability to respond with great competence to the exigencies of the moment does not always leave you with the resources to dole out your formidable talents in measured fashion for more routine matters.

Harold, my congenial fellow woodsman and log splitter, some of whose handiwork will warm this house next winter, I eyed you with all of the suspicion uniquely and appropriately directed to the suitor of one's first born daughter. By now, you are far less a stranger than a comfortable and treasured member of our confusing and noisy family. While Alisa is an expert in liveliness, you Harold seem to specialize in steadiness, she in now, you in then. May each corrupt each other, but only just a little, so that you don't lose these, your very real strengths.

You both know how to work hard. No matter what you do that is a quality that will surely stand you in good stead. Neither of you appears to view yourself as a finished product. That too, I find admirable. It has always seemed more important to me to try to be a *Lamdan*, one who keeps on learning, than a scholar whose learning has already arrived. Don't let your curiosity about important things die as you become engrossed by the routines of living. Don't let your search for the perfectly set table distract you from a concern for a larger vision which will energize both your lives over the years. Your commitments to Torah and Chochma, Jewish wisdom, will nourish you more than Julia Child. Yuppie heaven is ultimately not a very interesting place.

The Midrash assures us that making a proper match, one that will really hold together, is as great a miracle as the splitting of the Red Sea. If it was such miracle at the time of our ancestors, how much greater a miracle it must be in our own days when many expect so much more from marriage and invest in it so much less.

As you may have discovered already, it is either a great act of faith or an illusion to believe that men and women are really both members of the same species. In the face of the inevitable strains, what will serve you best is what can only be thought of as a moral resolve, your commitment to stick to your marriage and make it work. That determination is what you need more than anything else to carry you over the bumps. Off you go on a formidable journey together. I hope it will be a wonderful one. We your family and friends are very proud of you today, proud of your qualities as Jews, as students of secular culture, and as very honorable *mentchen*.

And there is every reason to believe that we will be even more proud in the course of time.

So, may you go forth in joy and be led forth in peace. May the mountains and the hills before you break into singing and all the trees of the field clap their hands. Though you are two persons, there is now only one life before you. May you find happiness in the time to come and may your days be good and long upon the earth.

Your father and soon to be father-in-law.

Thursday, January 14, 1988

Dear Alisa:

I never planned these letters as part of a package when I first started writing them. It seems to me that this is likely to be the last of the four I will have written you on special occasions—the last, not because there will be no further special occasions between us, but rather, because now the cycle is complete. (It is for the same reason that I address it to you rather than you and Harold. I in no way want to minimize the profound affection and respect I feel for him.) I first wrote you when I was a young parent just about to have a new-born and now, it is you who are a young parent about to have a new-born. It is you who are now more or less in the situation I was in some twenty-six years ago when you first surfaced. The decisions we had to make about your life are now for you and Harold to make about your nearly born child.

In many respects, it is a very different world today than the one into which you were born. Politically, the sixties were full of turmoil and hope. We were confident that we could change the world and make it better. We knew who the good people were and who the bad ones. Now everything is much more muddled and our chances of affecting the system seem much more remote.

Jewish life then was much more bland, but more genial. The world around us was so much more obviously hostile to Jews that we could not yet afford to harass each other. Israel was a tiny country, only a few miles wide and the Wall could only be seen in sentimental pictures of old Jerusalem.

Digital watches and VCRs didn't exist. Hand-held calculators cost a fortune and at that they were as big as Kleenex boxes. Computers lived in large laboratories at universities and didn't come home at night. Students were ashamed to tell their classmates they were going into law or medicine unless they claimed they were doing it to serve the poor. Teaching and the Peace Corps were the preferred professions, and no one, simply no one, would admit to wanting to go into business.

Into all of this, you appeared. I still remember clearly how terrified I was with the thought of bringing this expensive stranger into my house and had only the vaguest notions of what I was supposed to do with it. You already seem to know what to do with babies, something I never quite learned. I have argued that it is programed into your feminine hardware (feminine software would probably be the more felicitous phrase) but since Harold, too, appears to know significantly more about these things than I, an ostensibly experienced father, perhaps it is only my own soft or hardware that is deficient.

In other respects, too, I think you have an advantage over me. You seem to have fewer illusions. I was determined to be an outstanding parent, an obviously outrageous goal. You are more likely to want to be a good-enough parent. I do not believe you will want less for your child than I did for you, but rather, that you may know more about the limits of parenting that I did. Your aspirations for your child may be better tempered by your child's aspirations for itself. My parenting was grounded in a plan, albeit, not a very clear plan. Yours is more likely to be grounded in your child. I am probably overstating the case, because though part of me thinks I should have done that too, another part of me hopes that you and Harold also have in your heads and hearts some kind of grand notion about the kind of person you want your child to be and the values you want that child to have. I have never been able to escape from the old dilemma. To be altogether person-centered is to assume that only your child knows what one kind of person to become. That is patently a fraud, the same as the other notion which assumes that you can make any child turn out just the way you want if you only try hard enough. As with most anything else in this world, there is undoubtedly a middle ground which makes most sense of all.

As I look around at zealous and pure types, whether Jews, vegetarians or Republicans, it has become increasingly clear to me that any good idea carried to its logical conclusion is probably wrong. (I just met someone who wanted to impose the death penalty on people who hurt animals.) It is very easy for people with noble concerns to run amok. Avoid fads, whether of child rearing, Judaism or politics and you will probably be better parents for it.

If you are like us, part of the baggage of childhood that you bring with you into parenthood is the notion that since you are much nicer people than your parents, you and your children will get on much better with each other than you did with your parents. No chance. Undoubtedly you will not make the same mistakes we did. Rather, like us, you will make your own new and improved mistakes. Just don't assume that by doing the opposite of what we did, you will be more likely to be right. In the process of developing your own style of childrearing, do your best not bend over backwards so far you fall on your faces.

You and I have spoken of the old Greek theory of knowledge, reworked by the Midrashic literature, that all knowledge is known *in utero* but that an angel comes along at birth, strikes the child under the nose, leaving the crease that we all have, and causing the child to forget, so that learning is really recalling. Knowing with exquisite precision how to exasperate parents is one piece of wisdom that never has to be recalled. It always seems to sneak past the angel. Be confident that whatever your weaknesses, your children will find you out at once and immediately leap for the jugular, just as you and your brothers and sisters did. It is part of what parenting is all about. May you manage not to take it any more personally than necessary. It is important to understand your contribution to the mess but not to assume responsibility for all of it.

In particular, be sure to hold your psychic breath throughout those difficult adolescent years and hang on, no matter what. You were about thirteen and at the beginning of it all. There was something we wanted you to do that you didn't want to do, though what it was I have forgotten. You were in your nightgown on the stairs between the second and third floor when you declared, "I am now an autonomous, responsible adult and able to make my *own* decisions." And your teddy-bear was under your arm, an irony that somehow eluded you.

You will probably have forgotten your own adolescence by the time your child reaches that age. May you at least recollect enough to know that a lot of love and dogged determination will carry you through better than clever psychological insights.

Children are often hard on a marriage. In the course of raising them, it will be important for you and Harold to make a special effort to be nice to one another—for quite some time, particularly since, as we have learned from you and your sibs, there is no light at the end of the tunnel. But we have also learned that things really do become more manageable with the passage of years. In the short run, you should take comfort in knowing that you really will sleep again.

Do not assume that life will ever come together in a neat package, but in the long run, there will be some very satisfying resting spots.

Yes, raising children is hard, but it is also the most gratifying activity there is. If you raise them in order to get gratification, you will get none at all, but if you do it because there are few, if any, tasks more important, then child-rearing can provide a measure of extraordinary satisfaction that only those who have raised children can know. I am grateful to you for providing some of those choice satisfactions. It is true that there were times in the past when I would have or maybe did mumble the old curse, "May you have children like you." It turns out that I can still say the same words but now they have turned into a blessing. Alisa, may you have children like you.

With a love that is eager to discover new dimensions,
Your child's alarmingly and perhaps enduringly inexperienced

Grandfather

Rabbi Herbert A. Friedman (1918–2008)

The career of Herbert A. Friedman epitomized a life of service in the highest degree. Few leaders have played a more prominent role in Jewish affairs during the past half-century. He served as rabbi in Denver and Milwaukee, and he was the executive chairman, executive vice president and vice chairman of National United Jewish Appeal for twenty years. Beyond that, beginning with service as a chaplain in Europe during World War II and as director of the Wexner Jewish Heritage Foundation for more than twenty years, his career was interwoven with major events in the Jewish world. In his will he writes about those critical times and about the events on the American and world Jewish scenes in which he actively participated. He writes, too, about his beliefs and about his hopes for the reader, making his ethical will, abridged here, both illuminating and inspiring.

Opinions, Actions and Conclusions: A Legacy

I hope my years will roll on, but prudence warns that this should not be taken for granted. Therefore, in this eighth decade of my life, let me start to leave my legacy of opinions and conclusions, beginning with four subjects: What I believe, what I have done, what I have learned, and what my dream is for you.

I. What I Believe

1. *I believe in the uniqueness of the Jewish people.* Even as we share the quality of human-ness with all others of the species *homo sapiens*, still we are absolutely different in so many ways. And if we were not different, we probably would have disappeared as have all the others who started on the path when we did. Let me bring to mind three elements of our uniqueness. First there is the covenantal nature of our birth as a nation, in which we were linked to a God and a moral code. Next, this was succeeded by the acceptance of an eternal destiny through the concept of redemption by a Messiah, for both themselves and all mankind, in which a better world would be born for all humans to enjoy. How incredible! And lastly, there came the

notion that this moral covenant and Messianic redemption must also be linked with a specific land—a homeland, gained and lost, gained and lost—but the very dreaming of which provided the strength to endure the passage of the centuries. Now the land is gained again, in our own time. How miraculous!

2. *I believe in Israel's gift to mankind.* Alongside our uniqueness and separateness and particularity, a special quality of universalism exists in a measure which no other people or nation on earth, large or small, possesses. We are a people which truly believes in the brotherhood of man, whose sacred books stress that all men come from one father.

3. *I believe the Diaspora is an integral part* of the creative genius of the Jewish people, and our history offers plentiful proof of this thesis. The Diaspora has been a fruitful hinterland, providing intellectual spark and charismatic personalities. The American Jewish future is as yet unknown. But if it finds its way and maintains its Jewish identity in the midst of unprecedented freedom, there is the possibility that it will outstrip all previous Diasporas in terms of what it might achieve for Jewish creativity and continuity. So, here are the four seminal, simple beliefs that have directed my deeds and ruled my life: The Chosenness of the Jewish people; its linkage to a land; its universal message for all mankind; and the creativity of its ever-loyal Diaspora.

II. What I Did

1. *Helped Create the State.* According to my theory of what constitutes a meaningful life, action is the indispensable ingredient. Otherwise, one is not a participant, merely a theorist or even worse, just an observer, a couch potato. When the moment comes for action it must be seized immediately, or it will be lost for good. I have been very fortunate in my life since many opportunities for action did come my way. I seized them all and have been richly rewarded with a wonderful feeling that my days have been well spent. Other times, I saw certain needs and created the action scenarios myself, not waiting for others to do so.

It took me years to position myself so that I could do something about these inadequacies, but I set out on a course and stuck with it doggedly, finally reaching the point where, at the end of the war, I was in Germany, a chaplain, an American army officer, and was recruited by David Ben Gurion himself, into the Haganah. I worked actively in that role for three years in Europe, 1945–1947, smuggling Jews and guns, people and weapons, both needed to fight the inevitable War of Independence. Trains, trucks, food, camps, guides, ships—all had to be organized in a sweeping orchestration which brought the surviving remnant of Jews from as far away as the Russian republics in Asia down to the French Mediterranean coast— with Germany at the heart of the operation—for here the quarter million people we moved were housed as they came from the east, and were staged for transfer to Palestine. How many working Haganah men do you think were involved in this massive migration? Perhaps 200 on land and another 200 at sea. Can you believe it? The accumulation and shipping of weapons was also done by fewer than 100 people. It was the greatest period of my life.

2. *Helped Gather in the Exiles from the Four Corners of the Earth.* This opportunity came through the position I held as the Chief Executive Officer of the National UJA for two decades: Morocco was taken over by Moslem rule in 1955 when the French departed, following which the first pogrom took its casualties. We started to move small groups of Jews illegally across to Gibraltar, then we pushed for larger groups, openly, on French ships to Marseilles. One third of a million were transmigrated.

Yemen sent 50,000 on an airlift, and Iraq expelled 120,000 who were also flown to Israel within the 15-month limit allowed.

We moved 2000 per week for 50 weeks straight, from the Rumanian port of Constanza on the Black Sea to Haifa. A total of almost 400,000 Rumanian Jews were moved in less than a decade.

And so it continued, as the sovereign state of Israel in the greatest humanitarian effort in the entire history of the Jewish people gathered its children, from country after country, through the double dedication of its won citizens and free Diaspora Jewry.

3. *Helped Awaken the Sleeping Giant—American Jewry* [Following the Suez Operation in 1956] Two major efforts were required—one, a nationwide general educational campaign had to be developed to define and affirm the basic relationship which must prevail between American Jewry and Israel—the lesson to be taught was the unbreakable linkage between the people of Israel and the land of Israel; and a small cadre of young leaders had to be identified, recruited, inspired and educated, so that their youthful enthusiasm could be turned loose on the larger community, to help shape the deeper understanding and loyalties so necessary. The Young Leadership movement which I started myself at the UJA, thirty years ago, has since been duplicated in every individual Federation in the country, as well as most national organizations. The educational network of thousands of speeches every year spread far and wide the doctrine of unity of people and land.

4. *Lived There for Seven Years.* One of the most poignant episodes of our seven years of life in Jerusalem occurred one day when the two boys and I were walking up the long promenade to the entrance of the Israel museum. Our family policy was to speak English at home, so that the boys, David and Charles, having come to Israel when they could hardly read or write, would learn proper English, and to speak Hebrew in public, on the street and in school. We were therefore, speaking Hebrew as we strolled up the promenade. My voice is resonant and penetrating. My Hebrew was not as good as theirs. They were apparently embarrassed by my errors. Suddenly, they stopped and suggested in firm tones that I would do better to speak English, even in public. In an instant my mind flicked backward forty years, when I was walking one day with my father, across the Yale campus, and even though his English was fluent, still a Vilna-born accent must have been discernible, for I turned and asked him not to speak so loudly as to be overheard by fellow students on our same path. Wow!

The story symbolizes the turning of the wheel of Jewish history. From Vilna to Connecticut to Jerusalem—three generations of wandering Jews, struggling with new languages, cultures, mores, repeating the same experiences in each generation, of adjustment and renewal, yet always advancing. No wonder others are envious of us.

III. What I Have Learned

1. Life without risk is stagnant. It is safer, but less productive. *Be fearless, take chances;* you may get hurt, but you may win the lottery.
2. When you take chances, you must learn how to live with failure. Failures will inevitably occur. Get back up on the horse.
3. It is often necessary to fight, and that means even war. Evil like Hitler must be fought against. Independence and freedom must be fought for. Just as war may sometimes be necessary, peace is always necessary and must follow war. Genuine solutions to problems are never achieved by war. They must be achieved by the diplomatic negotiations and compromises which follow afterwards.
4. Separate the important from the less-important. You cannot support every project, taste every sensation, read every book. Prioritize. Do a few things very well. Decide what is the longest-lasting, broadest in scope, most seminal. Concentrate on those; drop the others.
5. Planning and execution go together; dreaming is not enough. You must be capable of great dreams otherwise you are a pedestrian dullard; but you must then be able to draw a blueprint by which the dream can be brought to realization, otherwise you are a BATLAN—a lovely Hebrew word meaning "idler, loafer, impractical, inefficient, ineffective"—just an idle dreamer.
6. To inspire means to demand. You can make the strongest plea in the most beautiful language, with poetic examples and historic analogies which may result in a standing ovation because the audience is simply swept away by the colour of your words and the majesty of your power. But when it is over, and the people are dispersing, you will hear the questions in the foyer: What was that all about? What was its purpose? What did the speaker want? If you have not demanded anything, have not cast a challenge which requires a response, have not provoked them to action, then you have failed, no matter how stirring was your oratory. A leader inspires and demands.

IV. What Is My Dream For You?

1. *Learn how to catch history by the tail and ride with it.* Don't be caught unawares, don't be left behind. This means thinking ahead. Develop the art of prediction, which is based on an analysis of the past, plus some crystal-ball gazing, plus good luck. Most people are afraid to do it, but it is not hard, once you habituate yourself. Set scenarios for yourself; it's wonderfully enjoyable ... an exciting game!

2. *Learn how to catch your own children (and grandchildren) by the tail.* Everyone understands that the major challenge facing the great and powerful Jewish community in America is the struggle against the indifference which comes from ignorance and leads to easy assimilation and intermarriage in this permissive society which has no barriers against Jews. Everyone also understands that the remedy lies in replacing ignorance with knowledge, but the remedy is difficult to apply. Children must be saturated, from an early age, with the "naturalness" of being Jewish by what they learn and do in school, at home, and with their friends. A day school education is the best process, and more and more parents are turning to it thus improving the schools at the same time. But the majority of children are not in day schools, and these children must get as much Jewish education as you can give them, plus reinforcement at home through Shabbat and holiday observances, plus summer camp with other Jewish kids, plus trips to Israel beginning around age 10, plus a year in Israel later on, plus, plus, plus ...

   This is your effort to combat intermarriage, but if it happens in your family, then you must start all over again with your non-Jewish son-in-law or daughter-in-law, seeking to transmit Jewish feelings and knowledge to them, urging conversion, if this be possible. And whether there is conversion or not, then at least your grandchildren must be given a Jewish identity and be brought up as Jews. Sit your grandchildren on your lap and tell them the story of their people, as you practice the holidays with them. Catch them, hold them, don't let them slide away. You can do it, with love and tact and a strong determination. My dream is that, like the little Dutch boy who kept his finger in the dike to keep the sea at bay, each one of you will become the keeper of an unassimilated people, which lives with its two identities, American and Jewish, in separate harmony.

3. *Be generous with money.* We in the middle class indulge ourselves. We give ourselves almost everything we want. Always remember that part of your budget, part of your cost of living must be the three-fold responsibility of supporting the infrastructure of your local community, maintaining Israel's strength, and helping individual Jews in need, be they Russians or Ethiopians or anyone. You all know the word *tzedakah*, and the concepts behind it. You have the same obligation to perform *tzedakah* as to put bread on your own table.

4. *Be aware of the needs of all humanity*, not just the Jews. While we are very particularistic, tribal, ethnic and, some say, even clique-ish, nevertheless we also possess a parallel streak of universalism in our mission which mandates us to care for all people. This streak is responsible for our liberal sentiments toward minorities, underprivileged, homeless, and other underclasses of mankind. All of this is subsumed in the phrase *Tikkun Olam*, which requires us to work for improvements in society as a whole. It is an important part of authentic Judaism, which put Heschel in the front ranks of the civil rights marches with Martin Luther King and caused Elie Wiesel to take up the cause of the Cambodians. These are good role models to follow.

5. *Be civilized, kind and understanding.* If you are looking for a role model, take the prophet Micah [chap 6 verse 8]: "He has told you, O man, what is good, and what God requires of you: Only to do justice and to love mercy, and to walk humbly with your God."

6. *Do your duty and keep your faith in Israel—the people and the land. Duty* and *courage* are fierce and fiery words. They moved Moses and David and Ezra and the Maccabees. And may they move you, the sons and daughters of Israel, today. Vision and perseverance are perhaps even more important words because they give sustenance for the long, long, endurance required to face a future with confidence.

Stephen Wise showed how the possession of the vision itself created the characteristics which would guarantee its attainment.

"Vision," he said, "looks inward and becomes duty. Vision looks outward and becomes aspiration. Vision looks upward and becomes faith."

Prodded by a sense of duty, ennobled by a sense of aspiration, sustained by a sense of faith, our little lives acquire a dimension of incredible strength, so that we each become like a small nuclear engine, driving with enormous power toward our goal—a free people in a warm, safe prosperous Israel, and a creative, proud Diaspora sharing the fruits of a good society with all neighbors, in a peaceful world, working for the betterment of all humanity. This is your dream to have and to hold, to cherish and make real, to give to your children as the most precious gift in the world. This is my dream for you. Make it come true.

Rabbi Stanley J. Garfein

The ethical will of Rabbi Stanley Garfein is unique in more than one respect: The first draft was addressed orally to his congregation, Temple Israel in Tallahassee, Florida, on Yom Kippur day in 1972. It was part of his sermon for the memorial service that day. In it, he urges the congregants "to revive the custom of the ethical will ... and to include in it our funeral instructions ... because the kind of funeral one has should reflect the values he admires in life."

Many rabbis of all streams in Judaism have waged an on-going battle against the modification or abandonment of traditional Jewish funeral practices. This will, therefore, in addition to declaring the wishes of the writer about his own funeral arrangements, is instructional to all, like all true ethical wills.

Finish Your Final Business

Yom Kippur, 5733
September 18, 1972

Dear Friends,

In traditional Judaism, death was not a subject that people avoided.

Death was looked upon as part of the whole fabric of life. There was a time to live and a time to die.

Among most of *our* members, however, there *does* seem to be a reluctance to talk about the end of physical life. Of our entire congregation, only one or two have given me instructions about the conduct of their funerals.

This is unfortunate, because it leaves one's final business unfinished. It's like not taking out life insurance, because of the fear of death. But, once you face the necessity of protecting your family, an emotional load is lifted from your shoulders. Without *your* direction at the time of death, there is likely to be great confusion among your next of kin. Family and friends must play guessing games as to what you really wanted in terms of funeral arrangements. Petty power struggles sometimes break out over who is to decide what.

Traditionally, this wouldn't have happened. Mourning procedures among Jews were standardized. When death actually had occurred, *and not a moment before*, the Chevra Kaddisha, or burial society, came in and took over. Last rites were performed with dispatch and simplicity.

The members of the burial society were usually laymen, who offered their services without charge. Such participation in the burial of the dead fulfilled an important mitzvah. Perhaps it is due to the professionalization of undertaking, and the disappearance of lay burial societies, that death became distant and not talked about.

Another tradition that has fallen by the way is the ethical will. We're of course familiar with *regular* wills that dispose of *material* possessions. An ethical will on the other hand, provided *spiritual* instruction for one's family. It is a sad commentary on our modern sense of values that people can't wait to open a regular will, but don't even *expect* an ethical will.

I would *urge* each of us to revive the custom of the ethical will. Moreover. I would like to suggest that we include our funeral instructions in the ethical will; *for the kind of funeral one has should reflect the values he admired in life.* Finally, may I recommend that we not merely lock our ethical wills in safe deposit boxes. A will is not likely to be found there till sometime after the funeral. Instead, one should distribute copies to his executor, to his next of kin, and to his rabbi.

In order to provide an example of what I mean, here is a draft of my ethical will.

To My Dear Ones Who Survive Me, Shalom Aleichem!

You know how I've always tried to plan ahead and avoid last minute confusion. Permit me now to offer this guidance in the making of my funeral arrangements.

Let two Jewish principles govern planning: (1) simplicity, and (2) expression of true feelings.

Following the Jewish tradition, the coffin should be the least expensive there is. I do not ask that it be all wood, as that might be costlier. Nor do I require a vault, unless that be a cemetery rule.

The funeral should be as soon after death as possible. If embalming is not required by civil law you may dispense with it.

Leave any pulpit robes to my successor. Remove all jewelry, so that it may be used by the living.

Clothe my body in casual, informal garments. Cover my shoulders with my tallit, and my head with the yarmulke I've worn at the pulpit.

Keep the casket closed. I have no desire to be viewed. I prefer to do without statements like: "He looks better now than he has in many-a-year." Remember me instead as I was in life.

Prior to the funeral, let there be no visitations at home or in the mortuary, except for consultations regarding arrangements.

Do not bring in anyone from outside the congregation to conduct the funeral. Our congregation is blessed to be able to count three rabbinical colleagues in our membership.[1] They have been good friends and supportive resources to the congregation. Please call on them to aid in the services. Also since I've always felt that laypeople should be highly involved in the conduct of worship, I'd like the Worship Committee to read a service from one of my *Rabbi's Manuals*.

If the Board of Trustees consents, let the service be at the temple, and last not more than twenty minutes.

The tone of the Psalms and prayers that are selected should match the nature of the death, be it sudden and tragic, *or* in the fullness of time, with the cup of fulfillment running over.

In place of a eulogy, I would feel honored if three or four excerpts from my sermons would be read. For I spent a large portion of my life in the preparation of my sermons. They reveal the concerns of my rabbinate.

In place of flowers, let contributions be made to Temple Israel, the Tallahassee Federation of Jewish Charities, or the United Fund of Leon County. I have no objection to flowers for the living, but I do object to banks of flowers at a funeral. Let there be no camouflage of the reality of death.

As a lover of music and singing, I would like our Organist and Soloist to render the "Twenty-third Psalm" and the "El Male Rachamim." These selections and any background music should fit the mood of the occasion, be it tragic or grateful.

Let the Worship Committee decide on whether or not to have pallbearers. Except for the hearse, do not rent special cars to go from home to the temple to the cemetery.

The service of committal at the Jewish cemetery should be short and traditional. I want no artificial grass concealing the earth. Lower the casket before Kaddish.

After Kaddish, I would consider it an honor if my friends would each shovel some of the good earth into my grave. I deem this a meaningful custom, because earth so beautifully symbolizes the ongoing cycle of life. Viewed from the perspective of the totality of God's creation, death is just a necessary phase of this ongoing cycle of life. Individual mortality is thus transcended by nature's immortality. I find *this* concept of immortality very appealing.

When the committal is over, and my family returns home, light the shivah (seven day) candle. I would appreciate it if the Sisterhood would provide a simple mourners' meal. Round rolls or bagels, and hard boiled eggs, symbolize the ongoing cycle of life. They thus bear a message of comfort.

Avoid other gifts of food, heavy feasting, levity or casual conversation. I think it is undignified. It distracts the mourners from expressing their grief. Don't try to distract the mourners with nervous, idle chatter. Instead, make them feel comfortable about expressing their feelings.

For five nights following the funeral and not including Sabbath or Holy Day, I would appreciate having a minyan at home led by the Worship Committee. I would, of course, have you abide by the traditional diminution of mourning should a Holy Day occur.

Let calls on the bereaved family be distributed over several weeks. It is cruel for everyone to pile in at once the day of the funeral, only to abandon the mourners during the subsequent, trying weeks of bereavement.

I do hope that my family will say Kaddish with special fervor at Sabbath services for eleven months following my funeral. I ask that they not attend purely social gatherings for at least thirty days, except if a Holy Day occurs in this period.

Most of these requests I make not just because they're traditional, nor because I would appreciate being offered respect in such ways. I make these requests because I'm convinced that it is psychologically good for the mourners to work through their grief, instead of denying it with false heroics. The practices of our tradition serve to make us face reality, when we most want to deny it. This is good for the sake of subsequent mental health.

At the end of eleven months, dedicate a low, flat stone at my grave. Let my name be inscribed in English and Hebrew, with dates of birth and death according to the Hebrew and civil calendars. If my dear ones can find a verse from the Psalms that applies to me, I would feel privileged to have it inscribed on the stone.

On the yahrzeit, light a candle at home and say Kaddish with special fervor at synagogue services. These observances are important to me. I do not, however, require a perpetual memorial cast in bronze.

This will has been reviewed by Vivian. Should there be any questions about the execution of its details, the Worship Committee shall defer to her wishes. Should she be unable to render a decision for any reason, the authority shall pass to either one of her dear parents.

Here ends the list of my wishes. By carrying them out, your expression of grief will be intense at first, and then gradually taper off, so that you can return to the routine of the living and function therein.

I am now prepared for the end of life, whenever that may be. Whatever awaits me beyond the grave is God's decision to make. "Into His hands do I commit my spirit."

I know that whenever I leave this world I shall be far from perfect. But I do feel a sense of satisfaction from the fact that my hands have not been idle, and I have achieved some good not only for myself but also for others.

To Vivian, Rebecca, and Susanna, let me say: I could never have functioned as well without your love, affection, encouragement, and help. How can I express in words the love and gratitude I feel?

God has granted me strength in sorrow, inspiration when I needed fresh ideas, good cheer during hours of celebration, and a wonderful family and friends, with whom I could share life's experiences.

May He bless you all, and help you fulfill your highest hopes.

With the achievements of medical sciences in the area of organ transplantation, a new opportunity for expression of brotherly love is made possible. Parallel progress in the preservation of donated transplantable body parts makes possible humane world-wide networks. As expected, and as underscored by Rabbi Garfein, contemporary halakhah has responded positively to these significant developments. This part of his will was also first conveyed in a sermon on Yom Kippur day, in 1989. This groundbreaking testament is suffused with a remarkably sensitive, enthusiastic spirit.

Organic Immortality

Yom Kippur, 5750/1989

The yearning to transcend the limitations of the flesh has been a major concern of humanity ever since we first became aware of the reality of death. There are actually a number of ways by which we may live beyond the grave: In the good we do, in the children we leave behind, in the tasks we hand over to others to complete. Then there is the belief shared by some of us that our individual consciousness, or soul, persists beyond the body's demise.

During the past year, I have become increasingly aware of and interested in the possibilities for immortality available through organ transplant. Last year, so many of us waited with Lew Rosenau, and prayed for him to receive the gift of a new heart. Ever since, I have realized what a direct contribution of continuing life one person can give to another. Each one of us can agree to pass on parts of his or her own life, when one is no longer in need of them. We can donate *parts* of *ourselves* to those who seek them to sustain and reinvigorate their lives.

Robert Test has beautifully described the possibilities of organic immortality in his poem "To Remember Me." He wrote:

> The day will come when my body will lie upon a white sheet neatly tucked under four corners of a mattress located in a hospital busily occupied with the living and the dying. At a certain moment a doctor will determine that my brain has ceased to function and that, for all intents and purposes, my life has stopped.
>
> When that happens, do not attempt to instill artificial life into my body by the use of a machine. And don't call this my deathbed. Let it be called the Bed of Life, and let my body be taken from it to help others lead fuller lives.
>
> Give my sight to the man who has never seen a sunrise, a baby's face or love in the eyes of a woman.
>
> Give my heart to a person whose own heart has caused nothing but endless days of pain.
>
> Give my blood to the teenager who was pulled from the wreckage of his car. So that he might live to see his grandchildren play.

Give my kidneys to one who depends on a machine to exist from week to week.

Take my bones, every muscle, every fiber and nerve in my body and find a way to make a crippled child walk. Explore every corner of my brain. Take my cells, if necessary, and let them grow so that, someday, a speechless boy will shout at the crack of a bat and a deaf girl will hear the sound of rain against her window.[2]

Organ transplants do *not* fall into the proscribed realm of mutilation of the body, which Jewish law forbids. Quite the contrary. No less an authority than Dr. Moses Tendler, an orthodox Rabbi, says that organ transplants are procedures that take precedence over all other legal considerations, because they save or uplift human life. Tendler, who is Chairman of the Biology Department of Yeshiva University of New York City and Chairman of the Bio-Ethics Commission of the Rabbinical Council of America, says "If one is in the position to donate an organ to save another's life, it's obligatory (a mitzvah) to do so. Even if the donor never knows who the beneficiary will be. The basic principle of Jewish ethics—'The Infinite Worth of the Human Being'—also includes donation of corneas, since eyesight restoration is considered a life-saving operation." He adds, "It is given that the donor must be brain dead in accordance with the standards set by the Harvard University criteria and the President's Commission on brain death."[3]

During a seminar for ministers, we saw slides of what someone could see before and after a corneal implant. His sight before the operation revealed what appeared to be a crater caused by an explosion. The same scene after the implant was actually a beautiful seascape, showing the surf hitting the shore beneath a rocky cliff under a blue sky. Such an operation must seem like the resurrection of the dead for those who are fortunate enough to benefit from it.

Now 15,000 corneal transplants are performed annually from 100 eye banks across the United States.

It is estimated that more than 80,000 kidneys and 200,000 corneas have been transplanted world wide in the past 20 years. Add to this number 5,300 bone marrow, 700 liver, 400 pancreas and 800 heart transplants.

These are impressive numbers because of the lives that have been saved and the improved *quality* of life they have given to the suffering.

Not unusual is the story of the death of a young boy and his gift of life to another. A 15-year-old on his bicycle was struck by a car. He sustained severe head injuries and extensive brain damage. His doctor determined that there was no hope for the boy. He was declared clinically brain dead. Naturally, the boy's parents were in shock.

The doctor approached the parents and gently told them that they could donate their son's organs for transplant with the potential of their son helping others to live. The family chose to donate. Their decision was a difficult one.

Both parents told the hospital chaplain that this is what their son would have wanted because he was "that kind of boy."

They found comfort in knowing that their son's eternity was of the spirit and of the body.

Often the hospital personnel is less than comfortable asking a family in the first shock of bereavement to consider donating organs from the body of their dear one. Sometimes, precious time elapses before a transplant occurs, time that may be needed for the transplant to be effective. That is why a uniform donor card is available. This obviates time consuming seeking of permission. A prospective donor fills it out as he would draw up a will or insurance application. It is kept with the driver's license in one's wallet. In the event of death, *after all efforts to save life have been tried*, a hospital is empowered to contact the organ network to make known the availability of any organs the donor has designated, and which are deemed usable by others in need. The donor card actually lists what the donor is willing to give.

After transplants have occurred, funeral and burial proceed in accordance with Jewish tradition. But one *additional* form of immortality, the gift of life, exists to comfort the mourners.

According to our tradition, whosoever saves one life is credited as if she/he saved the entire world.

This is because the person whose life is saved may go on to have a family, and so create a potential universe of others. How much more, then, do we save when we offer ourselves to aid *more* than one person? Let me share with you the result of the donation of one young man's body to aid the life of others. After all was said and done, the nurse at the hospital in charge of transplants wrote the family. In her letter, she said:

> I would like to thank you again for your kindness and generosity in donating your son's organs to people in need of a transplant.... The liver was transplanted into a 27-year-old Pittsburgh man who had undergone a previous transplant one month prior. He had been attending school, but the severity of his liver disease the past few months prior to his first transplant had restricted him to staying at home. He is now doing very well. The kidney was transplanted into a 26-year-old male who is married and has three small children. He is also doing very well. The heart was transplanted into a 34-year-old male in Minnesota who is doing just fine.... Both corneas were transplanted. One went to an 88-year-old female and the other went to a 79-year-old female.
>
> I know there is nothing I can say that will lessen the grief over your son's death. However, I hope you will find some comfort in knowing that because of your kindness and generosity, other people can have healthier and happier lives.

Yet, even though people know what marvelous things can be done through this most personal and meaningful of donations, there are waiting lists for transplants all over the country because of the present *lack* of donors.

If anyone would like to explore the possibility of his or her own organ donation, please see me or please see Karen Kuperberg, our temple member who is part of the transplant network.

The biblical Elisha, disciple and successor of Eliyahu Hanavi, was not only a prophet but also a great miracle worker; he restored the life of a boy by giving him what we know today as CPR (2 Kings 4:8–37). We may not share Elisha's ability to perform miracles, but today, we can share his capacity to restore and redeem life. On this Shabbat Shabbaton, this Sabbath of Sabbaths, let us live up to the legacy of the prophet Elisha. Let us make real and concrete our highest longings to preserve and enhance life. Let us all take a moral inventory of ourselves to see if we offer this day more than our songs, more than our prayers, more than our confessions, more than our fasting, more than our deepest remorse. Let us look deep inside to see if this day we might offer our very selves to salvation of life itself.

The philosopher writes that atonement is granted "... only to those who strive for the good. Without our moral work in repentance, God would be unable to redeem us." As the gates begin to close, let us offer to share the gift of life that each of us holds dear; then will our prayers for repentance be answered, not only because of the words of our lips, but by the work of our hands as well.

"Heal us, O Lord, and we shall be healed.

Save us, and we shall be saved."

Amen!

Rabbi Monroe Levens

Rabbi Monroe Levens (1908–1982) was the widely known spiritual leader of Tiferet Israel Synagogue in San Diego, California, for more than three decades. He was an innovative leader and a force in setting high standards in Jewish education for both children and adults. He filled leadership roles in Jewish life and in the general community as well. His ethical will, dealing in part with his views on life after death, is at once thought-provoking and instructional. Asking forgiveness for possible inadvertent wrongs is a recognized practice in Jewish life; it is directed to family and friends either orally or, as here, in writing. This was written in 1973.

Farewell

This is my farewell. If I have done any harsh thing to anyone in this world, I am sorry and ask to be forgiven. Of one thing I am certain: I have always enjoyed the respect, love and confidence of my brothers. And that is something, a sort of portable treasure, to take along with me wherever I go, if I go anywhere.

It is idle to speculate about death. It is one of the "secret things" that "belong to God." But whatever else it may be, it is the end of earthly existence. However, I do not believe it is the end of the spirit or the soul. And as for immortality, I think it is for us ourselves to determine that question. I believe we are as deathless as we desire or deserve to be. And so it is possible that I may be going somewhere, spiritually.

Life here is a great and wonderful adventure. It may be a greater and more thrilling adventure there. The spirit is at least as real, though mysterious, as the atom whose secret we have only recently penetrated. Whatever doubts I have had and I have had many even as a rabbi, I have always been a worshipper at the shrine of the wonder of life and the universe.

To be skeptical requires no special skill or intellectual insight. Cynicism is an expression of mental and emotional frustration. The fact that life is and always will be an enigma is no reason for despair but a challenge to faith.

And faith is the thing we supremely need, not the blind, unthinking acceptance of the beast of the field, not resignation, but the questioning, constructive faith which makes life livable and robs death of its terror.

My interest in Judaism, more than a perfunctory attachment, is a powerful and unshatterable allegiance to the Jewish people and the Jewish historic cause which is the cause of an emancipated humanity set free from the shackles of false ideologies and destructive idolatries.

I have a very intense, even prophetic, conviction that the new Israel is destined to loom large in the affairs of the world.

From my Jewish faith I have learned two things which have been the constant theme of my service as a rabbi: that you cannot build up your happiness on the unhappiness of another and second, that you get out of life no more, no less than what you put into it.

I am not afraid to go. Of course, life with all its burdens and reverses, is sweet, and friendships, especially the joys of unforgettable family relations, are precious. I have left many things undone and tasks unfinished as all of us do when the summons comes, but in terms of years, even more than the biblically allotted three score and ten, I have lived my life and should be satisfied. I have had moments of triumph and moments of defeat. I have suffered hardships and have weathered many a storm. I have loved and I have lost. But I believe, if they could be measured in a scale, the joys would outweigh the sorrows.

Rather than fear of the inevitable or regret in going, mine is a feeling of intellectual curiosity. I have experienced many things here, probably everything that can be experienced in this mundane sphere, except this one thing, the final curtain. Instead of dreading it, I find myself asking, "What, if anything, is it?"

The question may never be answered. It may be complete extinction, total irrevocable oblivion. And that is something or rather a vast, impenetrable nothing, about which we cannot speculate or argue either for or against. But if there is a God, and I believe there is, a Supreme and Inscrutable Intelligence, I think He is the God of Life not death.

Therefore with the poet, I will wrap the draperies of my couch about me and lie down, I hope to pleasant dreams.

Faithfully yours,
Monroe J. Levens

Part Five

Three Wills from Classics of Modern Jewish Literature

"Some things are true whether they happened or not."

Elie Wiesel

All the other wills in this collection were actually written by parents to their children. These three are works of fiction. We include them because they are classics of modern Jewish Literature and because they contain powerful and important spiritual truths, even though they are works of fiction.

Yossel Rakover Speaks to God

By Zvi Kolitz

Yossel Rakover Speaks to God has had a curious history. It originally appeared in a collection of stories and parables inspired by the Holocaust by Zvi Kolitz that was entitled *The Tiger Beneath the Skin*. Seven years later; a Yiddish version appeared in Israel in the literary journal, *Die Goldene Keit*. The editor of that magazine was under the misapprehension that this was an actual last will and testament that was somehow retrieved from the rubble of the Warsaw Ghetto. Then it appeared in a Hebrew translation in a collection of personal testimonies by Holocaust survivors called *This I Believe*. The Yiddish version was in turn translated into French by Arnold Mandel where it was discovered by Emanuel Levinas, the distinguished Jewish philosopher. He made it the basis of his radio broadcast: *Aimer la Thora plus quie Dieu*. And this in turn became the basis for a book length commentary by a Jesuit, Franz Jozef von Beeck, which was recently published by Loyola University Press.

In all of its wanderings, the story has had a profound impact upon its readers. It has been included in services for *Yom Hashoah* in many places and it has been studied as a superb expression of the depth of the pain of a people that has the awesome right to take its God to court.

Strictly speaking, it is not really an ethical will for it is addressed to God, not to one's children and it is fiction, not fact. But we have decided to include it because it is an eloquent example of how a human being makes an accounting of his life and a summation of his faith at the end of his days.

Warsaw April 28, 1943

I, Yossel, son of David Rakover of Tarnopol, a Hasid of the Rabbi of Ger and a descendant of the great, pious, and righteous families of Rakover and Meisel, inscribe these lines as the houses of the Warsaw ghetto go up in flames. The house I am in is one of the last unburned houses remaining. For several hours an unusually heavy artillery barrage has been crashing down on us, and the walls around are disintegrating under the fire. It will not be long before the house I am in is transformed, like almost every other house of the ghetto, into a grave for its defenders. By the dagger-sharp, unusually crimson rays of the sun that strike through the small, half-walled-up window of my room through which we have been shooting at the enemy day and night, I see that it must now be late afternoon, just before sundown, and I cannot regret that this is the last sun that I shall see. All of our notions and emotions have been altered. Death, swift and immediate, seems to us a liberator, sundering our shackles; and beasts of the field in their freedom and gentleness seem to me to be so lovable and dear that I feel a deep pain whenever I hear the evil fiends that lord it over Europe referred to as beasts. It is untrue that the tyrant who rules Europe now has something of the beast in him. He is a typical child of modern man; mankind as a whole spawned him and reared him. He is merely the frankest expression of its innermost, most deeply buried instincts.

In a forest where I once hid, I encountered a dog one night, sick and hungry, his tail between his legs. Both of us immediately felt the kinship of our situations. He cuddled up to me, buried his head in my lap, and licked my hands. I do not know if I ever cried so much as that night. I threw my arms around his neck, crying like a baby. If I say that I envied the animals at that moment, it would not be remarkable. But what I felt was more than envy. It was shame. I felt ashamed before the dog to be, not a dog, but a man. That is how matters stand. That is the spiritual level to which we have sunk. Life is a tragedy, death a savior; man a calamity, the beast an ideal; the day a horror, the night—relief.

When my wife, my children and I—six in all—hid in the forest, it was the night and the night alone that concealed us in its bosom. The day turned us over to our persecutors and murderers. I remember with the most painful clarity the day when the Germans raked with a hail of fire the thousands of refugees on the highway from Grodno to Warsaw. As the sun rose, the airplanes zoomed over us. The whole day long they murdered us. In this massacre, my wife with our seven-month-old child in her arms perished. And two others of my five remaining children also disappeared that day without a trace. Their names were David and Yehuda, one was four years old, the other six.

At sunset, the handful of survivors continued their journey in the direction of Warsaw, and I, with my three remaining children, started out to comb the fields and woods at the site of the massacre in search of the children. The entire night we called for them. Only echoes replied. I never saw my two children again, and later in a dream was told that they were in God's hands.

My other three children died in the space of a single year in the Warsaw ghetto. Rachel, my daughter of ten, heard that it was possible to find scraps of bread in the public dump outside the ghetto walls. The ghetto was starving at the time, and the people who died of starvation lay in the streets like heaps of rags. The people of the ghetto were prepared to face any death but the death of hunger. Against no death did they struggle so fiercely as against death by starvation.

My daughter, Rachel, told me nothing of her plan to steal out of the ghetto, which was punishable by death. She and a girl friend of the same age started out on the perilous journey. She left home under cover of darkness, and at sunrise she and her friend were caught outside the ghetto walls. Nazi ghetto guards, together with dozens of their Polish underlings, at once started in pursuit of these two Jewish children who had dared to venture out to hunt for a piece of bread in a garbage can. People witnessing the chase could not believe their eyes. One might think it was a pursuit of dangerous criminals, that horde of fiends running amok in pursuit of a pair of starved ten-year-old children. They did not endure very long in the unequal match. One of them, my child, running with her last ounce of strength, fell exhausted to the ground, and the Nazis then put a bullet in her head. The other child saved herself, but, driven out of her mind, died two weeks later.

The fifth child, Yacob, a boy of thirteen, died on his Bar Mitzvah day of tuberculosis. The last child, my fifteen-year-old daughter, Chaya, perished during a *Kinderaktion*—children's operation—that began at sunrise last Rosh Hashona and ended at sundown. That day, before sunset, hundreds of Jewish families lost their children.

Now my time has come. And like Job, I can say of myself, nor am I the only one that can say it, that I return to the soil naked, as naked as the day of my birth.

I am forty-three years old, and when I look back on the past I can assert confidently, as confident as a man can be of himself, that I have lived a respectable, upstanding life, my heart full of love for God. I was once blessed with success, but never boasted of it. My possessions were extensive. My house was open to the needy. I served God enthusiastically, and my single request to Him was that He should allow me to worship Him with all my heart, and all my soul, and all my strength.

I cannot say that my relationship to God has remained unchanged after everything I have lived through, but I can say with absolute certainty that my belief in Him has not changed a hair's breadth. Previously, when I was well off, my relation to God was as to one who granted me a favor for nothing, and I was eternally obliged to Him for it. Now my relations to Him are as to one who owes me something, owes me much, and since I feel so, I believe that I have the right to demand it of Him. But I do not say like Job that God should point out my sin with His finger so that I may know why I deserve this; for greater and saintlier men than I are now firmly convinced that it is not a question of punishing sinners; something entirely different is taking place in the world. More exactly it is time when God has veiled His countenance from the world, sacrificing mankind to its wild instincts.

This, however, does not mean that the pious members of my people should justify the edict, saying that God and His judgments are correct. For saying that we deserve the blows we have received is to malign ourselves, to desecrate the Holy Name of God's children. And those that desecrate our name desecrate the name of the Lord; God is maligned by our self-deprecation.

In a situation like this, I naturally expect no miracles, nor do I ask Him, my Lord, to show me any mercy. May he treat me with the same indifference with which He treated millions of His people. I am no exception, and I expect no special treatment. I will no longer attempt to save myself, nor flee any more. I have three more bottles of gasoline. They are as precious to me as wine to a drunkard. After pouring one over my clothes, I will place the paper on which I write these lines into the empty bottle and hide it among the bricks filling the window of this room. If anyone ever finds it and reads it, he will, perhaps, understand the emotions of a Jew, one of millions, who died forsaken by the God in whom he believed unshakably. I will let the two other bottles explode on the heads of the murderers when my last moment comes.

There were twelve of us in this room at the outbreak of the rebellion. For nine days we battled against the enemy. All eleven of my comrades have fallen, dying silently in battle, including the small boy of about five—who came here only God knows how and who now lies dead near me, with his face wearing the kind of smile that appears on children's faces when dreaming peacefully—even this child died with the same epic calm as his older comrades. It happened early this morning. Most of us were dead already. The boy scaled the heap of corpses to catch a glimpse of the outside world through the window. He stood beside me in that position for several minutes. Suddenly he fell backwards, rolling down the pile of corpses, and lay like a stone. On his small, pale forehead, between lock of black hair, there was a spattering of blood. Meanwhile I still live, and before my death I wish to speak to my Lord as a living man, a simple, living person who had the great but tragic honor of being a Jew.

I am proud that I am a Jew not in spite of the world's treatment of us, but precisely because of this treatment. I should be ashamed to belong to the people who spawned and raised the criminals who are responsible for the deeds that have been perpetrated against us.

I am proud to be a Jew because it is an art to be a Jew, because it is difficult to be a Jew. It is no art to be an Englishman, an American or a Frenchman. It may be easier, more comfortable, to be one of them, but not more honorable. Yes, it is an honor to be Jew.

I believe that to be a Jew means to be a fighter, an everlasting swimmer against the turbulent, criminal human current. The Jew is a hero, a martyr, a saint. You, our enemies, declare that we are bad? I believe that we are better and finer than you, but even if we were worse, I would like to see how you would look in our place.

I am happy to belong to the unhappiest of all people of the world, whose precepts represent the loftiest and most beautiful of all morality and laws. These important precepts which we possess have now been even more sanctified and immortalized by the fact that they have been so debased and insulted by the enemies of the Lord.

I believe that to be a Jew is an inborn trait. One is born a Jew exactly as one is born an artist. It is impossible to be released from being a Jew. That is our godly attribute that has made us a chosen people. Those who do not understand this will never understand the higher meaning of our martyrdom.

> Nothing is more whole than a broken heart, a great rabbi has said, and there is no people more chosen than a people continually persecuted.

If I ever doubted that God once designated us as the chosen people, I would believe now that our tribulations have made us the chosen one.

I believe in You, God of Israel, even though You have done everything to stop me from believing in You. I believe Your laws even if I cannot excuse Your actions. My relationship to You is not the relationship of a slave to his master but rather that of a pupil to his teacher. I bow my head before Your greatness, but will not kiss the lash with which You strike me.

Those that condemn murder orally, but rejoice at it in their hearts ... Those who meditate in their foul hearts: It is fitting, after all, to say that he is evil, this tyrant, but he carries out a bit of work for us for which we will always be grateful to him!

It is written in Your Torah that a thief should be punished more severely than a brigand, in spite of the fact that a thief does not attack his victim physically and merely attempts to take his possessions stealthily.

The reason for this is that the brigand in attacking his victim in broad daylight, shows no more fear of man than of God. The thief on the other hand fears man, but not God. His punishment, therefore, is greater.

I should be satisfied if You dealt with the murderers as with brigands, for their attitude towards You and towards us is the same.

But those who are silent in the face of murder, those who have no fear of You, but fear what people might say (fools! they are unaware that the people will say nothing!), those who express their sympathy with the drowning man but refuse to rescue him—punish them, O Lord, punish them, I implore You, like the thief, with a doubly-severe sentence!

And these are my last words to You, my wrathful God: Nothing will avail You in the least. You have done everything to make me renounce You, to make me lose my faith in You, but I die exactly as I have lived, crying:

"Eternally praised be the God of the dead, the God of Vengeance, of truth and of law, Who will soon show His face to the world again and shake its foundations with His almighty voice.

"Hear, O Israel, the Lord our God the Lord is One.

"Into your hands, O Lord, I consign my soul."

Four Generations—Four Wills

By Y. L. Peretz

Yehudah Leib Peretz (1852–1915) was one of the giants of Yiddish Literature. He lived on the borderline between two worlds, one that seemed destined to disappear, and one that seemed in the process of being born. He wrote exquisite stories about the world of the Hassidim, though he thought that that world would not last much longer. And he wrote out of a passionate faith in Socialism and Secularism which he thought were going to become dominant in Jewish life. This story about the changes that take place within a Jewish family in four generations was intended to make readers pause and take stock of the precious spiritual values that could be lost in the transition from traditional faith to modernity.

I

When Reb Eliezer-Chaikils departed from this world, the following note was found under his pillow:

"It is my will that my children shall continue as partners in my lumber-business.

"My unmarried son Benjamin (long may he live!) is to inherit my books; my other sons and sons-in-law got their books when they married.

"My spouse (long may she live!) is to have her own quarters in the house; let her take in a poor orphan, so as not to be lonely; let her make her own *Kiddish* and *Havdalla* and do her own housekeeping.

"She is to share as an equal partner with other heirs.

"Moreover...."

The rest was illegible. The note was apparently damp, when put under the pillow, and the letters had become blurred.

II

Reb Benjamin, son of Reb Eliezer-Chaikils, wrote a more detailed will:

"Now the time has come when I am about to return what has been entrusted to me by Him who is the keeper of all trusts.

"A human being is ever in awe of the Divine Presence and His judgment. I go from this world, however, without sadness and with

203

absolute faith in the God of Mercy, who will do with me in accordance with His justice and His great compassion.

"I know that what has been entrusted to me has been stained in the course of time. It has been spoiled. It...."

Let us pass over his confession and his moral precepts for his children and read on:

"My feet are growing colder, my mind is becoming more and more confused, and yesterday a strange thing happened to me: while studying I dozed off and had a dream. The book dropped from my hand and I awoke. I knew immediately that this was no ordinary experience but that the call had come for me....

"Whatever was in truth mine in this world, I shall be leaving only for a time and, when the full span of years shall elapse, even to the number of a hundred and twenty, it will follow me and I shall be deemed worthy of seeing it within the holy splendor of the Divine Presence—Amen! May this be the will of God!

"Whatever does not follow me was never really mine, and God is my witness that I leave it behind without any anguish of soul.

"As to my wealth I leave no will with regard to its disposal. I am confident that the members of my family will either live together in peace and harmony, or else will divide up in accordance with right and justice and nobody will in any way try to take advantage of another.

"I ask of my household, namely, of my wife (long may she live!) and of my sons and sons-in-law (long may they live!), that they deduct the tithe for charity twice in the following manner: Immediately after my death, they are to make a generous estimate of my possessions, movable goods, household furnishings, office equipment, promissory notes, unsecured debt due me, etc., and they are to make the first deduction of one-tenth the estate's total value for the benefit and salvation of my soul and they are to distribute this sum among the poor.

"Of the remainder, namely, of the net inheritance, let there be a second deduction. Let each of my heirs give one-tenth to the poor in his own behalf, just as it was customary for me to give of all profits.

"On both occasions, let them add to each tithe three percent to make up for any possible errors in figuring.

"Both tithes are to be given as charity for those poor people only who are not related to us.

"I leave it to the judgment of my heirs how much to give to poor relatives, but none of such contributions are to come from the portion designated for charitable purposes, because money for charity is not meant for enjoyment and, if one gives to relatives, it is like giving to oneself.

"On my tombstone let there be inscribed merely my name, the name of my father of blessed memory, the date of my death, and nothing more.

"I beg my sons and sons-in-law not to devote themselves entirely to the vanities of this world, not to vie with big business, because the bigger the businessman the smaller the Jew in him. Let them not enter into extensive commercial transactions nor scatter their little capital to all the four corners of the earth, because God helps, where he wills, and a little business can prosper as much as a big one.

"This admonition is meant primarily for my dear son Mordechai because I have seen that he has a great longing for wealth.

"I beg my children to continue the custom of deducting each year before the Jewish New Year one-tenth profit of the preceding twelve months for the benefit of the poor and, even if (God forbid!) there should ever be a loss, let them nevertheless give charity, since the loss is doubtless a trial sent from heaven.

"I beg them most urgently to study every day at least one portion of the *Gemara* and a page of wisdom literature.

"Let them travel at least once a year to a saintly rabbi.

"The women should read in *Yiddish Kav-Hayoshor* as well as the *Tseena-Ureena* on Sabbaths and holidays.

"On the anniversary of my death, let the men study Torah all day and women distribute charity—privately, without public display."

III

When Moritz Benditsohn (a son of Benjamin) died, this document was found, written in Polish:

"A telegram is to be sent to Paris and the funeral services are to be delayed until my son arrives.

"I bequeath ten thousand as a trust fund, the interest of which is to be distributed each year among the poor.

"I bequeath ten thousand for a bed in the new hospital, on condition that the bed be named for me.

"During the burial ceremony, charity is to be distributed.

"Contributions are to be sent to all Hebrew Schools: the teachers and the school children are to follow the bier.

"A learned scholar is to be engaged to say Kaddish for me.

"The tombstone is to be ordered abroad in accordance with the specifications which I append.

"A sum of money is to be set aside as a trust fund for the specific purpose of keeping the grave and the tombstone in perfect shape.

"The business is to be called 'Moritz Benditsohn's Son.'

"Regarding the..."

We omit the balance sheet of the estate, the list of debts to be collected, and the good advice, how best to continue the business.

IV

"I Moritz Benditsohn's son, leave this world neither in happiness nor in sadness but because of emptiness.

"Aristotle uttered profound wisdom: Nature hates a void.

"The world is a stupendous machine. Every wheel has its specific function, its separate purpose. If a wheel is spoiled or is used up prematurely, it is no longer a part of the machine; it makes the transition from something to nothing.

"I cannot live any longer, because I have nothing more to do on earth. I am fit for nothing, because I have lived my life. I have drained to the last drop all the joy apportioned to me. I have consumed and used up everything that I needed.

"I have been taught a great deal but I have not been taught how to live without consuming life.

"I have nothing in the world to keep me back or to hold me bound to life. I have never lacked a thing that was of any value for me. I took everything without a care, without worrying, without effort—as though it were mine for the mere asking: things and people, men and women.

"All the men smiled upon me and yet I did not have a single friend; all the women liked to kiss me and yet I could get along without every one of them.

"I inherited a fortune and it grew and increased without my effort, regardless of my will.

"It grew until it outgrew me.

"My heart often wept within me: 'O, that something were lacking! O, that I were compelled to do something!' The doctors recommended for me: walks, games, sports … not life but a substitute for life, a pretending to live, a pretending to work, Ersatz.

"Many lands have I seen but none that I could call my own. Many places did I admire but to none did I feel intimately attached—I played with words as with balls.

"I changed peoples and languages as one changes gloves.

"The whole world was mine but I was too small to hold it in my grasp; my hands were too small to embrace it; I was no world conqueror.

"Whatsoever I might have been able to conquer, came to me ready-made, bequeathed to me by others.

"Everything was done for me, everything was bought for me; whatever remained to be gotten, my wealth got for me.

"Everything—the smile on my friend's face, the kiss of red lips, the Kaddish for my father…. At best, I overpaid, but I never learned to give of myself, to sacrifice for others.

"The little things seemed to be petty; the great things, too gigantic; and nothing seemed worth living for.

"I die because I am barren, physically and spiritually. I have nothing within me that lives and that creates life … I have long been lifeless, I have long been without the zest of living; now I have become completely disgusted with everything.

"I have been treated as a peasant treats a pig; I have been fattened. But the peasant, when the hog is sufficiently fattened, slaughters it. I am summoned to do my own slaughtering, however, and I haven't even the courage to refuse.

"The arsenic is on the table; the last drink to make drunk; the drink from which I shall not emerge sober.

"Shall I leave word behind about my wealth? For what? My wealth was my misfortune.

"Is there anyone I want to thank?

"No. I paid everybody for everything.

"Yes—even for this last drink."

The Will of Nissim Laniado

By Avraham Sutzkever

"The Will of Nissim Laniado" purports to be the will of a devout Sephardic Jew. In it, the aged Laniado reveals his fervent devotion to the idea of the Ingathering of Israel and the dawn of a new world which it presages.

The idea among Jews of a messianic age in latter days stems from scriptural references (Isa. 2:2–4; Mic. 4:1–4; Gen. 49:1), elaborated to some extent in Talmudic literature and in later writings. Jewish conceptions about the coming of an age of peace, justice and plenty for mankind refer variously to such ideas as *biat hamashiah*—coming of the messiah, *yemot hamashiah*—messianic times, *olam haba*—the world to come. These and other notions have not attained the status of dogma in Judaism but have been cherished among many Jews as a symbol of hope for a world perfected. Eastern Jews, Sephardim like Nissim Laniado, kept true to the vision and prophecies of the Ingathering of Exiles; though scattered to the far reaches of Africa and Asia for nearly two millennia, they survived—to be borne "on wings of eagles" to the Land of Promise in our own day. In Avraham Sutzkever's poem, these ideas are present in symbol and allusion: the blossoming almond symbolizes hopes for the speedy coming of the desired era (Jer. 1:11–12); the Great Shofar, mentioned in daily and High Holiday prayers, will signal the start of the hoped-for messianic times.

The poet, Avraham Sutzkever (1913–2010), a leading figure in Yiddish literature, resides in Israel. He lived through the Holocaust, first in the Vilna ghetto then escaping to fight with the partisans. After the war he reached Israel where, from 1949 till recently, he was editor of *Die Goldene Keyt*, the respected Yiddish literary magazine. The subject matter of his poetry is wide-ranging; he writes of the Holocaust, but also of the beauty he sees everywhere. Having lived through the Holocaust and living now in the resurrected Land of Israel, who can write with more feeling than he about intimations of a messianic era for mankind?

In a corner of old Meah She'arim
Where they deal in cinnamon and sighs—
On a carpet all laden with volumes
A manuscript greeted my eyes.

Its little blue pages were spotted,
Like small speckled pieces of sky.

Its edges were mildewed and moldy
From the countless damp nights gone by.

My attention was drawn to the pages
As if they *meant* to attract and engage.
A host of motifs otherworldly
Thrummed beneath the pale ink on each page.

I rendered the text into Yiddish
In poetic meter and rhyme,
To preserve the Will of a Sephardi
From extinction by passage of time.

My children, this Will of your father
Must seem to you strange and bizarre.
But reality for Nissim Laniado
Is different from others' by far.

My eyes, dim and nearly extinguished,
Rashi letters no longer discern;
But a third, a new eye will soon open
To watch over me now in its turn.

When my pains at last leave my body
Like ripe fruits that fall from the tree,
This third eye in me will then open—
You will know when this happens to me.

Shed no tears when this happens; but open
Shutters wide to the evening sky,
Let a minyan of stars robed in starlight,
Bowed, recite the Tehillim on high.

Next day—if no war is searing
Our land with its terrible heat,
When my soul takes flight toward Heaven
To the Merciful Judgment Seat—

Your father, the Elder of Sephardim,
Entreats you to do this with care:

Bring my body to the banks of the Jordan
And immerse it seven times there.

But if illness or war should prevent this,
Or if drought is abroad in the land—
Then I shall be equally grateful
If you ritually cleanse me in sand.

After this, I ask that you hasten
To clothe me as I dressed in life:
In the homemade shift of white linen
Sewn for me by your mother, my wife.

Over this, pray, put on me my kaftan,
The one striped in light greenish-gold;
Then, in the tallit embroidered with silver,
My body completely enfold.

Remember to cover the tallit,
With the mantle that shimmers and glows,
Like the waves of a fiery sunset,
In colors of crimson and rose.

Drape my shawl well about me
With its fringes like sun-yellow wheat;
In my pocket—a handkerchief folded,
As though the heart beneath it still beats.

Put on me my cap, my stockings
And slippers, the purplish pair,
Just as, on eves of Shabbat and Yom Tov,
Laniado—man and boy—used to wear.

In one pocket of my over-mantle
Put a full flask of raisin wine.
My own T'nakh, printed in Cremona,
In the other pocket of mine.

Next you will choose the location
For building your father his home—
In the dry, sunny sands of Judea
Or here, in our graveyard's moist loam.

Dig my grave in the earth like a well,
Then into it, *erect*, lower me,
So that, standing, I may dream of Him,
And of that which is certain to be.

Remember, before closing my dwelling
As around me at graveside you stand,
Place a stout branch of blossoming almond
For a walking-stick into my hand.

And now I reveal the intention
Of my Will, for the hour draws nigh:
There is no real death in the world!
All my days, all my nights testify!

For a sleep is not everlasting.
In latter days a Great Trumpet will sound,
Like the trumpet of winds in grasses
When the rainstorm touches the ground—

The voice will demand: 'Laniado,
Laniado, how long? End your sleep!
The shepherd must gather together his flock,
And you are his wandering sheep!'

Many years will elapse, perhaps thousands,
But happen it will, for it must!
And meanwhile the swords will be dancing
As cities fall and others rise on their dust—

Then, thus dressed I will join that procession,
That is what your father intends,
So there's no lapse between now and tomorrow;
And...."

Here the manuscript ends.

Translated by Nathaniel Stampfer

Part Six

A Guide to Writing Your Own Ethical Will

The following section contains suggestions for writing an ethical will. The presentation here is neither lengthy nor exhaustive. It doesn't need to be. Our observation has been that writing a *tzava'ah*, (will, instruction) is something that most often comes quite easily, possibly because the impulse to write it is deeply human as well as sanctified by tradition. In our practical experience, a small number of strategies prove sufficient for stimulating remembrances and feelings and for outlining useful writing procedures.

There is no *one* way in which to write an ethical will. Feel free to write yours in whatever style or tone you want to. But as every writer knows, the hardest thing is to get started. And so we offer these suggestions and guidelines based on our experiences and on the wills in this collection. These are only a number of topic headings under which you can structure what you wish to say; you may choose other topic headings, as you wish. The topical index will help you to see how many famous and ordinary Jewish people have dealt with ethical issues in their lives and in their ethical wills.

Step I:
How to Decide on Topics: Some Suggestions

Getting started can be challenging. Here are some introductory sentences to help you enter this rewarding effort.

- These were the formative events of my life ...
- This is the world from which I came ...
- These are some of the important lessons that I have learned in my life ...
- These are the people who influenced me the most ...
- These are some of the favorite possessions that I want you to have and these are the stories that explain what makes these things so precious to me ...
- These are causes for which members of our family have felt a sense of responsibility, and I hope you will too ...
- Some of the scriptural passages that have meant the most to me ...
- These are the mistakes that I regret having made the most in my life that I hope you will not repeat ...
- This is my definition of true success ...
- This is how I feel as I look back over my life ...
- I would like to ask your forgiveness for ... and I forgive you for ...
- I want you to know how much I love you and how grateful I am to you for ...

Step II:
How to Organize and Write What You Want to Say

Having selected and completed some of the topics suggested above, and/or written down a number of your own, write each of these at the top of a separate sheet of paper. Treat each statement as a topic sentence and expand it into a paragraph or develop it into a section of any number of related paragraphs. Many or all of your topics may warrant such development. Some topics may require more than one page. In that case, attach same-topic pages to each other. (An alternate plan for organizing your writing is on the following page.)

Arrange the pages in sequence, that is, in the order in which you wish the parts to be in the final form. Rearrange the parts until you arrive at the sequence you desire. Read all the parts through for coherence, making needed changes or corrections. If you have used quotations, now is a good time to check their accuracy.

Rewrite or type the entire manuscript. It is recommended that this be considered a *draft* of the final document. It is useful to set it aside for a few days or weeks then re-read and edit it from the perspectives presented in the next section.

Alternate Plan for Organizing Your Writing

Briefly fill in some or all of these statements, or others you wish, on a single sheet. This serves as an outline for expansion on separate sheets of paper. Then proceed as suggested in step II.

OPENING	THE FAMILY
I write this to you, my _____ in order to _____	1. My parents, siblings, antecedents were/are ... 2. Events that helped shape our family ...
RELIGIOUS OBSERVANCES, INSIGHTS 1. The ritual(s) of most meaning to me ... 2. Specific teachings from Jewish source(s) that move me most ...	PERSONAL HISTORY 1. People who strongly influenced my life ... 2. Event(s) that helped shape my life ...
ETHICAL IDEALS AND PRACTICES 1. Ideals that found expression in my life ... 2. I would like to suggest to you the following ...	CLOSING 1. My ardent wishes for you ... 2. May the Almighty ...

Step III:
How to Personalize and Strengthen the Links

Special Words

Some words are worth a thousand pictures. Are there such words and expressions, loaded with special meaning for you and your family? Your use of these in your ethical will are bound to resonate for your loved ones. In re-reading your draft, therefore, consider including some of these to evoke important memories and insights. If some of these like Bar Mitzvah, Seder, Shabbat, Brit, Kiddush, Confirmation, Israel, are associated with specific events in the life of the family, perhaps these special events ought to be remembered in your ethical will.

Favorite Sayings

Are there favorite sayings often used in the family that should be preserved? One family recalls that their mother used to tell the children at meal time *Est Kinderlach, vet ihr hobn koyach tzum lernen*. (Yiddish for "Eat children, so you can have strength to study well.") It is for them a deeply cherished recollection which they have in turn transmitted to their children.

Anecdotes

Do you have or wish to find a suitable anecdote to help illustrate a point you have made in the draft of your ethical will? Here is an example:

> A skier, separated from his comrades in a blizzard, became lost and disoriented. He fought valiantly to stay awake and moving, against the bitter wind and the blinding snow. But after several hours, his strength ebbing, feeling his struggles to be in vain, he lay down to comforting sleep but certain death.
>
> But as he moved to lie down, he stumbled over an object in the snow. Glancing at the object that had made him fall, he realized to his suprise that the object was a *man*. He cleared the snow from the face and body, placed his ear to the man's chest, and detected a heartbeat. Quickly, he began massaging the limbs of the other vigorously to restore circulation, and in so doing, he restored his own. When the man returned to consciousness, he helped him to his feet.
>
> Supporting each other, the two walked on ... until they reached safety together.

This story has appeal in the context of an ethical will because it underscores the ethical view that brotherly love demonstrated by kind deeds, charity, encouragement, volunteerism, etc., is as basic as any necessity for maintaining human life and preserving the human image in man.

How Much Is Enough?

How much or how little to elaborate on any idea is an individual matter. There are ethical wills in this volume that are brief; they simply list the ideas dearest to their writers and of motivating force in their lives. Others are longer because they expand the major ideas and explain how they were expressed in the lives of their writers. If you choose to list several ideas or principles, however, keep in mind that they should be able to stand alone. Here are several examples:

- Reality can be an extension of our dreams.
- What each of us does is significant and makes a difference.
- Collectively and individually we are always *emerging* and are capable of becoming more than we are.
- Each of us can find his and her human-Jewish fulfillment and personal perfection only in concert with others in a community of action.
- We are all responsible, ultimately, for one another.
- When we identify with the ideas and causes of the Eternal People and with the institutions which give them continuity, a touch of immortality becomes our own.

Note that each of these statements is a complete sentence and expresses a single idea. Each can, of course, be elaborated upon and discussed. But whether to do so or not is up to you. Although it is often true that "more is less," it is not always true. It is not true of an ethical will if you have the desire to elaborate.

Important Dates—Yahrzeit

If there are yahrzeit dates which you wish to have observed, you may want to request this in your ethical will, as some of the writers of wills found in this book have done. Surely, reciting the Kaddish on the anniversary of a relative's death and at Yizkor memorial prayers are among the links that bind the generations.

If some of these elements are to be added to the draft, it may be possible to do so without re-writing or retyping the entire draft. When you feel the text is ready, consider the section that follows.

Step IV:
How to Prepare the Ethical Will Document in Other Formats

The great majority of ethical wills are prepared in written or printed form, on paper. Although some have been audio or video taped, the favored mode has been the written. In this form it is durable, easily reproduced and framed. Keep in mind, too, that even if recorded, your text needs to be written out first.

If written or typed, it is advisable to use acid-free paper. Many documents written on acid-free paper have remained in superb condition for hundreds of years. Such papers are widely available in specialty stores. Also, if the ethical will is to be written by hand, a fountain pen should be used rather than a ball point because the ink in ballpoint pens is usually oil-based and very often causes the ink to "bleed" through the paper. These precautions will help preserve the valuable document against time and environmental factors.

In this vital process of linking the generations, however, there *is* an important place for an audio or video format after the ethical will has been written, that is, preserving and transmitting cherished songs, poems, stories, and beloved *zemirot* (Sabbath table songs) that might otherwise be forgotten. These can be prepared with home recording equipment or in a professional setting. The coming generations can be depended on to transfer the cherished recordings into whatever new formats are developed in the future.

Step V:
How to Convey the Ethical Will

Each individual can decide when it is the right time to present an ethical will to loved ones. Some prefer to present it soon after writing; others prefer to review and revise it over time, even over a period of years. Some leave this spiritual legacy to be given after their death, often as a codicil to the material will; some do both—presenting one while alive and a second loving message as a codicil. Either way, the will should be reviewed and updated over a period of time.

Step VI:
Some Other Considerations

If you have written a *living* will,[1] tell your children what is in it and where it can be found. If you have made a decision about donating your organs after death, they should be told about it. In both these matters you should first discuss the details with rabbinic authorities or the clergyman of your faith.

If you have divided your goods among your survivors, you may want to explain to them the reasoning behind your distribution.

And if there is any more unfinished business between you and them, this is the time to resolve it and make peace.

Topical Index

This index is provided to help you see how many famous and ordinary Jewish people have dealt with ethical issues in their lives and in their ethical wills. The page numbers listed below refer to the first page of the will that addresses the topic.

afterlife; xxx, 144, 175, 188, 193, 203

America; xxi, 89, 101, 147, 150, 159, 161, 175

bequests; xxiii, 89, 107, 141, 183, 203

books; xxv, 38, 64, 89

burial (see funeral)

business advice; xxiii, 3, 9, 120, 203

charity; 9, 18, 25, 28, 55, 96, 101, 107, 135, 139, 141, 156, 175, 203

children, grandchildren; xxiii, 9, 28, 34, 114, 130, 163, 175

earning a living; xxiii, 9, 144

ethical conduct

honesty; 9, 25, 55, 110, 114, 125, 128

love of fellow-man; 61, 66, 68, 122, 123, 125, 130, 141, 147, 161, 175, 188, 193

rules of conduct (hanhagot); 9, 28, 34, 110, 114, 128, 130, 159, 175

speech, care, reticence in; 9, 18, 25

family unity; 18, 61, 89, 96, 101, 107, 110, 114, 117, 120, 137, 144, 159, 163, 175, 183, 193, 203

funeral / mourning practices

eulogy; 3, 34, 38, 81, 96, 101, 107, 116, 135, 152, 183, 203

burial; 34, 38, 89, 139, 183, 203

mourning; 89, 156, 183

Kaddish, yahrzeit, yizkor; 89, 104, 114, 156, 183, 203

gratitude

to God; 18, 89, 104, 141, 183

to family; 34, 104, 123, 130, 141, 163, 193

hanhagot (see rules of conduct under ethical conduct)

holocaust; 39–52, 78, 159, 161, 175, 193, 197

individuality, personal traits of survivors; xxiii, 18, 25, 28, 114, 122, 125, 130, 144, 159, 163, 175, 203

intermarriage, advice, concern about; 110, 141, 156, 175

Israel; 55, 73, 84, 135, 141, 150, 156, 159, 163, 175, 193, 203

Jewish education, for the young; 28, 110, 130, 159, 163

Jewish heritage, preserving; xxiii, 18, 28, 34, 61, 73, 89, 94, 101, 107, 110, 114, 120, 144, 156, 159, 163, 175

love for children; xxiii, 3, 18, 28, 50, 52, 73, 89, 112, 125, 130, 141, 150, 152, 163

organ donation; 188

prayer; 9, 73, 112, 183, 197

religious duties

people to God; 3–38, 55, 66, 68, 73, 89, 96, 112, 114, 117, 120

person to person; 3, 110, 114, 130, 141, 175

retribution; 39–52, 197

synagogue; 73, 120, 138, 141, 147

Torah study; xxiii, 9, 25, 28, 55, 141, 156, 203

Torah study for daughters; 28, 163, 203

trust in God; 9, 28, 89, 114, 117, 122, 130, 141, 150, 161, 175, 193, 197, 203

war; xxiii, 78, 81, 82, 83, 123, 125, 128, 159

Yiddish; xiv, 89, 107, 110, 116, 208, 215

Credits

The will of William Lewis Abramowitz printed by permission of Lee Abramowitz-Halzel.

Sholom Aleichem's will reprinted by permission of the Sholom Aleichem family. Epitaph translated by Bel Kaufman. Copyright © 1983 by Bel Kaufman and used with permission.

Amanut Publishing, Ltd.; Noam Grossman, from *Noam: Ner Neshama lezecher Noam Grossman shenafal be-hare yehuda*, Tel Aviv, 1948. Copyright © 1948 by Anna and Reuben Grossman. Translated for this edition by Nathaniel Stampfer.

American Jewish Archives: Benjamin M. Roth, "An Ethical Letter: Benjamin Roth to His Son, 1854," translated by Albert H. Friedlander in *American Jewish Archives*, Vol. VI, No. 1, 1954. Reprinted by permission of *American Jewish Archives*.

Joshua Chachik Publishing House, Ltd.: Zippora Birman, Theodor Herzl, Edmond de Rothschild, Meir Dizengoff, Alter Ya'akov Sahrai, Moshe Sofer, Hirsch Zaddok from *Sefer Hama'alot* edited by Eliezer Steinman, Tel Aviv, 1956. Copyright © 1956 by Joshua Chachik Publishing House, Ltd. Translated for this edition by Nathaniel Stampfer.

Crown Publishers: Avraham Kreizman, "For you I shall continue to live," translated by Eliezer Whartman, and Eldad Pan, "Life is worth little unless...," translated by Sidney Greenberg from *A Treasury of Comfort* edited by Sidney Greenberg, New York, 1954. Copyright © 1954 by Sidney Greenberg. Used by permission of Crown Publishers, Inc.

C.Y.C.O. Publishing House: A Mother's Will, A Polish Jew, Berl Tomshelski, Shulamit Rabinovitch, Shulamit Rabinovitch's Husband, "On the Walls of Bialystok Prison" from *Kiddush Hashem* edited by Sh. Niger, New York, 1948. Copyright © 1948 Louis La Med Literary Foundation. Translated for this edition by Nathaniel Stampfer.

The will of Herbert A. Friedman printed by permission of its author.

The will of Randee Rosenberg Friedman printed by permission of its author.

The wills of Stanley J. Garfein printed by permission of their author.

Richard J. Israel, "Four Letters to My Child," reprinted in *The Hadassah Magazine Jewish Parenting Book*, edited by Roselyn Bell, New York, The Free Press, 1989, pp. 353–363. Reprinted by permission of Richard J. Israel.

Jewish Frontier Association: Hayim Greenberg from *Inner Eye: Selected Essays of Hayim Greenberg*, Vol. II, edited by Sholomo Katz. Copyright © 1964 by

Notes

Preface

1. *Hebrew Ethical Wills*, by Israel Abrahams, Jewish Publication Society, Philadelphia, 1926.

Introduction to the Revised Edition

1. Abraham Joshua Heschel, *The Earth Is the Lord's: The Inner World of the Jew in Eastern Europe* (Woodstock, VT: Jewish Lights, 1995), 107.

What I Have Learned Since I Began Collecting Ethical Wills

1. From "The Letter to Willie from His Father," from *The Caine Mutiny* by Herman Wouk. ©1951 by Herman Wouk. Used by permission of Doubleday, a division of Bantam Doubleday Dell Publishing Group, Inc.

Solomon Kluger

1. In hasidic lore the expression "provisions for the journey" refers to the good deeds accumulated during a person's lifetime, since these sustain him during life after death.

2. These passages constitute a brief, clever homily based on a play on words, namely, the three meanings of the word *ma'alot*. virtues, ascents, and steps. Paraphrased, the homily reads, "Do not speak of my virtues *[ma'alot]*, for what good is a 'Song of Ascents' *[Shir Hama'alot*, Pss. 120–134]; one does not ascend the altar by these steps *[ma'alot].*"

3. The expression "acts of true kindness," *hesed shel emet*, is reserved in Jewish tradition for kindnesses done for the deceased, since they are done without expectation of any reward.

4. i.e., in white shroud and prayer shawl.

5. Kaddish is customarily recited the first eleven months after the death. The reason for this is that according to mystic lore, the dead who are sinful require twelve months to become purified in Gehinnom; the Kaddish, which helps alleviate the sufferings of the deceased during that process, is therefore recited only *eleven* months for loved ones in order not to categorize them as sinful. The author here states clearly that he wishes to have the Kaddish recited for the full year since no man knows what grievous sins he may have unwittingly committed. Also, leap years in the Hebrew calendar contain an extra month, and the writer provides for such an eventuality as well.

6. In ancient Jewish law, capital punishment could be imposed for specified offenses by one of four modes of execution: stoning, burning, slaying (by the sword), and strangulation. So many strictures surrounded its application, however, that capital punishment was seldom employed, and was abolished entirely forty years before the destruction of the Second Temple (Babylonian

Talmud, *Makkot* 7a). Nevertheless Rabbi Kluger requests the symbolic stoning after death in case he had been inadvertently culpable during his lifetime. His choice of stoning over the other modes on grounds that it was the most severe refers to the gravity of the offenses that call for stoning, for stoning was reserved for such transgressions as blasphemy, rebelliousness, and idolatry, all of which deny the existence of God, a sine qua non of Judaism (Babylonian Talmud, *Sanhedrin* 49b).

Moshe Yehoshua Zelig Hakohen

1. *Kelippa* is the "husk" which in kabbalistic thought refers to the force of evil which may overlay the force of good.

2. Over the destruction of the Temple and for the restoration of Israel.

Mordekhai Mottel Michelsohn

1. Transposition of Mal. 2:10.

Edmond James de Rothschild

1. An allusion to Rosh Pina, one of the earliest settlements which Rothschild maintained, and to the verse, "The stone which the builder rejected is become the chief cornerstone [*rosh pina*]" in Psalm 118:22.

Yitzhak Ben Nehemia Margalit

1. Babylonian Talmud, *Baba Batra* 73a

2. Genesis 43:29.

3. A double allusion: To Jacob's blessing of Ephraim and Manasseh the sons of Joseph, Genesis 48:16; and to the fact that the son, Nehemia, is named after the writer's deceased father.

4. Paraphrase of Deuteronomy 4:25.

Nissen Sheinberg

1. The usual custom calls for lighting of candles only at the head of the deceased.

2. The use of earth from Eretz Yisrael in Jewish burial reflects the belief that the sacred soil of the Holy Land atones. The custom as described in *Shulhan Arukh* (Code of Jewish Law) No. 362 is exactly as requested by Nissen Sheinberg.

3. Confessional prayer recited before death.

4. To avoid any practices resembling a wake, prohibited in Judaism.

5. *Shivah*, meaning seven, refers to the first seven and most intense days of mourning following burial.

6. Quorum of ten, the minimum required for public worship. Kaddish recitation, as well as Torah reading and the other elements of communal worship, require at least a minyan. Although private prayer is permitted in Judaism, communal worship is the ideal.

7. *Halla*, which in general usage refers to Sabbath loaves, has a second meaning—the Priestly Due, the share of bread dough given to the *kohen* by Jews in Temple days, as required by biblical law [Deut. 15:18–21]. Although priestly offerings are not observed today, the mitzvah is practiced in modified form so that the observance not be forgotten. The housewife removes a piece of dough the size of an olive and throws it into the fire while reciting the appropriate benediction. A contribution to charity is customary as well. If *halla* was taken from the dough, it should be taken from the bread. Hence the father's concern about bought bread.

8. Allusion to Ecclesiastes 1:2, "Vanity of vanities...."

Bernard L. Levinthal

1. Literally, in connection with which the rabbis would say, "a person like me...."

Rabbi Stanley J. Garfein

1. Rabbi Richard Rubenstein, Rabbi Joseph Levenson and Rabbi Ronald Goff

2. Robert Test, "To Remember Me," Mosaic Press, Cincinnati, Ohio.

3. The quotation from Rabbi Moses Tendler is an espousal of the viewpoint of his late father-in-law, Rabbi Moses Feinstein, one of the foremost halachic decisors of our day. This position is disputed by some authorities. The source for the viewpoint expressed is Rabbi Moses Feinstein, *Igrot Moshe*, *Yore Deah*, III:132.

A Guide to Writing Your Own Ethical Will

1. A "living will" is one which provides for those medical measures which one wishes to be taken or not taken in his/her behalf if physicians declare him/her to be in a persistent vegetative state with no likelihood of regaining consciousness.

Bible Study / Midrash

Passing Life's Tests: Spiritual Reflections on the Trial of Abraham, the Binding of Isaac *By Rabbi Bradley Shavit Artson, DHL*
Invites us to use this powerful tale as a tool for our own soul wrestling, to confront our existential sacrifices and enable us to face—and surmount—life's tests.
6 x 9, 176 pp, Quality PB, 978-1-58023-631-7 **$18.99**

Speaking Torah: Spiritual Teachings from around the Maggid's Table—in Two Volumes *By Arthur Green, with Ebn Leader, Ariel Evan Mayse and Or N. Rose*
The most powerful Hasidic teachings made accessible—from some of the world's preeminent authorities on Jewish thought and spirituality.
Volume 1—6 x 9, 512 pp, HC, 978-1-58023-668-3 **$34.99**
Volume 2—6 x 9, 448 pp, HC, 978-1-58023-694-2 **$34.99**

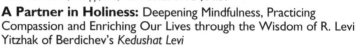

A Partner in Holiness: Deepening Mindfulness, Practicing Compassion and Enriching Our Lives through the Wisdom of R. Levi Yitzhak of Berdichev's *Kedushat Levi*
By Rabbi Jonathan P. Slater, DMin; Foreword by Arthur Green; Preface by Rabby Nancy Flam
Contemporary mindfulness and classical Hasidic spirituality are brought together to inspire a satisfying spiritual life of practice.
Volume 1— 6 x 9, 336 pp, HC, 978-1-58023-794-9 **$35.00**
Volume 2— 6 x 9, 288 pp, HC, 978-1-58023-795-6 **$35.00**

The Genesis of Leadership: What the Bible Teaches Us about Vision, Values and Leading Change *By Rabbi Nathan Laufer; Foreword by Senator Joseph I. Lieberman*
6 x 9, 288 pp, Quality PB, 978-1-58023-352-1 **$18.99**

Hineini in Our Lives
Learning How to Respond to Others through 14 Biblical Texts and Personal Stories
By Dr. Norman J. Cohen 6 x 9, 240 pp, Quality PB, 978-1-58023-274-6 **$18.99**

Masking and Unmasking Ourselves: Interpreting Biblical Texts on Clothing & Identity *By Dr. Norman J. Cohen* 6 x 9, 224 pp, HC, 978-1-58023-461-0 **$24.99**

The Messiah and the Jews: Three Thousand Years of Tradition, Belief and Hope
By Rabbi Elaine Rose Glickman; Foreword by Rabbi Neil Gillman, PhD
Preface by Rabbi Judith Z. Abrams, PhD 6 x 9, 192 pp, Quality PB, 978-1-58023-690-4 **$16.99**

The Modern Men's Torah Commentary: New Insights from Jewish Men on the 54 Weekly Torah Portions *Edited by Rabbi Jeffrey K. Salkin*
6 x 9, 368 pp, HC, 978-1-58023-395-8 **$24.99**

Moses and the Journey to Leadership: Timeless Lessons of Effective Management from the Bible and Today's Leaders *By Dr. Norman J. Cohen*
6 x 9, 240 pp, Quality PB, 978-1-58023-351-4 **$18.99**; HC, 978-1-58023-227-2 **$21.99**

The Other Talmud—The *Yerushalmi*: Unlocking the Secrets of *The Talmud of Israel* for Judaism Today *By Rabbi Judith Z. Abrams, PhD*
6 x 9, 256 pp, HC, 978-1-58023-463-4 **$24.99**

Sage Tales: Wisdom and Wonder from the Rabbis of the Talmud
By Rabbi Burton L. Visotzky
6 x 9, 256 pp, Quality PB, 978-1-58023-791-8 **$19.99**; HC, 978-1-58023-456-6 **$24.99**

The Torah Revolution: Fourteen Truths That Changed the World
By Rabbi Reuven Hammer, PhD 6 x 9, 240 pp, Quality PB, 978-1-58023-789-5 **$18.99**
HC, 978-1-58023-457-3 **$24.99**

The Wisdom of Judaism: An Introduction to the Values of the Talmud
By Rabbi Dov Peretz Elkins 6 x 9, 192 pp, Quality PB, 978-1-58023-327-9 **$16.99**

Or phone, fax, mail or email to: **JEWISH LIGHTS Publishing**
Sunset Farm Offices, Route 4 • P.O. Box 237 • Woodstock, Vermont 05091
Tel: (802) 457-4000 • Fax: (802) 457-4004 • www.jewishlights.com
Credit card orders: **(800) 962-4544** (8:30AM–5:30PM EST Monday–Friday)
Generous discounts on quantity orders. SATISFACTION GUARANTEED. Prices subject to change.

Congregation Resources

Relational Judaism: Using the Power of Relationships to Transform the Jewish Community *By Dr. Ron Wolfson* How to transform the model of twentieth-century Jewish institutions into twenty-first-century relational communities offering meaning and purpose, belonging and blessing.
6 x 9, 288 pp, HC, 978-1-58023-666-9 **$24.99**

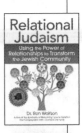

The Spirituality of Welcoming: How to Transform Your Congregation into a Sacred Community *By Dr. Ron Wolfson*
Shows crucial hospitality is for congregational survival and dives into the practicalities of cultivating openness. 6 x 9, 224 pp, Quality PB, 978-1-58023-244-9 **$19.99**

Jewish Megatrends: Charting the Course of the American Jewish Future
By Rabbi Sidney Schwarz; Foreword by Ambassador Stuart E. Eizenstat
Visionary solutions for a community ripe for transformational change—from fourteen leading innovators of Jewish life. 6 x 9, 288 pp, HC, 978-1-58023-667-6 **$24.99**

Inspired Jewish Leadership: Practical Approaches to Building Strong Communities *By Dr. Erica Brown*
Develop your leadership skills and dialogue with others about issues like conflict resolution and effective succession planning.
6 x 9, 256 pp, HC, 978-1-58023-361-3 **$27.99**

Building a Successful Volunteer Culture: Finding Meaning in Service in the Jewish Community *By Rabbi Charles Simon; Foreword by Shelley Lindauer; Preface by Dr. Ron Wolfson*
6 x 9, 192 pp, Quality PB, 978-1-58023-408-5 **$16.99**

The Case for Jewish Peoplehood: Can We Be One?
By Dr. Erica Brown and Dr. Misha Galperin; Foreword by Rabbi Joseph Telushkin
6 x 9, 224 pp, HC, 978-1-58023-401-6 **$21.99**

Empowered Judaism: What Independent Minyanim Can Teach Us about Building Vibrant Jewish Communities *By Rabbi Elie Kaunfer; Foreword by Prof. Jonathan D. Sarna*
6 x 9, 224 pp, Quality PB, 978-1-58023-412-2 **$18.99**

Finding a Spiritual Home: How a New Generation of Jews Can Transform the American Synagogue *By Rabbi Sidney Schwarz*
6 x 9, 352 pp, Quality PB, 978-1-58023-185-5 **$19.95**

Judaism and Health: A Handbook of Practical, Professional and Scholarly Resources
Edited by Jeff Levin, PhD, MPH, and Michele F. Prince, LCSW, MAJCS
Foreword by Rabbi Elliot N. Dorff, PhD
6 x 9, 448 pp, HC, 978-1-58023-714-7 **$50.00**

Jewish Pastoral Care, 2nd Edition: A Practical Handbook from Traditional & Contemporary Sources *Edited by Rabbi Dayle A. Friedman, MSW, MA, BCC*
6 x 9, 528 pp, Quality PB, 978-1-58023-427-6 **$40.00**

Jewish Spiritual Direction: An Innovative Guide from Traditional and Contemporary Sources *Edited by Rabbi Howard A. Addison, PhD, and Barbara Eve Breitman, MSW*
6 x 9, 368 pp, HC, 978-1-58023-230-2 **$30.00**

A Practical Guide to Rabbinic Counseling
Edited by Rabbi Yisrael N. Levitz, PhD, and Rabbi Abraham J. Twerski, MD
6 x 9, 432 pp, HC, 978-1-58023-562-4 **$40.00**

Professional Spiritual & Pastoral Care: A Practical Clergy and Chaplain's Handbook
Edited by Rabbi Stephen B. Roberts, MBA, MHL, BCJC
6 x 9, 480 pp, HC, 978-1-59473-312-3 **$50.00***

Reimagining Leadership in Jewish Organizations: Ten Practical Lessons to Help You Implement Change and Achieve Your Goals
By Dr. Misha Galperin 6 x 9, 192 pp, Quality PB, 978-1-58023-492-4 **$16.99**

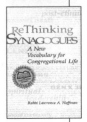

Rethinking Synagogues: A New Vocabulary for Congregational Life
By Rabbi Lawrence A. Hoffman, PhD 6 x 9, 240 pp, Quality PB, 978-1-58023-248-7 **$19.99**

Revolution of Jewish Spirit: How to Revive *Ruakh* in Your Spiritual Life, Transform Your Synagogue & Inspire Your Jewish Community
By Rabbi Baruch HaLevi, DMin, and Ellen Frankel, LCSW; Foreword by Dr. Ron Wolfson
6 x 9, 224 pp, Quality PB, 978-1-58023-625-6 **$19.99**

*A book from SkyLight Paths, Jewish Lights' sister imprint

Children's Books

Lullaby
By Debbie Friedman; Full-color illus. by Lorraine Bubar
A charming adaptation of beloved singer-songwriter Debbie Friedman's best-selling song *Lullaby*, this timeless bedtime picture book will help children know that God will keep them safe throughout the night.
9 x 12, 32 pp, Full-color illus., w/ a CD of original music & lyrics by Debbie Friedman
HC, 978-1-58023-807-6 **$18.99** *For ages 3–6*

Around the World in One Shabbat
Jewish People Celebrate the Sabbath Together
By Durga Yael Bernhard
Takes your child on a colorful adventure to share the many ways Jewish people celebrate Shabbat around the world.
11 x 8½, 32 pp, Full-color illus., HC, 978-1-58023-433-7 **$18.99** *For ages 3–6*

It's a ... It's a ... It's a Mitzvah
By Liz Suneby and Diane Heiman; Full-color illus. by Laurel Molk
Join Mitzvah Meerkat and friends as they introduce children to the everyday kindnesses that mark the beginning of a Jewish journey and a lifetime commitment to *tikkun olam* (repairing the world).
9 x 12, 32 pp, Full-color illus., HC, 978-1-58023-509-9 **$18.99** *For ages 3–6*

Also available as a Board Book: **That's a Mitzvah**
5 x 5, 24 pp, Full-color illus., Board Book, 978-1-58023-804-5 **$8.99** *For ages 1–4*

What You Will See Inside a Synagogue
By Rabbi Lawrence A. Hoffman, PhD, and Dr. Ron Wolfson; Full-color photos by Bill Aron
A colorful, fun-to-read introduction that explains the ways and whys of Jewish worship and religious life.
8½ x 10½, 32 pp, Full-color photos, Quality PB, 978-1-59473-256-0 **$8.99*** *For ages 6 & up*

Because Nothing Looks Like God
By Lawrence Kushner and Karen Kushner
Invites parents and children to explore, together, the questions we all have about God.
11 x 8½, 32 pp, Full-color illus., HC, 978-1-58023-092-6 **$18.99** *For ages 4 & up*

In God's Hands By Lawrence Kushner and Gary Schmidt
Each of us has the power to make the world a better place—working ordinary miracles with our everyday deeds.
9 x 12, 32 pp, Full-color illus., HC, 978-1-58023-224-1 **$16.99** *For ages 5 & up*

What Makes Someone a Jew? By Lauren Seidman
Reflects the changing face of American Judaism. Helps preschoolers and young readers understand that you don't have to look a certain way to be Jewish.
10 x 8½, 32 pp, Full-color photos, Quality PB, 978-1-58023-321-7 **$8.99** *For ages 3–6*

In Our Image: God's First Creatures
By Nancy Sohn Swartz God asks all of nature to offer gifts to humankind—with a promise that the humans would care for creation in return.
Full-color illus., eBook, 978-1-58023-520-4 **$16.95** *For ages 5 & up*
Animated app available on Apple App Store and the Google Play Marketplace **$9.99**

The Book of Miracles: A Young Person's Guide to Jewish Spiritual Awareness
Written and illus. by Lawrence Kushner
6 x 9, 96 pp, 2-color illus., HC, 978-1-879045-78-1 **$16.95** *For ages 9–13*

The Jewish Family Fun Book, 2nd Edition: Holiday Projects, Everyday Activities, and Travel Ideas with Jewish Themes By Danielle Dardashti and Roni Sarig
6 x 9, 304 pp, w/ 70+ b/w illus., Quality PB, 978-1-58023-333-0 **$18.99**

When a Grandparent Dies: A Kid's Own Remembering Workbook for Dealing with Shiva and the Year Beyond By Nechama Liss-Levinson
8 x 10, 48 pp, 2-color text, HC, 978-1-879045-44-6 **$15.95** *For ages 7–13*

*A book from SkyLight Paths, Jewish Lights' sister imprint

Spirituality / Prayer

Davening: A Guide to Meaningful Jewish Prayer
By Rabbi Zalman Schachter-Shalomi (z"l) with Joel Segel; Foreword by Rabbi Lawrence Kushner
A fresh approach to prayer for all who wish to appreciate the power of prayer's poetry, song and ritual, and to join the age-old conversation that Jews have had with God. 6 x 9, 240 pp, Quality PB, 978-1-58023-627-0 **$18.99**

Jewish Men Pray: Words of Yearning, Praise, Petition, Gratitude and Wonder from Traditional and Contemporary Sources
Edited by Rabbi Kerry M. Olitzky and Stuart M. Matlins; Foreword by Rabbi Bradley Shavit Artson, DHL
A celebration of Jewish men's voices in prayer—to strengthen, heal, comfort, and inspire—from the ancient world up to our own day.
5 x 7¼, 400 pp, HC, 978-1-58023-628-7 **$19.99**

Making Prayer Real: Leading Jewish Spiritual Voices on Why Prayer Is Difficult and What to Do about It *By Rabbi Mike Comins* 6 x 9, 320 pp, Quality PB, 978-1-58023-417-7 **$18.99**

Witnesses to the One: The Spiritual History of the *Sh'ma*
By Rabbi Joseph B. Meszler; Foreword by Rabbi Elyse Goldstein
6 x 9, 176 pp, Quality PB, 978-1-58023-400-9 **$16.99**; HC, 978-1-58023-309-5 **$19.99**

My People's Prayer Book Series: Traditional Prayers, Modern Commentaries *Edited by Rabbi Lawrence A. Hoffman, PhD*
Provides diverse and exciting commentary to the traditional liturgy. Will help you find new wisdom in Jewish prayer, and bring liturgy into your life. Each book includes Hebrew text, modern translations and commentaries from all perspectives of the Jewish world.

Vol. 1—The *Sh'ma* and Its Blessings
  7 x 10, 168 pp, HC, 978-1-879045-79-8 **$29.99**
Vol. 2—The *Amidah* 7 x 10, 240 pp, HC, 978-1-879045-80-4 **$29.99**
Vol. 3—*P'sukei D'zimrah* (Morning Psalms)
  7 x 10, 240 pp, HC, 978-1-879045-81-1 **$29.99**
Vol. 4—*Seder K'riat Hatorah* (The Torah Service)
  7 x 10, 264 pp, HC, 978-1-879045-82-8 **$29.99**
Vol. 5—*Birkhot Hashachar* (Morning Blessings)
  7 x 10, 240 pp, HC, 978-1-879045-83-5 **$29.99**
Vol. 6—*Tachanun* and Concluding Prayers
  7 x 10, 240 pp, HC, 978-1-879045-84-2 **$24.95**
Vol. 7—*Shabbat at Home* 7 x 10, 240 pp, HC, 978-1-879045-85-9 **$29.99**
Vol. 8—*Kabbalat Shabbat* (Welcoming Shabbat in the Synagogue)
  7 x 10, 240 pp, HC, 978-1-58023-121-3 **$24.99**
Vol. 9—Welcoming the Night: *Minchah* and *Ma'ariv* (Afternoon and
  Evening Prayer) 7 x 10, 272 pp, HC, 978-1-58023-262-3 **$24.99**
Vol. 10—Shabbat Morning: *Shacharit* and *Musaf* (Morning and
  Additional Services) 7 x 10, 240 pp, HC, 978-1-58023-240-1 **$29.99**

Spirituality / Lawrence Kushner

I'm God; You're Not: Observations on Organized Religion & Other Disguises of the Ego
6 x 9, 256 pp, Quality PB, 978-1-58023-513-6 **$18.99**; HC, 978-1-58023-441-2 **$21.99**

The Book of Letters: A Mystical Hebrew Alphabet
Popular HC Edition, 6 x 9, 80 pp, 2-color text, 978-1-879045-00-2 **$24.95**
Collector's Limited Edition, 9 x 12, 80 pp, gold-foil-embossed pages, w/ limited-edition silkscreened print, 978-1-879045-04-0 **$349.00**

The Book of Miracles: A Young Person's Guide to Jewish Spiritual Awareness
6 x 9, 96 pp, 2-color illus., HC, 978-1-879045-78-1 **$16.95** *For ages 9–13*

God Was in This Place & I, i Did Not Know: Finding Self, Spirituality and
Ultimate Meaning 6 x 9, 192 pp, Quality PB, 978-1-879045-33-0 **$16.95**

Honey from the Rock: An Introduction to Jewish Mysticism
6 x 9, 176 pp, Quality PB, 978-1-58023-073-5 **$18.99**

Invisible Lines of Connection: Sacred Stories of the Ordinary
5½ x 8½, 160 pp, Quality PB, 978-1-879045-98-9 **$16.99**

The Way Into Jewish Mystical Tradition
6 x 9, 224 pp, Quality PB, 978-1-58023-200-5 **$18.99**

Meditation / Yoga

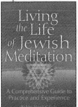

Living the Life of Jewish Meditation: A Comprehensive Guide to Practice and Experience *By Rabbi Yoel Glick*
Combines the knowledge of Judaism with the spiritual practice of Yoga to lead you to an encounter with your true self. Includes nineteen different meditations.
6 x 9, 272 pp, Quality PB, 978-1-58023-802-1 **$18.99**

Mussar Yoga: Blending an Ancient Jewish Spiritual Practice with Yoga to Transform Body and Soul
By Edith R. Brotman, PhD, RYT-500; Foreword by Alan Morinis
A clear and easy-to-use introduction to an embodied spiritual practice for anyone seeking profound and lasting self-transformation.
7 x 9, 224 pp, w/ over 40 b/w photos, Quality PB, 978-1-58023-784-0 **$18.99**

The Magic of Hebrew Chant: Healing the Spirit, Transforming the Mind, Deepening Love
By Rabbi Shefa Gold; Foreword by Sylvia Boorstein
Introduces this transformative spiritual practice as a way to unlock the power of sacred texts and make prayer and meditation the delight of your life. Includes musical notations. 6 x 9, 352 pp, Quality PB, 978-1-58023-671-3 **$24.99**

The Magic of Hebrew Chant Companion—The Big Book of Musical Notations and Incantations 8½ x 11, 154 pp, PB, 978-1-58023-722-2 **$19.99**

Aleph-Bet Yoga: Embodying the Hebrew Letters for Physical and Spiritual Well-Being
By Steven A. Rapp; Foreword by Tamar Frankiel, PhD, and Judy Greenfeld; Preface by Hart Lazer
7 x 10, 128 pp, b/w photos, Quality PB, Lay-flat binding, 978-1-58023-162-6 **$16.95**

Discovering Jewish Meditation, 2nd Edition
Instruction & Guidance for Learning an Ancient Spiritual Practice
By Nan Fink Gefen, PhD 6 x 9, 208 pp, Quality PB, 978-1-58023-462-7 **$16.99**

The Handbook of Jewish Meditation Practices
A Guide for Enriching the Sabbath and Other Days of Your Life
By Rabbi David A. Cooper 6 x 9, 208 pp, Quality PB, 978-1-58023-102-2 **$16.95**

Jewish Meditation Practices for Everyday Life: Awakening Your Heart, Connecting with God *By Rabbi Jeff Roth*
6 x 9, 224 pp, Quality PB, 978-1-58023-397-2 **$18.99**

Ritual / Sacred Practices

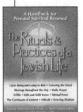

God in Your Body: Kabbalah, Mindfulness and Embodied Spiritual Practice
By Jay Michaelson 6 x 9, 272 pp, Quality PB, 978-1-58023-304-0 **$18.99**

Jewish Ritual: A Brief Introduction for Christians
By Rabbi Kerry M. Olitzky and Rabbi Daniel Judson
5½ x 8½, 144 pp, Quality PB, 978-1-58023-210-4 **$14.99**

The Rituals & Practices of a Jewish Life: A Handbook for Personal Spiritual Renewal
Edited by Rabbi Kerry M. Olitzky and Rabbi Daniel Judson
6 x 9, 272 pp, Illus., Quality PB, 978-1-58023-169-5 **$18.95**

The Sacred Art of Lovingkindness: Preparing to Practice
By Rabbi Rami Shapiro 5½ x 8½, 176 pp, Quality PB, 978-1-59473-151-8 **$16.99***

Mystery & Detective Fiction

Criminal Kabbalah: An Intriguing Anthology of Jewish Mystery & Detective Fiction *Edited by Lawrence W. Raphael; Foreword by Laurie R. King*
All-new stories from twelve of today's masters of mystery and detective fiction—sure to delight mystery buffs of all faith traditions.
6 x 9, 256 pp, Quality PB, 978-1-58023-109-1 **$16.95**

Mystery Midrash: An Anthology of Jewish Mystery & Detective Fiction
Edited by Lawrence W. Raphael; Preface by Joel Siegel
6 x 9, 304 pp, Quality PB, 978-1-58023-055-1 **$16.95**

*A book from SkyLight Paths, Jewish Lights' sister imprint

Theology / Philosophy

Believing and Its Tensions: A Personal Conversation about God, Torah, Suffering and Death in Jewish Thought
By Rabbi Neil Gillman, PhD Explores the changing nature of belief and the complexities of reconciling the intellectual, emotional and moral questions of Gillman's own searching mind and soul. 5½ x 8½, 144 pp, HC, 978-1-58023-669-0 **$19.99**

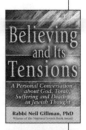

God of Becoming and Relationship: The Dynamic Nature of Process Theology *By Rabbi Bradley Shavit Artson, DHL* Explains how Process Theology breaks us free from the strictures of ancient Greek and medieval European philosophy, allowing us to see all creation as related patterns of energy through which we connect to everything. 6 x 9, 208 pp, HC, 978-1-58023-713-0 **$24.99**

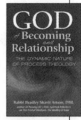

The Way of Man: According to Hasidic Teaching
By Martin Buber; New Translation and Introduction by Rabbi Bernard H. Mehlman and Dr. Gabriel E. Padawer; Foreword by Paul Mendes-Flohr
An accessible and engaging new translation of Buber's classic work—*available as an eBook only.* eBook, 978-1-58023-601-0 Digital List Price **$14.99**

The Death of Death: Resurrection and Immortality in Jewish Thought
By Rabbi Neil Gillman, PhD 6 x 9, 336 pp, Quality PB, 978-1-58023-081-0 **$19.99**

Doing Jewish Theology: God, Torah & Israel in Modern Judaism *By Rabbi Neil Gillman, PhD*
6 x 9, 304 pp, Quality PB, 978-1-58023-439-9 **$18.99**; HC, 978-1-58023-322-4 **$24.99**

From Defender to Critic: The Search for a New Jewish Self
By Dr. David Hartman 6 x 9, 336 pp, HC, 978-1-58023-515-0 **$35.00**

The God Who Hates Lies: Confronting & Rethinking Jewish Tradition
By Dr. David Hartman with Charlie Buckholtz 6 x 9, 208 pp, Quality PB, 978-1-58023-790-1 **$19.99**

A Heart of Many Rooms: Celebrating the Many Voices within Judaism
By Dr. David Hartman 6 x 9, 352 pp, Quality PB, 978-1-58023-156-5 **$19.95**

Jewish Theology in Our Time: A New Generation Explores the Foundations and Future of Jewish Belief *Edited by Rabbi Elliot J. Cosgrove, PhD; Foreword by Rabbi David J. Wolpe; Preface by Rabbi Carole B. Balin, PhD*
6 x 9, 240 pp, Quality PB, 978-1-58023-630-0 **$19.99**; HC, 978-1-58023-413-9 **$24.99**

Maimonides—Essential Teachings on Jewish Faith & Ethics: The Book of Knowledge & the Thirteen Principles of Faith—Annotated & Explained
Translation and Annotation by Rabbi Marc D. Angel, PhD
5½ x 8½, 224 pp, Quality PB, 978-1-59473-311-6 **$18.99***

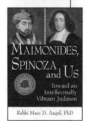

Maimonides, Spinoza and Us: Toward an Intellectually Vibrant Judaism
By Rabbi Marc D. Angel, PhD 6 x 9, 224 pp, HC, 978-1-58023-411-5 **$24.99**

Our Religious Brains: What Cognitive Science Reveals about Belief, Morality, Community and Our Relationship with God
By Rabbi Ralph D. Mecklenburger; Foreword by Dr. Howard Kelfer; Preface by Dr. Neil Gillman
6 x 9, 224 pp, HC, 978-1-58023-508-2 **$24.99**

Your Word Is Fire: The Hasidic Masters on Contemplative Prayer
Edited and translated by Rabbi Arthur Green, PhD, and Barry W. Holtz
6 x 9, 160 pp, Quality PB, 978-1-879045-25-5 **$16.99**

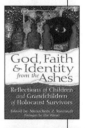

God, Faith & Identity from the Ashes
Reflections of Children and Grandchildren of Holocaust Survivors
Almost ninety contributors from sixteen countries inform, challenge and inspire people of all backgrounds. *Edited by Menachem Z. Rosensaft; Prologue by Elie Wiesel*
6 x 9, 352 pp, HC, 978-1-58023-805-2 **$25.00**

I Am Jewish
Personal Reflections Inspired by the Last Words of Daniel Pearl
Almost 150 Jews—both famous and not—from all walks of life, from all around the world, write about many aspects of their Judaism.
Edited by Judea and Ruth Pearl 6 x 9, 304 pp, Deluxe PB w/ flaps, 978-1-58023-259-3 **$19.99**
Download a free copy of the *I Am Jewish* Teacher's Guide at www.jewishlights.com.

**A book from SkyLight Paths, Jewish Lights' sister imprint*

Ecology / Environment

A Wild Faith: Jewish Ways into Wilderness, Wilderness Ways into Judaism
By Rabbi Mike Comins; Foreword by Nigel Savage
6 x 9, 240 pp, Quality PB, 978-1-58023-316-3 **$18.99**

Ecology & the Jewish Spirit: Where Nature & the Sacred Meet
Edited by Ellen Bernstein 6 x 9, 288 pp, Quality PB, 978-1-58023-082-7 **$18.99**

Torah of the Earth: Exploring 4,000 Years of Ecology in Jewish Thought
Vol. 1: Biblical Israel & Rabbinic Judaism; Vol. 2: Zionism & Eco-Judaism
Edited by Rabbi Arthur Waskow Vol. 1: 6 x 9, 272 pp, Quality PB, 978-1-58023-086-5 **$19.95**
Vol. 2: 6 x 9, 336 pp, Quality PB, 978-1-58023-087-2 **$19.95**

The Way Into Judaism and the Environment *By Jeremy Benstein, PhD*
6 x 9, 288 pp, Quality PB, 978-1-58023-368-2 **$18.99**; HC, 978-1-58023-268-5 **$24.99**

Graphic Novels / Graphic History

The Adventures of Rabbi Harvey: A Graphic Novel of Jewish Wisdom and Wit in the
Wild West *By Steve Sheinkin*
6 x 9, 144 pp, Full-color illus., Quality PB, 978-1-58023-310-1 **$16.99**

Rabbi Harvey Rides Again: A Graphic Novel of Jewish Folktales Let Loose in the
Wild West *By Steve Sheinkin*
6 x 9, 144 pp, Full-color illus., Quality PB, 978-1-58023-347-7 **$16.99**

Rabbi Harvey vs. the Wisdom Kid: A Graphic Novel of Dueling Jewish Folktales in
the Wild West *By Steve Sheinkin*
6 x 9, 144 pp, Full-color illus., Quality PB, 978-1-58023-422-1 **$16.99**

The Story of the Jews: A 4,000-Year Adventure—A Graphic History Book
By Stan Mack 6 x 9, 304 pp, Illus., Quality PB, 978-1-58023-155-8 **$18.99**

Grief / Healing

Facing Illness, Finding God: How Judaism Can Help You and Caregivers Cope
When Body or Spirit Fails *By Rabbi Joseph B. Meszler*
6 x 9, 208 pp, Quality PB, 978-1-58023-423-8 **$16.99**

Grief in Our Seasons: A Mourner's Kaddish Companion *By Rabbi Kerry M. Olitzky*
4½ x 6½, 448 pp, Quality PB, 978-1-879045-55-2 **$18.99**

Healing and the Jewish Imagination: Spiritual and Practical Perspectives on
Judaism and Health *Edited by Rabbi William Cutter, PhD*
6 x 9, 240 pp, Quality PB, 978-1-58023-373-6 **$19.99**

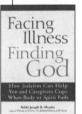

Healing from Despair: Choosing Wholeness in a Broken World
By Rabbi Elie Kaplan Spitz with Erica Shapiro Taylor; Foreword by Abraham J. Twerski, MD
5½ x 8½, 208 pp, Quality PB, 978-1-58023-436-8 **$16.99**

Healing of Soul, Healing of Body: Spiritual Leaders Unfold the Strength & Solace
in Psalms *Edited by Rabbi Simkha Y. Weintraub, LCSW*
6 x 9, 128 pp, 2-color illus. text, Quality PB, 978-1-879045-31-6 **$16.99**

Judaism and Health: A Handbook of Practical, Professional and Scholarly Resources
Edited by Jeff Levin, PhD, MPH, and Michele F. Prince, LCSW, MAJCS
Foreword by Rabbi Elliot N. Dorff, PhD 6 x 9, 448 pp, HC, 978-1-58023-714-7 **$50.00**

Midrash & Medicine: Healing Body and Soul in the Jewish Interpretive Tradition
Edited by Rabbi William Cutter, PhD; Foreword by Michele F. Prince, LCSW, MAJCS
6 x 9, 352 pp, Quality PB, 978-1-58023-484-9 **$21.99**

Mourning & Mitzvah, 2nd Edition: A Guided Journal for Walking the Mourner's
Path through Grief to Healing *By Rabbi Anne Brener, LCSW*
7½ x 9, 304 pp, Quality PB, 978-1-58023-113-8 **$19.99**

Tears of Sorrow, Seeds of Hope, 2nd Edition: A Jewish Spiritual Companion
for Infertility and Pregnancy Loss *By Rabbi Nina Beth Cardin*
6 x 9, 208 pp, Quality PB, 978-1-58023-233-3 **$18.99**

A Time to Mourn, a Time to Comfort, 2nd Edition
A Guide to Jewish Bereavement *By Dr. Ron Wolfson; Foreword by Rabbi David J. Wolpe*
7 x 9, 384 pp, Quality PB, 978-1-58023-253-1 **$21.99**

When a Grandparent Dies: A Kid's Own Remembering Workbook for Dealing
with Shiva and the Year Beyond *By Nechama Liss-Levinson, PhD*
8 x 10, 48 pp, 2-color text, HC, 978-1-879045-44-6 **$15.95** *For ages 7–13*

Social Justice

Where Justice Dwells
A Hands-On Guide to Doing Social Justice in Your Jewish Community
By Rabbi Jill Jacobs; Foreword by Rabbi David Saperstein
Provides ways to envision and act on your own ideals of social justice.
7 x 9, 288 pp, Quality PB, 978-1-58023-453-5 **$24.99**

There Shall Be No Needy
Pursuing Social Justice through Jewish Law and Tradition
By Rabbi Jill Jacobs; Foreword by Rabbi Elliot N. Dorff, PhD; Preface by Simon Greer
Confronts the most pressing issues of twenty-first-century America from a deeply
Jewish perspective. 6 x 9, 288 pp, Quality PB, 978-1-58023-425-2 **$16.99**

There Shall Be No Needy Teacher's Guide 8½ x 11, 56 pp, PB, 978-1-58023-429-0 **$8.99**

Conscience
The Duty to Obey and the Duty to Disobey
By Rabbi Harold M. Schulweis
Examines the idea of conscience and the role conscience plays in our relationships
to government, law, ethics, religion, human nature, God—and to each other.
6 x 9, 160 pp, Quality PB, 978-1-58023-419-1 **$16.99**; HC, 978-1-58023-375-0 **$19.99**

Judaism and Justice: The Jewish Passion to Repair the World
By Rabbi Sidney Schwarz; Foreword by Ruth Messinger
6 x 9, 352 pp, Quality PB, 978-1-58023-353-8 **$19.99**

Spirituality / Women's Interest

Embracing the Divine Feminine: Finding God through the Ecstasy of
Physical Love—The Song of Songs Annotated & Explained
Annotation and Translation by Rabbi Rami Shapiro; Foreword by Rev. Cynthia Bourgeault, PhD
Restores the Song of Songs' eroticism and interprets it as a celebration of the love
between the Divine Feminine and the contemporary spiritual seeker.
5½ x 8½, 176 pp, Quality PB, 978-1-59473-575-2 **$16.99***

The Women's Haftarah Commentary
New Insights from Women Rabbis on the 54 Weekly Haftarah Portions,
the 5 Megillot & Special Shabbatot
Edited by Rabbi Elyse Goldstein
Illuminates the historical significance of female portrayals in the Haftarah and the
Five Megillot. 6 x 9, 560 pp, Quality PB, 978-1-58023-371-2 **$19.99**

The Women's Torah Commentary
New Insights from Women Rabbis on the 54 Weekly Torah Portions
Edited by Rabbi Elyse Goldstein
Over fifty women rabbis offer inspiring insights on the Torah, in a week-by-week format.
6 x 9, 496 pp, Quality PB, 978-1-58023-370-5 **$19.99**; HC, 978-1-58023-076-6 **$34.95**

The Divine Feminine in Biblical Wisdom Literature
Selections Annotated & Explained
Translation & Annotation by Rabbi Rami Shapiro; Foreword by Rev. Cynthia Bourgeault, PhD
5½ x 8½, 240 pp, Quality PB, 978-1-59473-109-9 **$18.99***

New Jewish Feminism: Probing the Past, Forging the Future
Edited by Rabbi Elyse Goldstein; Foreword by Anita Diamant
6 x 9, 480 pp, HC, 978-1-58023-359-0 **$24.99**

The Quotable Jewish Woman
Wisdom, Inspiration & Humor from the Mind & Heart
Edited by Elaine Bernstein Partnow
6 x 9, 496 pp, Quality PB, 978-1-58023-236-4 **$19.99**

*A book from SkyLight Paths, Jewish Lights' sister imprint

Spirituality

Amazing Chesed: Living a Grace-Filled Judaism
By Rabbi Rami Shapiro Drawing from ancient and contemporary, traditional and non-traditional Jewish wisdom, reclaims the idea of grace in Judaism.
6 x 9, 176 pp, Quality PB, 978-1-58023-624-9 **$16.99**

Jewish with Feeling: A Guide to Meaningful Jewish Practice
By Rabbi Zalman Schachter-Shalomi (z"l) with Joel Segel
Takes off from basic questions like "Why be Jewish?" and whether the word *God* still speaks to us today and lays out a vision for a whole-person Judaism.
5½ x 8½, 288 pp, Quality PB, 978-1-58023-691-1 **$19.99**

Perennial Wisdom for the Spiritually Independent: Sacred Teachings— Annotated & Explained *Annotation by Rabbi Rami Shapiro; Foreword by Richard Rohr*
Weaves sacred texts and teachings from the world's major religions into a coherent exploration of the five core questions at the heart of every religion's search.
5½ x 8½, 336 pp, Quality PB, 978-1-59473-515-8 **$16.99**

A Book of Life: Embracing Judaism as a Spiritual Practice
By Rabbi Michael Strassfeld 6 x 9, 544 pp, Quality PB, 978-1-58023-247-0 **$24.99**

Bringing the Psalms to Life: How to Understand and Use the Book of Psalms
By Rabbi Daniel F. Polish, PhD 6 x 9, 208 pp, Quality PB, 978-1-58023-157-2 **$18.99**

Does the Soul Survive? 2nd Edition: A Jewish Journey to Belief in Afterlife, Past Lives & Living with Purpose *By Rabbi Elie Kaplan Spitz; Foreword by Brian L. Weiss, MD*
6 x 9, 288 pp, Quality PB, 978-1-58023-818-2 **$18.99**

Entering the Temple of Dreams: Jewish Prayers, Movements and Meditations for the End of the Day *By Tamar Frankiel, PhD, and Judy Greenfeld*
7 x 10, 192 pp, illus., Quality PB, 978-1-58023-079-7 **$16.95**

First Steps to a New Jewish Spirit: Reb Zalman's Guide to Recapturing the Intimacy & Ecstasy in Your Relationship with God
By Rabbi Zalman Schachter-Shalomi (z"l) with Donald Gropman
6 x 9, 144 pp, Quality PB, 978-1-58023-182-4 **$16.95**

Foundations of Sephardic Spirituality: The Inner Life of Jews of the Ottoman Empire
By Rabbi Marc D. Angel, PhD 6 x 9, 224 pp, Quality PB, 978-1-58023-341-5 **$18.99**

God & the Big Bang: Discovering Harmony between Science & Spirituality
By Dr. Daniel C. Matt 6 x 9, 216 pp, Quality PB, 978-1-879045-89-7 **$18.99**

God in Our Relationships: Spirituality between People from the Teachings of Martin Buber
By Rabbi Dennis S. Ross 5½ x 8½, 160 pp, Quality PB, 978-1-58023-147-3 **$16.95**

The God Upgrade: Finding Your 21st-Century Spirituality in Judaism's 5,000-Year-Old Tradition *By Rabbi Jamie Korngold; Foreword by Rabbi Harold M. Schulweis*
6 x 9, 176 pp, Quality PB, 978-1-58023-443-6 **$15.99**

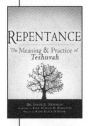

The Jewish Lights Spirituality Handbook: A Guide to Understanding, Exploring & Living a Spiritual Life *Edited by Stuart M. Matlins*
6 x 9, 456 pp, Quality PB, 978-1-58023-093-3 **$19.99**

Judaism, Physics and God: Searching for Sacred Metaphors in a Post-Einstein World
By Rabbi David W. Nelson
6 x 9, 352 pp, Quality PB, inc. reader's discussion guide, 978-1-58023-306-4 **$18.99**
HC, 352 pp, 978-1-58023-252-4 **$24.99**

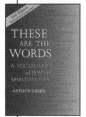

Repentance: The Meaning and Practice of Teshuvah
By Dr. Louis E. Newman; Foreword by Rabbi Harold M. Schulweis; Preface by Rabbi Karyn D. Kedar
6 x 9, 256 pp, HC, 978-1-58023-426-9 **$24.99**; Quality PB, 978-1-58023-718-5 **$18.99**

The Sabbath Soul: Mystical Reflections on the Transformative Power of Holy Time
Selection, Translation and Commentary by Eitan Fishbane, PhD
6 x 9, 208 pp, Quality PB, 978-1-58023-459-7 **$18.99**

Tanya, the Masterpiece of Hasidic Wisdom: Selections Annotated & Explained
Translation & Annotation by Rabbi Rami Shapiro; Foreword by Rabbi Zalman Schachter-Shalomi (z"l)
5½ x 8½, 240 pp, Quality PB, 978-1-59473-275-1 **$18.99**

These Are the Words, 2nd Edition: A Vocabulary of Jewish Spiritual Life
By Rabbi Arthur Green, PhD 6 x 9, 320 pp, Quality PB, 978-1-58023-494-8 **$19.99**

Inspiration

The Chutzpah Imperative: Empowering Today's Jews for a Life
That Matters *By Rabbi Edward Feinstein; Foreword by Rabbi Laura Geller*
A new view of chutzpah as Jewish self-empowerment to be God's partner and
repair the world. Reveals Judaism's ancient message, its deepest purpose and most
precious treasures. 6 x 9, 192 pp, HC, 978-1-58023-792-5 **$21.99**

Judaism's Ten Best Ideas: A Brief Guide for Seekers
By Rabbi Arthur Green, PhD A highly accessible introduction to Judaism's greatest contributions to civilization, drawing on Jewish mystical tradition and the
author's experience. 4½ x 6½, 112 pp, Quality PB, 978-1-58023-803-8 **$9.99**

Into the Fullness of the Void: A Spiritual Autobiography *By Dov Elbaum*
One of Israel's leading cultural figures provides insights and guidance for all of us.
6 x 9, 304 pp, Quality PB, 978-1-58023-715-4 **$18.99**

The Bridge to Forgiveness: Stories and Prayers for Finding God and Restoring Wholeness
By Rabbi Karyn D. Kedar 6 x 9, 176 pp, Quality PB, 978-1-58023-451-1 **$16.99**

The Empty Chair: Finding Hope and Joy—Timeless Wisdom from a Hasidic Master,
Rebbe Nachman of Breslov *Adapted by Moshe Mykoff and the Breslov Research Institute*
4 x 6, 128 pp, Deluxe PB w/ flaps, 978-1-879045-67-5 **$9.99**

The Gentle Weapon: Prayers for Everyday and Not-So-Everyday Moments—
Timeless Wisdom from the Teachings of the Hasidic Master Rebbe Nachman of Breslov
Adapted by Moshe Mykoff and S. C. Mizrahi, together with the Breslov Research Institute
4 x 6, 144 pp, Deluxe PB w/ flaps, 978-1-58023-022-3 **$9.99**

God Whispers: Stories of the Soul, Lessons of the Heart *By Rabbi Karyn D. Kedar*
6 x 9, 176 pp, Quality PB, 978-1-58023-088-9 **$16.99**

God's To-Do List: 103 Ways to Be an Angel and Do God's Work on Earth
By Dr. Ron Wolfson 6 x 9, 144 pp, Quality PB, 978-1-58023-301-9 **$16.99**

Happiness and the Human Spirit: The Spirituality of Becoming the Best You Can Be
By Rabbi Abraham J. Twerski, MD
6 x 9, 176 pp, Quality PB, 978-1-58023-404-7 **$16.99**; HC, 978-1-58023-343-9 **$19.99**

Life's Daily Blessings: Inspiring Reflections on Gratitude and Joy for Every Day, Based
on Jewish Wisdom *By Rabbi Kerry M. Olitzky* 4½ x 6½, 368 pp, Quality PB, 978-1-58023-396-5 **$16.99**

Restful Reflections: Nighttime Inspiration to Calm the Soul, Based on Jewish Wisdom
By Rabbi Kerry M. Olitzky and Rabbi Lori Forman-Jacobi
4½ x 6½, 448 pp, Quality PB, 978-1-58023-091-9 **$16.99**

Sacred Intentions: Morning Inspiration to Strengthen the Spirit, Based on Jewish Wisdom
By Rabbi Kerry M. Olitzky and Rabbi Lori Forman-Jacobi
4½ x 6½, 448 pp, Quality PB, 978-1-58023-061-2 **$16.99**

Saying No and Letting Go: Jewish Wisdom on Making Room for What Matters Most
By Rabbi Edwin Goldberg, DHL; Foreword by Rabbi Naomi Levy
6 x 9, 192 pp, Quality PB, 978-1-58023-670-6 **$16.99**

The Seven Questions You're Asked in Heaven: Reviewing and Renewing Your
Life on Earth *By Dr. Ron Wolfson* 6 x 9, 176 pp, Quality PB, 978-1-58023-407-8 **$16.99**

Kabbalah / Mysticism

Ehyeh: A Kabbalah for Tomorrow
By Rabbi Arthur Green, PhD 6 x 9, 224 pp, Quality PB, 978-1-58023-213-5 **$18.99**

The Gift of Kabbalah: Discovering the Secrets of Heaven, Renewing Your Life on Earth
By Tamar Frankiel, PhD 6 x 9, 256 pp, Quality PB, 978-1-58023-141-1 **$18.99**

Jewish Mysticism and the Spiritual Life: Classical Texts, Contemporary
Reflections *Edited by Dr. Lawrence Fine, Dr. Eitan Fishbane and Rabbi Or N. Rose*
6 x 9, 256 pp, HC, 978-1-58023-434-4 **$24.99**; Quality PB, 978-1-58023-719-2 **$18.99**

Seek My Face: A Jewish Mystical Theology *By Rabbi Arthur Green, PhD*
6 x 9, 304 pp, Quality PB, 978-1-58023-130-5 **$19.95**

Zohar: Annotated & Explained *Translation & Annotation by Dr. Daniel C. Matt*
Foreword by Andrew Harvey 5½ x 8½, 176 pp, Quality PB, 978-1-893361-51-5 **$18.99**
(A book from SkyLight Paths, Jewish Lights' sister imprint)

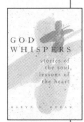

About Jewish Lights

People of all faiths and backgrounds yearn for books that attract, engage, educate, and spiritually inspire.

Our principal goal is to stimulate thought and help all people learn about who the Jewish People are, where they come from, and what the future can be made to hold. While people of our diverse Jewish heritage are the primary audience, our books speak to people in the Christian world as well and will broaden their understanding of Judaism and the roots of their own faith.

We bring to you authors who are at the forefront of spiritual thought and experience. While each has something different to say, they all say it in a voice that you can hear.

Our books are designed to welcome you and then to engage, stimulate, and inspire. We judge our success not only by whether or not our books are beautiful and commercially successful, but by whether or not they make a difference in your life.

For your information and convenience, at the back of this book we have provided a list of other Jewish Lights books you might find interesting and useful. They cover all the categories of your life:

Bar/Bat Mitzvah	Life Cycle
Bible Study / Midrash	Meditation
Children's Books	Men's Interest
Congregation Resources	Parenting
Current Events / History	Prayer / Ritual / Sacred Practice
Ecology / Environment	Social Justice
Fiction: Mystery, Science Fiction	Spirituality
Grief / Healing	Theology / Philosophy
Holidays / Holy Days	Travel
Inspiration	Twelve Steps
Kabbalah / Mysticism / Enneagram	Women's Interest

Stuart M. Matlins, Publisher

Or phone, fax, mail or email to: **JEWISH LIGHTS Publishing**
Sunset Farm Offices, Route 4 • P.O. Box 237 • Woodstock, Vermont 05091
Tel: (802) 457-4000 • Fax: (802) 457-4004 • www.jewishlights.com
Credit card orders: (800) 962-4544 (8:30AM–5:30PM EST Monday–Friday)
Generous discounts on quantity orders. SATISFACTION GUARANTEED. Prices subject to change.

For more information about each book, visit our website at www.jewishlights.com.